HOT TARGET
COWBOY

JUNE FAVER

sourcebooks
casablanca

Published by Sourcebooks Casablanca, an imprint of Sourcebooks, Inc.
P.O. Box 4410, Naperville, Illinois 60567-4410
(630) 961-3900
Fax: (630) 961-2168
sourcebooks.com

Printed and bound in the United States of America.
OPM 10 9 8 7 6 5 4 3 2 1

Also by June Faver

DARK HORSE COWBOYS
Do or Die Cowboy

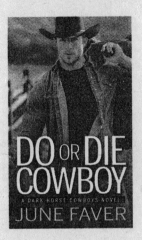

Chapter 1

COLTON GARRETT WAS LATE.

He hated to be late for anything, but most especially anything having to do with his father. He could already see the disapproval in "Big Jim" Garrett's eyes and hear his huff of impatience.

As the oldest of the Garrett sons, Colt was somehow expected to set a good example for the others. To be perfect, it seemed.

Colt heaved a sigh as he pulled his truck in at the auction barn and located a parking space. He knew his dad would already be there with his youngest brother, Beau.

Well, Colt's tardiness couldn't be helped. Just as he was preparing to leave the ranch and had barely climbed into his truck, his middle brother, Tyler, called, and he could hardly hang up on him.

Tyler, a rising country-western star, was on his first tour with his recently formed band. As a newlywed, Ty missed his bride, Leah, but since Leah's eight-year-old daughter, Gracie, attended the local elementary school, Leah couldn't exactly run off and join him on the road. Ty was lonesome and didn't want to make Leah feel bad, but getting everything off his chest to his big brother had apparently done him a lot of good…or at least that's what Ty had said.

Colt climbed out of his truck and stomped through the unpaved parking area, roiling up a layer of dust on his freshly polished boots. He frowned, realizing he would have to give them another shine if he planned to go to the weekly dance at the Eagles Hall in Langston that evening.

He had hoped to enjoy a few beers at the bar and a few dances with some of the local talent. Friday nights were meant for dancing and an end to the seemingly endless toil of keeping up with the sprawling Garrett ranch.

Colt entered the auction barn, looking around for his dad and his youngest brother.

The smell of fresh hay and animals mingled with Texas dust was a familiar aroma to a working cowboy.

"Hey, Colt!" Evan Burke greeted him. "Going to be at the Eagles tonight?"

"You betcha," Colt responded. "Hey, have you seen my dad?"

Evan rolled his eyes. "Hard to miss Big Jim. He's on the other side of the show barn, inspecting some stock. He was lookin' for you earlier."

"Yeah, I imagine he still is." He gave Evan a clap on the shoulder and strode off to meet his fate. Not that Big Jim was anyone for his sons to fear, but he had a way of expressing his displeasure that left the unfortunate offender with no doubt as to their shortcomings. Colton didn't like to be that person.

As the oldest of the three brothers, Colton was also the biggest. He was six foot four like his dad and had the shoulders of a linebacker. Making his way through the milling crowd was slow going, but at least he could see over most of them. He started when he heard a feminine yelp.

"Watch it!"

He had smacked into someone and turned just in time to grab her before she rebounded onto the ground. He was staring into the face of the most beautiful female he had ever laid eyes on, much less held in his arms. "Um, sorry," he said.

She made a growl in the back of her throat. "Honestly! Colton Garrett, you need to watch where you're going. You could kill a girl just by stomping all over her."

Perplexed, he gazed into her dark eyes, seeking some recognition, but was unable to place this lovely young woman. "I didn't mean to step on you… Uh, do I know you?"

She huffed again. "Oh, for Pete's sake. Of course you do." She pushed away and gave him a scowl before tossing her long, dark hair and striding off.

Colt gazed after her, trying to place her in the long line of girls he had known over the course of his lifetime there in Langston. He was certain the long-legged beauty hadn't been in his graduating class in school. He would have surely remembered her.

She was tall, with legs up to her neck. Her butt was round, and Colt couldn't stop staring as her rear moved with each step in her faded Wranglers. She wore a sleeveless Western shirt that snapped up the front and showed off her slim but well-toned arms to advantage. And her breasts…oh, yeah. She had 'em. *Dang!* Now he was standing in the milling throng of mostly male farmers and ranchers with a hard-on like a horny teenager.

Colt swept off his Stetson and held it waist high to cover his state while he raked his fingers through his hair.

But he couldn't tear his gaze from the unknown female. Her long, straight hair had been topped with a white-straw cowboy hat, and she wore an attitude as though she had a permanent case of get-the-hell-away-from-me.

Colt sighed. Casting back in his memory, he couldn't think of any particular girl who had disliked him so openly. In fact, having been an all-star athlete in the local high school had made him pretty popular. Most of the local girls he knew had fallen all over themselves to make sure he was aware they found him attractive and totally desirable as a boyfriend. Of course, a lot of that had to do with the size of his father's ranch. Girls who grew up in farm and ranch territory knew that God wasn't making any more prime Texas real estate, and being a future heir to a considerable chunk of that land would have made him popular with the local female population even if he wore thick glasses and had buck teeth and a face full of zits.

Being a Garrett in this part of the world was generally thought to be a good thing. Why this particular girl didn't think so was a puzzle to Colt. But he had no time to find out.

He followed along in the direction the mystery girl had taken, all the while keeping an eye out for Big Jim or Beau.

The latter individual hailed him with the wave of a hand. "Hey, Bubba."

Colt cringed at the nickname. "Don't call me that," he admonished.

His youngest brother gazed up at him, his intense blue eyes, a Garrett characteristic, twinkling with mischief. "How about Mud? That's what I'm thinking your name is. You better go make nice with Dad. He sent me to find you." He grinned. "Or, I should say, to 'see if you had gotten your lazy ass out of bed yet.'"

Colt drew in a deep breath and let it out, shaking his head as he did so. "I'm in trouble?"

"Not so much. Dad's got his eye on some horses. He wants you to take a look at the lot of 'em and give your opinion."

Colt gazed at Beau with an exaggerated look of surprise. "Me? He wants my opinion?" He placed his hand on his broad chest.

Beau gave him a shove. "Don't be an ass. Of course he does. The opinion of the lowly little brother counts for nothin'...but you..." He gave Colt another nudge. "You da big expert."

Colt grinned, emitting a wry chuckle. "And you da lil' bro who gets off easy."

Beau raised his brows. "You think it's been easy growing up in your shadow?"

Colt grunted. "You think it's been easy breaking ground and paving the way for you two losers?"

The brothers kept up their good-natured teasing as they strolled toward the show barn.

Colt put his Stetson back on his head and looked around. "Hey, do you know who that girl is up ahead? The one with the long, dark hair?"

"And that bodacious backside?"

They both stared at the aforementioned rear with due reverence and fascination.

"Yup, that's the one."

"That, big bro, is Joe Dalton's little sister. None other than the lovely Misty Dalton. What do you think? Pretty hot, huh?"

Colt felt as though he'd been sucker-punched. Joe's little sister... She couldn't be more than nineteen or

twenty to his twenty-eight. *Too young. Way too young.*
"Why haven't I seen her around before?"

"Roll your tongue back in your head, Colt. You're
gonna trip on it."

Colt took a long look. "She knew who I was, but I
couldn't place her."

"You graduated and were off at college before she hit
high school. No reason you would have noticed her...
Hell, she's a couple of years younger than me. For you,
she would practically be jailbait."

"Shut up." Colt continued to fill his eyes with the
rare beauty.

She walked with a certain graceful bearing that he
found appealing, like a queen among her subjects. Head
high, back straight. Her wide-set dark eyes flicked around
the crowd as though she too searched for someone.

Colt felt a tug of something he was surprised to
recognize as jealousy. He hoped she wasn't looking
for her boyfriend...or, worse still, her husband. He
cleared his throat. "Do you know if she's married or
going with someone?"

Beau gave him a sharp glance. "Man, you're not kidding, are you? Is this a case of that 'love at first sight'
thing I've heard about?"

Colt chuckled. "Well, it seems to have worked out
for Ty."

Beau cocked his head to one side and stroked his
chin. "Sure did," he muttered.

Misty Dalton scanned the churning crowd for either
one of her brothers. Joe was dead set on selling off the

Dalton stock, no matter what she or her little brother, Mark, thought about it. With their dad so very ill, she supposed they didn't have much choice, but it killed her to see the pain in Mark's eyes over losing his beloved Appaloosa stallion. He was only twelve years old and had raised the horse from a colt.

This was just too much misery for one so young to bear. At least she had gotten to enjoy a childhood with both parents.

When their mother was alive, things had been different. Her mom had been a cheerful, churchgoing woman, a "treasure above rubies," according to her dad.

But when her mom was killed, riding on the church bus to a women's retreat, everything changed. The remaining family members seemed to have stopped functioning when they buried their matriarch. They slogged through their days with no particular plan or ambition. Misty was only fifteen at the time, and somehow it had fallen to her, as the surviving female in the household, to shop for groceries and produce simple meals, to wash dishes and do laundry. At first, Joe shouldered a lot of the responsibility for the ranch, while their father had fallen into the bottle, deadening his pain with liquor to make it through the sleepless nights. Now, he was dying of liver disease and stomach cancer. *Not fair. The whole thing is just not fair.*

Misty pressed her lips together and swept the hall with her gaze again, searching for Mark or Joe. She blew out an exasperated breath when she spied the Garrett brothers. *Big assholes.* She compared the two, walking side by side.

Beau, the younger one, had gone to school with Joe.

She guessed he was okay. Not bad to look at. Despite being tall and broad-shouldered, he almost appeared downright puny standing next to the other one. *Colton. Mr. Everything at Langston High.*

She could see his eyes from where she stood. Bright blue, almost turquoise, set in his tanned face. Ringed with black lashes all around to match his dark, dark hair. He wore an expensive Western shirt and Wranglers that fit just right, showing off his muscular thighs. Sitting on his head was a soft gray Stetson. *Absolutely freakin' perfect, Mr. Check Me Out, I'm a Hot Cowboy.*

She knew her brother Joe had looked up to his friend Beau's big brother. Idolized him, in fact. Colton Garrett went out for all sports and seemed to do well in all of them, and like in all small towns, Langston citizens were very supportive of their athletes. She recalled all the games where her entire family had sat together on the sidelines, cheering on the local boys.

She pressed her lips together. Those had been good days, but then her family had fallen apart.

Yes, Colton Garrett had been everything Joe Dalton aspired to be. An athlete. A scholar. And rich.

Too bad Joe had never been any of those things, and if Fred Hamilton, the president of the bank, had anything to say about it, the Daltons would be penniless and tossed off their land soon enough.

Poor Dad. He hadn't been able to work much the past couple of years. Joe was doing his best, but it seemed to be too big of a task for him to take on all the responsibility for the ranch by himself. Joe just wasn't cut out for ranching, much to the disappointment of their father.

Paco and Rosa Hernandez, the older couple who had

lived on the ranch for as long as she could remember, helped out a lot. Paco would till the fields and tend the stock, but he was getting old too. She huffed out a sigh. The Hernandezes were drawing no salary for all their hard work, just food and a place to live... This was the situation since the Daltons had fallen on such hard times. They were indeed like family, and Misty loved them dearly.

Sadly, the one who loved the ranch the most was way too young to take over.

Mark had a deep and abiding kinship with the ranch and the stock. He seemed to have a natural affinity for all the animals and some kind of sixth sense about the crops. Too bad it would all be gone before long.

Misty spotted Mark leaning against the metal wall and motioned for him to join her.

He pushed away from the wall and approached, his gaze cast down and his lips tight with anger and sorrow.

She looped an arm around his neck, giving him an awkward hug. "Let's gut up and get this over with."

"I hate him. He didn't have to put my horse in with the others. He knows how much I love Sam."

"I know how you must feel, but I'm pretty sure Joe is trying to sell off everything we can while we still own it." She gave him a surreptitious kiss on his temple and pulled him along with her. "Be brave, honey. Let's go say goodbye and hope we get top dollar. We sure do need it."

Mark made a scoffing sound deep in his throat. "I wish I was dead."

"No, you don't. I need you. Be strong now."

He fell into step beside her as they made their way into the big show barn where the auction would take place and then out the side door where the various lots of horses were grouped for the prospective bidders to inspect.

———•~~~•———

Although Colton's attention had been captured by the lovely Misty Dalton, the minute he entered the show barn, he was forced to pay homage to his father.

Big Jim stood by the railing with one eyebrow raised as his sons approached. "Well, good afternoon, Colt. Glad to see you could make it."

"It's barely 10 a.m., Dad. Gimme a break."

"Give me a break," Big Jim insisted. "I wanted you to take a look at the horses out back. I'm particularly interested in two different lots. Go check them out, and then tell me what you think."

"Sure." Colt thought he was getting off easy and wondered what it was about the horses that had his father so excited.

"Check out lots 236 and 211. Looks like some good stock there." Big Jim pounded him on the shoulder and moved away from the railing. "Beau and I are going to the cattle barn. I'm lookin' to add a little breeding stock to the herd." He put his hand on Beau's shoulder but kept his gaze fastened on Colton. "You might want to think about investing in some stock too, Son."

Beau laughed. "Yeah, you can afford it."

"I'll keep that in mind." Colt watched his father and brother head out behind the show barn to the area where cattle were being offered in lots for inspection before the auction. He blew out a breath, headed for the area marked *Horses,* and stepped outside where portable fences cordoned off the different lots of horses grouped for sale.

He found lot 236 and gave his approval. There were six beautiful Arabs being offered. Just the kind of horse to catch his dad's eye. One stallion and five fillies. The stallion was antsy, dancing a little on his fine hooves, his neck arched as he looked over the crowd. *Yes, perfect for Big Jim Garrett.*

Colt moved down the line to locate the other horses Big Jim had deemed worthy. At the very end of the line, he found lot 211. This was a mixed lot with a big Appaloosa stallion, a roan gelding, a couple of Appaloosa fillies, and two sorrel fillies. Not a bad lot at all.

A young boy was leaning against the fence, stroking the stallion's neck. Silent tears were running unchecked down his face.

Cute kid. He had dark hair in need of a trim and a few freckles scattered across his nose. His clothes were worn, and his boots were scuffed.

"Hey, son," Colt said. "This looks like a good horse. What can you tell me about him?" He reached to give the horse's nose a stroke.

The boy sniffed. "He is a great horse. His name is Sam. I raised him from the time he was a foal."

"Good job. And now you're selling him?"

"No," the boy moaned. "My big brother is. He says we need the money and we can't afford the feed anymore."

Colt felt a tightness invade his chest. "That's too bad. What's your name, boy?"

"Mark," he answered. "Mark Dalton. I'm only twelve. If I was older I could get a job and pay for his feed."

At the name *Dalton*, Colt sucked in a breath. Mark had the same coloring as Misty. Maybe a younger sibling? "My name is Colton Garrett. You can call me Colt. Maybe we could work something out." He chatted with the boy for a bit and then returned to the auction barn.

From the entrance, he glanced back and saw Misty approaching the boy. She handed him a canned soft drink and gave him a hug.

Colt could see the pain on her face as well. He recalled the boy's words that they couldn't afford to buy feed for their stock. *Sad state for a family.*

"Well, hell," Big Jim exploded. "When I suggested you might want to buy some stock, I didn't mean for you to buy the lot I was interested in."

Colt grinned at him. "My mistake, Dad. I thought you would be satisfied with those fine Arabs and leave the other lot for me."

"Mistake, my ass!" Big Jim was grumbling, but he finally admitted he was glad Colton had invested in some horses on his own. Why this particular lot, Colt couldn't explain.

"Dunno, Dad. That big Appaloosa looked like he could sire a few good foals, and the Appaloosa fillies are fine too."

"I'm glad you broke loose with some of that money you've been sitting on forever." Big Jim shook his silvered head, piercing his son with the intensity of his blue eyes. "I've paid you for working on the ranch since you were in grade school. I've never seen a kid hoard cash the way you do. I'm just glad you finally found something to invest in."

"I have other horses," Colt said, a defensive note in his voice.

"Gifts. Every one of your horses has been a gift."

Colt grinned. "You can give me those Arabs anytime you want."

Big Jim snorted. "Not a chance. I'm going to the cattle auction now, unless you want to buy the lot I'm planning to bid on."

Colt slapped Big Jim on the shoulder. "No, you go ahead. Maybe Beau will bid on them." He watched as Big Jim shook his head and made his way to the cattle area.

"Colt?"

He turned to find Mark Dalton gazing up at him. "Hey, son."

"Did you mean what you said?" the boy asked.

Colt regarded him seriously. "Sure did. Are you agreeable?"

A grin split Mark's face. "Are you kidding? Yes." He stuck out his hand.

Colt shook it, somberly. "So, we're partners, right?"

The boy nodded.

"And you'll ride the bus out to the Garrett ranch after school to give Sam some exercise and do other jobs for me?"

Another gleeful nod.

"I'll drive you home after your work is done. I'm going to pay you, and you can buy Sam back from me anytime you see fit."

"Yes!" Mark shook hands enthusiastically.

"Deal," Colt said. "See you Monday afternoon." He turned to watch Mark race out of the show barn, a grin plastered across his face.

"I don't know what you're planning, but you better not break my brother's heart."

Colton whirled around to find Misty Dalton gazing up at him. Not an ounce of trust in those dark eyes. "I assure you I had no such intentions."

"He's had enough pain and disappointment to last a lifetime. I won't let you hurt him again." Her lower lip trembled, and Colt had to stop himself from reaching out to stroke her cheek. Her skin was alabaster white, setting off the large, dark eyes to perfection.

He reached for her hand instead. "I understand how you feel about your little brother. I have two of them, and I feel the same way." Her hand felt small tucked inside his large one.

She lifted her chin slightly, still skewering him with her dark gaze. "But you're big enough to stop anyone who tried to hurt them." She wrested her hand from his grasp.

He nodded. "I am, but I respect your feelings, and I would never do anything to cause Mark any pain. I grew up on a ranch, and my dad paid me for my chores. I'll do the same for Mark. It will be good for him and good for me too."

"But why are you doing this?" she persisted.

He heaved a sigh. "Why not? Can't I just take an interest in Mark? He was so heartbroken at losing the horse. I wanted to help him."

Her expression softened. "Okay," she said reluctantly.

He was curious as to why this family was in financial trouble. Not being able to afford to feed one's stock was indeed a problem. "I'm sorry you had to sell your horses, but be secure in the knowledge that they will be well cared for at the Garrett ranch."

She nodded, pressed her lips together, and suppressed a shiver. "Good to know… My father is ill, and it pained him to agree to sell, but my brother Joe convinced him it was for the best."

Colton considered the young woman in front of him. He had to admire her courage as well as her beauty. "I'm sorry your father is ill," he said. "I wish him a speedy recovery."

Her lips twitched. "He's on hospice."

The full weight of her pronouncement settled heavily on him. "Tough break. Will you and your brothers be okay?"

She shook her head. "I don't think so." She turned away, grimacing.

"Well, I hope to see you again sometime." Colton raised a hand, but she walked away from him so, he thought, he wouldn't see her tears.

Chapter 2

COLTON AND BEAU WALKED INTO THE EAGLES HALL together and paid the entrance fee. They were early. The band was just setting up, but the parking lot was filling with trucks, and people were streaming inside the hall, some couples and some stag.

The brothers gazed around the huge room lined with tables and a dance floor close to the raised stage. They headed for the bar, and Colton paid for the first round. He took a slow draw on his longneck and leaned back against the bar to survey the gathering crowd.

He recognized many of the local residents. Whether they were fellow ranchers, people he knew from school or church, or some of the tradespeople from around town, he could count a lot of familiar faces. But there were also people from the surrounding area. Due to the fact that a popular band from Amarillo was gathering on stage and it was known to draw quite a crowd, he figured some of the crowd had even driven from the city.

When he glanced in the mirror over the bar, he was in for a surprise. At the opposite end, Misty Dalton stood gazing somberly down at the longneck in front of her. Raising it to her lips, she tilted her head back, took a long swallow, and then set it back on the bar. She resumed her quiet contemplation of the bottle.

Colton picked up his beer and joined her. "Are you old enough to be drinking?"

She glanced at him, a flash of dark fire in her eyes, but her voice was soft when she spoke. "Of course I am. My twenty-second birthday was this past Wednesday."

"You've got a baby face." He raised his bottle in a silent toast. "Happy birthday, Misty. I hope you had a good one."

Her shoulders sagged. "Not so much." She took another swig of the beer.

Colton leaned both forearms on the polished wood of the bar. "Well, we should celebrate. It's not every day one turns twenty-two." He mentally calculated the difference in their ages. Six years wasn't so bad. "How about tomorrow night? I'll take you to dinner at the steak house."

She glanced up again. "Aw, you don't have to do that."

"I'd like to take you to dinner. I can pick you up at six."

Her dark eyes seemed to be assessing him. "I don't know what my dad would say."

"It's just dinner," he said. "You know, to celebrate your birthday."

She nodded. "That would be nice. I'll see how Dad is feeling tomorrow." She met his gaze shyly. "I can call you if he's feeling well enough to be left alone with my brothers."

Colt swallowed. There was an air of sadness that seemed to hang over her like a shroud tonight. Not the same spunky young woman who had challenged him earlier. "That will be fine. I hope you can work it out." He asked for her phone and punched his number in. He handed it back, hoping he would hear from her.

The band was tuning up their instruments, and one of the Eagle members stepped to the microphone to make announcements. He rattled off the name of the band and a list of upcoming events. By the time he finished, the band began to play their first number, a fast polka.

A few couples took to the floor and whirled around at a rapid clip. Colton watched Misty watching the dancers. He wanted to hold her in his arms, and the easiest way to accomplish that was on the dance floor.

When the song ended, the band started up a two-step, and he decided to make his move. "Would you like to dance?"

She shrugged. "I guess so." She set her bottle on the bar and strode out onto the dance floor, once again reminding him of a queen among her subjects. When she reached the center of the floor, she turned to him, and he gathered her in his arms.

Nice. He held her for a moment, realizing she felt perfectly matched to him. Tall and slender, she placed her hand in his and the other on his shoulder. He experienced a squeezing in his chest but set off dancing when he would rather be kissing her.

As Colt moved to the music, he couldn't tear his gaze away from Misty's face. Due to his size, people generally got out of his way on the dance floor, but he felt especially protective of his partner, making sure no one bumped into them. He wondered how, in the course of a few hours, he had become so interested in her.

It wasn't only her beauty but also her attitude that captured his interest. This girl had an inner strength she must have earned the hard way.

He wanted to know everything about her but was reluctant to pummel her with questions. He wanted to be in her life but knew he had no right to expect her to open up to him when she had so much going on with her family. He wanted to be the only man in her life, but right now, he was just her dance partner and perhaps her dinner companion the following night, if things played out in his favor.

As he danced, he dreaded the end of the song when he would have to let her go, but the next dance was a waltz.

She looked up at him, a sweet smile on her lips. "Oh, a waltz. Can we do this one too? I love to waltz."

"My pleasure," he said, surprised that his stomach was doing flip-flops like the first time he had ever asked a girl to dance. He swirled her around the dance floor, delighted when she grinned and leaned into the turns. Her long hair flowed out behind her in the wake of their turns, and she looked, for the first time, as though she had left her pain behind.

All too soon, the waltz came to an end, and Colton was left to escort Misty back to the bar. He placed his hand at her waist, enjoying the sensation of her warm skin just beneath the cotton shirt and the firm muscles as she walked. "Thanks for the dances," he murmured when they reached the bar.

She flashed him a smile. "I enjoyed it."

He took a few steps down the bar to where Beau stood, nursing his beer. "Man, you got it bad."

Colt expelled a breath. "I know. I can't figure out what happened to me."

Beau snorted with laughter. "I can. My big bro has finally fallen for a girl who isn't all goofy about him."

Colt snuck another glance at Misty. "You could be right."

"She's the first one who isn't worshiping at your shrine. How does that make your ego feel? I mean, now that you're like the rest of us mere mortals?"

Colton lifted his bottle to salute Beau. "You're enjoying this, aren't you?"

"You bet. It looked like you were about to gobble her up out there on the dance floor. Just glad you made it back without embarrassing yourself."

"Keep it up, Little Bro." Colton felt a stab of jealousy as another man came to ask Misty to dance. Her new dance partner must have been someone she knew because they immediately began to talk.

Beau inclined his head toward the twosome. "Got a little competition there, Bubba."

"Don't call me that." Colton watched as Misty danced in another man's arms. "I'm going to marry that girl."

Misty kept glancing at Colton while she danced with one of her former classmates. She loved to dance, but something about being held in Colton Garrett's strong arms had thrilled her to her toes. No, she didn't want to lose her head. It couldn't mean anything to the all-powerful Colt Garrett to be dancing with her, but for a moment there, it had felt so right. She could have stayed in his embrace all night.

She returned to the bar when the song was over and picked up the bottle of beer she had been sipping. She needed to make it last, because she shouldn't be spending any more money. Add that to the fact that she had never indulged in more than one serving of beer at a time, and those were on the sly from Joe's stash.

She was supposed to wait here for Joe and Mark, who had collected the check from the auction and were to pick her up for the ride home. She hoped her dad would be relieved and not worry so much about their finances.

His illness was enough for him to handle without being concerned for the ones he would leave behind.

Casting a quick glance down the length of the bar, she saw Colton staring at her. She swallowed hard, as a blush crept up her neck and painted her cheeks. *He can't possibly like me. Not really. Not like a girlfriend. We're too different. Too far apart.* She tilted the bottle to her lips, drained it, and then set it back on the bar.

"Can I buy you another?" It was Colton, his voice deep and rich, wrapping around her like a warm blanket.

"Um, no, thanks. I'm a total lightweight. I just wanted to buy a beer to prove I could." She smiled up at him, hoping she didn't sound like a complete idiot.

A smile touched his lips. "You do have that baby-faced thing going for you."

Misty shrugged. "My curse."

"There will come a time when you'll be glad for your young face." He gave her a wink and tilted his beer up to drain it. He nodded at the bartender and gestured with the bottle. "How about a soda then?" He was regarding her kindly.

The bluest eyes she had ever seen set fire to something in her chest. *He thinks I'm just a kid. The same way he's nice to Mark. That's it. He's just being nice to another kid.* She nodded. "Thanks."

He signaled to the bartender, who served her a soda in a can along with a mug of crushed ice and set another longneck in front of Colt.

"We could get a table, if you like," he offered.

"Um, I'm waiting for my brothers. They had to collect the check and drop off the trailer we borrowed to haul the horses." Her lips twitched before she pressed them together and released a sigh. "Now we just need to sell off the cattle before the ax falls."

"Ax?" Colt gazed at her, trying to keep his expression neutral.

Misty shrugged. "Before the bank forecloses on our land and gobbles up our cattle and equipment too."

The silence that followed settled heavily on her shoulders. She glanced up at Colt and found his gaze fastened on his beer.

A muscle twitched in his jaw. "Why don't we sit over there?" He pointed to a table close to the dance floor where she could keep an eye on the door. "That looks like a good vantage point. I'll wait with you for your brothers." He picked up her soda and his longneck. "Come along, Little Brother. Let's keep the beautiful lady company."

Beau gave him a funny look but followed along behind them.

The Garrett brothers seated themselves on either side of her at the table. She didn't figure anyone else would dare ask her to dance with such a formidable lineup surrounding her. Big, hunky maleness all around.

She grinned and took a sip of her soda.

Beau stood up and directed a formal bow at her. "Miss Dalton, may I have this dance?"

She giggled. He looked so serious. "Yes, you may," she said and put her hand in the one he offered.

Beau led her onto the dance floor and through a nice two-step. He was tall and broad-shouldered like Colton but less so. He didn't hold her the same way as Colton. He just wasn't Colton.

"Are you seeing anybody?" he asked.

"No. I've been too busy taking care of my dad."

He smiled at her. "Sorry to hear that about your dad. But Colt will be glad to hear you're not involved."

"What?" She stumbled.

"My brother Colton. You have figured out he likes you, haven't you?"

Misty swallowed hard. "Um, no...I didn't know that."

Beau smiled and twirled her under his arm. "Well, he does. I didn't want you to miss it, in case he's being too subtle for you."

She gazed back to where Colton was sitting, staring at her. He raised his beer to her and took another drink. "I, uh...I don't know what to say. Joe said all the girls were crazy over him when he was in school."

"They were," Beau agreed amiably. "But it didn't go to his head. He always had a lot of responsibilities around the ranch. He's a pretty serious guy."

She tried to absorb what he was telling her. She couldn't, really. She wondered if Colton had conspired with Beau to tell her this...and if it were true.

When the song finished Beau started to escort her back to the table, but Colton met them half way.

"My turn," he said, holding out his hand.

She considered what Beau had told her as she was wrapped in Colton's arms again. *Does he really like me, or was Beau teasing me?* Something she saw burning in the depths of Colt's eyes made her think Beau's words might be factual.

At last the band played a slow song and Colton could

draw Misty close. The house lights went down, lending an illusion of intimacy. She seemed to soften against him, her pretty face pressed against his shoulder. He buried his lips in her hair, inhaling the fragrance—something floral that he couldn't identify.

She circled her arm around his waist, snagging his belt loop with her thumb to hang on to. Her body melted against his, and he thought he had reached heaven, or at least a place nearby.

When the song ended, he reluctantly lifted his head and gazed into her beautiful eyes. Without thinking he leaned down and brushed his lips against hers. It was just the merest hint of a kiss, but she didn't draw back. He dipped his head for another, this time parting her sweet lips with his tongue. The kiss deepened as they stood in the middle of the dance floor and the band struck up another song. Couples danced around them, but he was oblivious to everything except the woman in his arms. When he pulled away, he felt slightly dazed. He glanced around and led her back to the table, hoping he hadn't ruined his chances with her.

For her part, Misty was quiet and somewhat subdued. As Colt seated her, Joe Dalton pulled up a chair opposite them.

"Oh, Joe," she said. "I didn't see you come in."

He let out a derisive snort. "You were otherwise occupied."

Colt frowned, narrowing his gaze at Joe.

Misty blushed as though being caught kissing Colton was a bad thing. "Where is Mark?" she asked.

"He went home with one of his school buds. The Tates took him for a sleepover."

She looked uncertain. "He didn't have a change of clothes."

Joe waved his hand at her. "You worry too much. He'll be fine." He lifted his longneck and chugged down his beer. "Like I'm fine with this nice fat check for the stock sale." He pulled it out of the breast pocket of his shirt, unfolding and displaying it for them to see. "Thank you, Garretts, for buying my horses."

"Thank Colt," Beau said. "He was the one who bought them."

Joe nodded to Colton, raising his beer in a salute but spilling some of it. He started to fold the check, but it slipped from his fingers, landing in the puddle in front of him.

Misty snatched the check and blotted the spilled beer off it. "They weren't your horses, Joe," she said gruffly. "And this isn't your money. It belongs to Dad, and I'll see that he gets it."

She folded the check and tucked it into her bra.

Joe leaned across the table, grabbing her shirt, but Colton's hand shot out to grip Joe's wrist.

"Not a good idea." Beau wagged his finger at Joe. "Do not make the big man mad."

Joe froze, glancing from Beau to Colt and back again. Slowly he uncurled his fingers from the fabric of Misty's shirt.

Colton pushed Joe's hand across to the other side of the table, giving him a stern glare.

"Okay, okay. I'm sure Little Sister will be persuaded to turn over the check later." He smirked, giving Colton and Misty the benefit of his smug expression.

"I think this money better make it to your father's

hands," Colt said, his voice low and deadly. It occurred to him that Joe had imbibed more than a few beers before he got to the Eagles Hall.

"We'll see," Joe said in a singsong voice. He drained his beer and stood up. "I'm going to the ranch, Misty. Come on." He jangled his keys in front of her.

Beau stood, grabbing the keys. "I think you've had a little too much alcohol to be driving anyone home tonight. I can drive you, and Colton can follow to pick me up."

"Nobody's driving me home. I'm perfectly capable of getting us back to the ranch. C'mon, Misty." He was slurring his words, but he made a swipe at Beau, snagging his keys in the process.

Misty frowned, pressed her lips together, but stood as if to leave with him.

Colton stood beside her. "I'll drive Misty home," he said, his hand on her arm.

Joe glowered at her, then turned and stomped across the floor, almost lurching into a couple. He pushed his way out of the hall and into the night.

Colt looked at Misty. "Sorry about that. I hope there won't be any trouble later."

She shook her head. "He'll be all right. But I do want to be sure this money gets in the bank. We can't afford to waste it." She patted her breast.

Colt grinned at her. "I think it's in a pretty secure place right now. Let's dance, and then I'll make sure you get home safely."

Chapter 3

MISTY LINGERED AT THE EAGLES HALL, DANCING MOSTLY with Colton and occasionally with Beau. She wanted to make sure Joe had a chance to get home and hoped he would be passed out and sound asleep by the time she was delivered by the Garretts. She didn't want to have any kind of ugly confrontation with Joe while he was drunk. Tomorrow, she would show her dad the check and get him to sign it for deposit only. Then she would make sure it got to the bank, hopefully without an all-out battle with Joe.

In the meantime, she was having a great evening being entertained by both charming brothers. After the interlude with Joe, both the Garretts seemed to step up to the task of taking her mind off her troubles.

When Colton led her to the dance floor, she was very aware of him, of his hands guiding her, of his very muscular arms surrounding her, of his granite-hard chest when he pulled her close for a slow dance.

Careful, girl. He's just being nice. You can't fall for him.

When she yawned, Colt pushed back from the table and stood up. He pulled her chair out. "Guess you're turning into a pumpkin. Time to take you home."

Reluctantly, she stood and smiled up at him. "Thanks to both of you for babysitting me tonight. I'm sure you had better things to do."

Colt took her hand and pressed a kiss against her palm. "Not me. This was the most fun I've had in a long time."

A shiver ran down her spine given the intensity of his gaze and the brush of his lips against her flesh. She swallowed hard. "Th—thanks. It was great fun for me."

He pressed her palm against his chest, and she could feel the reverberation of his heartbeat. Somehow, this steady rhythm reached out to annex her as a part of him.

A shiver spiraled through her body as she stared into the bluest eyes on the planet. All of her senses were completely aware of this man, as though someone had flipped a switch and suddenly she was alive.

Colt ran his other hand up and down her bare arm. "Cold?"

Misty shook her head, unwilling to search for the words to explain how she was feeling.

"I had a good time too, and now I'm out of here," Beau added. He scraped his chair back and rose to his feet. "But I think Colt got the best end of the deal. Goodnight. I'm going home." He winked at her and headed for the door.

Although the hall was full of people, Misty felt as though she was suddenly alone with Colton. He gazed down at her, holding her close but not close enough. A sudden ache washed through her. She wasn't sure what more she wanted from him, but she wanted more.

Rising on her tiptoes, she raised her chin, and a smile flickered on Colt's lips.

He wrapped both arms around her and lifted her against him. A brief glance before his lips met hers.

Misty circled his neck with her arms and enjoyed the best kiss she had ever received. Pressed so tightly against him, she could feel her heartbeat pulsing her body.

Colt's mouth was all she could think about as the kiss continued, his tongue caressing hers, inciting her entire body into a state of arousal she had never experienced before.

When at last he drew back, he held her for a moment, still gazing into her eyes as though asking a question before setting her back on her feet.

Silently, he took her hand, leading the way out of the Eagles Hall and into the cool night. They walked down the stairs together and stepped onto the pea gravel of the parking area, their boots making a crunching sound with each step.

Misty glanced up at the moon, sharply defined in the clear night sky. A million stars shone brightly to accompany it, but the moon took center stage, almost half full.

She looked at Colt, his handsome face bathed in moonlight.

"I hope you'll be able to have dinner with me tomorrow night." He arranged his Stetson on his head, throwing his expressive face into shadow. "We still need to celebrate your birthday in style."

"I hope so too," she said. "There was no other celebration. I didn't even tell Dad it was my birthday. I didn't want him to feel bad about forgetting it."

Colt huffed out a breath. "Too bad. I'm pretty certain we can do better." He lifted her hand to kiss the back of her fingers.

When they reached his truck, Colton held the passenger door open for her. He gave her a hand up into the cab, and when she was settled, slammed the door with a solid thunk.

Colt climbed in on the driver's side and reached behind him. He pulled a jacket from the back seat and wrapped it around Misty's shoulders.

She gave him a smile of acknowledgment as he started the big diesel motor. The truck roared to life as he revved the engine a couple of times, then put it in gear and drove out of the Eagles parking lot.

Once on the highway, it was as though theirs was the only vehicle on the road that night. It was a long, straight highway, bathed in moonlight, the darkness falling off on either side as they sped along.

A country station was playing softly on the radio, the only sound other than the diesel engine's soft whine.

Misty lolled her head back, and Colt reached for her hand. It felt nice. It felt as though someone cared, which hadn't happened for a long time.

When Colton turned onto the farm-to-market road leading to the Dalton ranch, Misty sat up, alert to see what was going on at the house.

The family truck was parked close to the house, so obviously Joe had made it home safely. All the lights were off, which gave her hope that he was sound asleep and wouldn't confront her about the check when she went inside. She heaved a sigh of relief.

Colton drew to a stop and put the truck in gear. He opened the door and reached out a hand to help her down.

Walking to the front door, her hand tucked in the crook of Colt's arm, she reflected that this had been a great day for the most part. Sad that they had to sell the horses, but great that they had received a significant amount of money from the sale. And best of all was the time she had spent with Colton. She had no idea what their relationship was, or if they had one, but for this moment in time, her insides were buoyant.

Colt's arm felt like steel with a warm layer of flesh over it. She couldn't imagine what he did to develop muscles like that, but whatever it was, she found the result thrilling.

At the front door, he gazed down at her tenderly before cupping her face in his big hands. He leaned down to kiss her and then wrapped her in his arms for a hug.

"Go on inside, Misty. I hope to see you tomorrow."

She expelled a sigh. "I'm not going in the house." At his puzzled expression, she went on. "In case Joe gets ugly, I'm just going to sleep in the little house out back."

"Then I'll see you to that door," he said.

She nodded, leading the way behind the main house, past the barn to the little cottage tucked away by itself, out of sight.

"What is this place?" Colton asked.

"My dad built it for the couple who live with us, Paco and Rosa Hernandez. They've been with my family since before I was born."

"And you're going to stay with them tonight?"

Smiling, she shook her head. "Just me. The Hernandezes moved into the big house when my dad became ill. Rosa is a great help, and Paco has completely taken over tending the livestock."

"And you're going to be okay out here all by yourself?" Colton's expression touched her deeply.

"Sure. Want to see inside? It's adorable. I've fixed it up some since it's been vacant." She opened the door and flicked on a small lamp. A soft glow spread around the room.

Colton looked oversized in the small space. "This is real nice, Misty. It looks homey."

She let out a giggle. "It looks girly. I've treated it like my own dollhouse. Being the only female, I guess I needed a place to be a girl."

He grinned at that, grabbing her and lifting her as he spun around in a circle. "You go ahead and be a girl all you want. I love your girly stuff." He stopped, gazing up at her. "In fact, I love everything about you." His voice had become husky on the last part.

The intensity in his eyes caused a warm flush to spread through her insides. Slowly, he lowered her until they were at eye level.

Without thinking, she wrapped her arms and legs around him, clinging to him and feeling the heat coil through her.

He held her tight against him, cupping her butt with one hand and her head with the other. The first kiss felt as though a lit match had landed on dry tinder. The next felt like a full-fledged forest fire.

She tugged at his shirt, and then clothing started falling to the floor, first his shirt and then hers. He tentatively stroked her shoulder, his fingers caressing her bra strap, as though asking permission to go on. Misty released the breath she hadn't known she'd been holding then met his gaze. The intensity scorched her.

He glanced around and headed through the door to the small bedroom. Once again, he hesitated. "Are you sure you want this?"

She nodded. "I need you." Her voice came out low and raspy, like the growl of a feral animal.

He set her on her feet and slid the bra strap from her shoulder, tracing the line first with his finger and then with his lips. His touch sent swirls of passion spiraling low in her belly.

Grinning, he unbuckled her belt, stripped it from its loops, and then dropped it beside the bed. "You can do me," he offered, spreading his arms.

Misty fumbled with the Western buckle, but suddenly it was open, and she pulled on it, as Colton had done, and then slid the belt from around his waist. Nerves got the best of her, and she giggled.

Colton gathered her in his arms and kissed her. He eased her back onto the bed then stood back gazing down at her. "I swear, Misty. You're so beautiful I just can't stop looking at you."

She felt a rush of heat, and a deep blush crept up from her neck. "I'm not beautiful," she denied. "I'm just…me."

"That's plenty good enough for me." Colton grabbed one of her boots and wrested it off before going after the other one. "I think you're beautiful, and nothing you say will change my mind." He pulled off her socks and held both of her bare feet in his hands. "Your feet are cold. Let me warm them up for you." He rested them against his rock-hard abs and rubbed them with both hands.

He couldn't possibly know how vulnerable she was or how starved for affection. Everything he did overwhelmed her, both physically and emotionally.

She sucked in a breath and reached to unfasten the waistband of her denims, but Colt was watching her intently. When she fumbled with the zipper, he kissed the sole of her foot and placed them both on the bed before leaning over her with an expression of such tenderness she almost cried out.

Colt finished opening the zipper and gently slipped the jeans off, devouring her with his gaze. "So beautiful," he whispered. He deftly removed his own boots and Wranglers before divesting himself of his underwear.

Misty tried not to stare, but she couldn't help herself. Her heartbeat pulsed in her ears, almost frightening in its strength.

Colton picked up his Wranglers and removed something from his wallet before stepping closer. When he climbed onto the bed beside her, every fiber of her being was on fire with anticipation. She didn't want to show him how inexperienced she was, but she yearned to be loved by this man, and she wasn't sure how to let him know.

All at once he was kissing her…touching her…setting her on fire. She arched against him, grazing her nipples against the dark hair swirling across his chest. A sound escaped her throat, and that was all it took to push Colton into overdrive. He touched her and kissed her, heightening her frenzy. He took a moment to don a condom before entering her.

Colton had teased and pleased her. Now he set about to bring all her hungry desires to a head. Rhythmic stroking hit all her nerve endings until she reached the pinnacle of desire and everything shifted into slow motion. She couldn't think. Couldn't breathe…could only feel the building of sensation that finally, deliciously, culminated in a detonation of passion.

She lay in his arms, exhausted and exhilarated at the same time. Never in her limited experience had she ever felt as though she were part of an explosion.

"Misty," he whispered, his lips against her temple. "That was amazing."

She nodded, not sure what to say. Her heart was still pounding in her ears, and she couldn't seem to catch her breath.

He held her for some time, gently stroking her hair and kissing her. "Misty, I didn't know we would be together like this, but this whole evening has been important to me. I feel that we have something special between us. I hope you feel the same."

She nodded, unable to form coherent speech.

He kissed her forehead. "I guess I better go. I don't think your father or brothers would like to find me here."

Misty felt a sudden sense of loss. She didn't want to even think of how bad it would be to have her brothers find her naked in Colton Garrett's arms…but she didn't want to let him go, either. "You're right." She tore herself out of his embrace. "I guess you had better leave."

"I'm hoping you'll be able to give me some good news tomorrow."

"Good news?" she asked.

"Dinner. If I'm lucky, your father will feel well enough for me to take you to dinner tomorrow."

She smiled, warming at the thought that she might be with him again. "Me too."

He climbed out of bed, retrieved his clothes, and pulled them back on. Leaning onto the bed, he gathered the comforter around her and kissed her. "Give me a call later. Let me know when we can get together." He handed her a card with his number on it, and she clasped it to her bosom. "You already have my cell number in your phone. This has the ranch number on it as well. Good night, Misty, and thanks for spending your evening with me." He gave her another quick kiss on the cheek and straightened.

She followed him to the door, dragging the comforter behind her. From the window, she watched him return to the truck and drive away. She also hoped her dad would have a good day tomorrow.

Returning to the bedroom, she gathered her clothing and picked up the check that had fallen from her bra. Her priorities reached out and gave her a mental smack on the head. "Yeah, I know what I have to do."

―――∾∾―――

Colton climbed in his truck and rolled as quietly as possible away from the Dalton homestead. He hated leaving Misty alone. All he had wanted was to stay with her, but he didn't want to cause any trouble with her family. Leaving her caused an ache in his chest.

He only knew one thing about the delicious Misty Dalton. He had to have more. No matter the consequences, he wasn't about to let her get away from him.

Turning onto the main highway, he heaved a sigh. *This one's a keeper.*

He didn't encounter any other vehicles on the stretch of highway between the Dalton and the Garrett ranches. His headlights cut a path through the darkness, making him feel like the only human left on the planet.

When he turned in at the big horseshoe-shaped gate marking the entrance to the private drive leading to the Garrett ranch house, he was thinking about the possibility of taking Misty to dinner and ways he could make it a special evening for her.

The big, rambling Spanish-style ranch house was quiet. Big Jim had apparently retired.

The lights were out in the wing that Leah, Gracie,

and Fern Davis—Leah's grandmother—were currently occupying while waiting for Ty to return from his tour and for their new house to be built.

Colton parked and got out of his truck as quietly as possible, but when he went into the house, he was surprised to find Beau watching a rerun of *The Walking Dead* in the front room.

"Hey, Bubba," he said in a soft voice.

"Don't call me that," Colton snapped. "It's after three in the morning. Isn't it past your bedtime, Little Brother?"

Beau chuckled. "But not yours. You must have gotten a little action from the lovely Misty Dalton."

"Shut up!" Colt huffed out a sigh. "I really like her, so just back off."

Beau continued to give Colton a hard time about being so obviously smitten with Misty. "I mean, Bro, you're supposed to be cool. Play hard to get."

"I don't want to play hard to get. I want her to know I'll be easy to get...for her." He opened the buttons on his shirt, intending to head for his bedroom.

"But you just met this girl," Beau protested.

Colton ignored his brother and made his way down the hall to his room as quietly as possible, hoping not to awaken anyone. He managed to strip out of his clothes and take a quick shower but decided to raid the refrigerator before climbing into bed. He pulled on his denims again and walked barefoot down the hall.

He turned on the light in the kitchen and was surprised when his dad joined him.

"Late night for you," Big Jim commented.

Colt shook his head, grinning. "Dancing at the Eagles Hall."

Big Jim slouched in the doorway, leaning against the frame. "Anyone special catch your eye?"

Colt narrowed his gaze. "And Little Brother has been shooting off his mouth, hasn't he?"

Big Jim snorted. "A little bird did happen to mention that you were dancing with one particular young lady."

"Guilty. A very pretty one at that." Colt reached in the refrigerator for a package of sliced turkey and the jar of mayonnaise. He opened the bread and took out four slices, laying them out on a plate.

"The Dalton girl?" Big Jim's forehead furrowed as he arched a brow. "She's a little young, don't you think?"

"I'm a few years older, but I don't think that's much of a difference."

Big Jim pushed away from the doorframe, standing with his feet as wide apart as his wide shoulders. He shoved his hands in the pockets of his Wranglers. His mouth was set firmly as though he was holding back on something.

Colton regarded his father, steeling himself for resistance. "Actually, I'm thinking she's just right for me. At least, everything about her seems that way to me." He recalled how perfectly their bodies had fit together and how sweet her lips had tasted. Swallowing hard, he slathered mayonnaise on all the bread and began dealing out slices of smoked turkey. "Do you have a problem with the Daltons, Dad?"

"Just be careful. I heard they were having some trouble financially. That girl might be looking at you to bail them out...you know, baiting the hook."

Colton felt his jaw tighten but tried to maintain an easy inflection to his voice. "She said they were having trouble. Her dad is sick…dying, in fact." He glanced at Big Jim and saw him flinch.

"I didn't know that. Sorry. What's going to happen to the kids when he passes?"

"Don't know. We didn't discuss it, but Misty is taking care of her father, and she seems to be taking care of her brothers as well."

Big Jim frowned. "That's a big load for someone so young."

Colton filled a tall glass with cold milk and returned the jug to the refrigerator. "You're right. She turned twenty-two this past week and didn't even tell her dad it was her birthday because she didn't want to upset him. I think she's a pretty special person."

Big Jim stood in the doorway, his face grim. "Sad."

Colton took his plate and glass to the table and seated himself. "Take a seat, Dad. If you have a lecture for me, we might as well be comfortable."

Big Jim stepped away from the doorway. "I didn't say I was going to lecture you." He pulled out a chair and settled his big frame in it, resting his forearms on the table. "I'm just concerned, that's all. I don't want you to get involved with the wrong kind of girl, Son."

"You haven't even met her." Colt leveled a questioning gaze at his father. "I think even you would be impressed."

Big Jim scowled. "I take it you intend to see this young lady again."

Colton nodded, stuffing a bite of sandwich in his mouth. He chewed and swallowed, eyeing his father. "If Mr. Dalton is doing well tomorrow, I'm going to take her to dinner. If not…" He shrugged. "There will definitely be another time."

Chapter 4

MISTY WOKE UP EARLY THE NEXT MORNING, BUT SHE felt she had been in bed too long. She jerked fully awake, and her feet hit the floor. She had pulled on her clothes after Colton left and now tidied the bed to erase all signs of their lovemaking. She couldn't erase the smile on her face and the lightness in her heart.

Hurrying into the main house, she rushed to her father's room. Quietly, she opened the door, relieved to see he was still asleep, a peaceful expression on his face.

She smiled, glad he was resting comfortably.

In the kitchen, she filled the teakettle with water and set it on the gas range to heat. Considering their meager stores of food, she opted to make oatmeal for her father's breakfast. She arranged a tea bag in his favorite mug and poured steaming-hot water over it. Stirring the oatmeal, she wished she had some fresh fruit to go with it, but settled for a few spoonfuls of brown sugar. She added another for good measure since her father's medication seemed to have affected his taste buds. "More is better," she whispered.

Misty added buttered toast and a jar of strawberry preserves to the tray and headed for her father's room. "Good morning, Dad," she called out.

There was an answering stir of the covers, and Arnold Dalton raised his head from the pillow. "Ah, there's my sunshine." His voice was weak and gravelly.

"Let me help you sit up." Misty set the tray on the nightstand and arranged the pillows behind him. She set the tray over him and tucked a paper towel in the neck of his pajamas. "Here's some honey for your tea, Daddy." She nudged a squirt bottle shaped like a bear toward him.

"It looks wonderful. Thanks, my darling." Arnold's face was sallow, but he managed a brief smile and a pat on her hand.

"Dad, we sold the horses at the auction yesterday. Do you remember?"

He looked puzzled for a moment but then nodded. "Yes, I remember."

"I'm going to deposit the check today, so I need you to sign it." She offered the check and a pen, which he took with a shaky hand.

"What does it say?" He indicated the words she had written on the back.

"I wrote 'for deposit only' and the account number… just in case it got…lost."

Arnold gave her a puzzled glance, then shrugged and signed it.

A wave of relief washed over her as she folded the check. Now, if she could get to the bank before it closed that afternoon, all would be well. She lifted the spoon and offered some oatmeal to her father. "Eat up, Daddy. You need your strength."

※

Big Jim Garrett hadn't slept well. He was concerned for his oldest son, Colton. Always the serious one, it wasn't at all like Colt to lose his head over a girl, especially one from the Dalton family.

He had known Arnold Dalton forever, it seemed. There was nothing remarkable about the man that he could bring to mind.

Arnold had never been particularly successful, but he had somehow managed to marry and produce three children while keeping his ranch in the black. Lately, however, things had been different. When his wife died, Arnold had sought solace in the bottle. He probably hadn't drawn a sober breath in years.

Big Jim heaved a sigh, remembering the pain when his own beloved wife had passed away. Tore the heart right out of the man, but he had responsibilities…three sons and a sprawling ranch to see to. He had dug in and eased his sorrow with hard work and devotion to the boys.

The result of all his hard work was that he had raised the three boys to manhood and had amassed even more land and cattle. Three fine sons…

And now the oldest was apparently smitten with the little Dalton girl. *Not acceptable.*

Big Jim had heard that the Dalton ranch was now heavily mortgaged and that the family was on the verge of losing its land.

As a rancher, Big Jim was always interested in acquiring more land. He had his own sons to provide for, and to his way of thinking, land was always the best investment. The boys would be coming into their own soon, and giving them their share of the Garrett ranching enterprise had always been his intention.

Of course, Tyler had his music career and a lovely new bride. Big Jim heaved a sigh. Although Ty had never expressed any thoughts of moving away from the land, there had been a time Big Jim thought he had lost his middle son for good. Fortunately, the rift between father and son had been healed with no permanent damage, and he knew he owed a big debt of gratitude to his lovely daughter-in-law, Leah. Now, Ty might not always be present to take on the day-to-day tasks involved in running the ranch, but he would help out when he was home. And Ty was building a house for his new family right there on the ranch. Yes, the boy had his head on straight and would always be a part of the land.

Big Jim's youngest offspring, Beau, had graduated from Texas Tech University in Lubbock with a degree in land management. He had never expressed any thoughts other than to be a part of the Garrett ranching enterprise.

Nor, for that matter, had Colton. Big Jim felt his oldest son was strong and steady. He was born and bred to be a rancher, and this land was what he knew like the back of his hand. Big Jim had no worries there...but he was concerned that Colt might not make a wise decision when it came to the fairer sex.

Colt had never been girl crazy. He had spent his school days as a leader, both scholastically and athletically. There had been girls, of course, but they were the popular girls. The class leaders. Girls from the best, most affluent families in the area. Colt hadn't been serious about any of them. Like Ty and Beau, he had also graduated from Texas Tech and dated his fair share of girls while there, but he had never brought anyone home.

Big Jim couldn't put his finger on why he was so troubled, but when Beau told him that Colt was acting uncharacteristically smitten, it had stirred a core of parental concern. He thought Colt was overdue in the romance department. If he was just going to have a fling, that would be okay, but somehow, Big Jim felt this Dalton girl had struck a chord. Somehow she had come to mean a lot to his son, and he wasn't sure this was a good thing.

Just the little rumblings he had heard about the Daltons and their current state of affairs had him worried. Maybe he could find a way to intervene.

"Where is it?" Joe demanded.

"What are you talking about?" Misty gazed at her brother, though she had a pretty good idea what he was after.

"The check. I know you have it, so hand it over." He glared at her, his hand extended as though to receive the object of his desires.

"Too late," she said. "While you were sleeping it off, I drove into town and deposited the check. You need to just chill and realize we have to be very careful with that money."

"You little bitch!" Joe screamed at her. "I need that money." He hit her with the back of his hand, sending her careening into the coffee table.

She fell on it, hard, causing it to collapse. Misty sucked in a breath and blew it out through her clenched teeth. Glaring up at him, her cheek throbbed and her hip ached from the collision with the coffee table.

"What's going on out here?" The hospice nurse stepped out of Arnold's room and into the hallway. She frowned at the scene before her. "You two stop right now. Don't upset Mr. Dalton. He's not feeling well to begin with."

Joe's jaw twitched as he huffed out a snort. "You better find a way to get me that money. My life depends on it." He shot one last hate-filled glare at Misty and stomped out of the house.

"Are you all right, Miss?" the nurse called.

Misty swallowed and picked herself up off the floor. "I—I'm okay." Her hands were shaking as she raked her fingers through her hair. At least Mark wasn't around to witness Joe being an ass.

She was glad she'd picked her baby brother up at the Tates' house when she had gone to the bank, but he was engrossed in playing a video game in his room and had his headphones on.

She heard Joe slam the door of the pickup and rev the motor. He tore out, the tires squealing.

Good. Just get away from me. She was angry over his outburst. Everything always had to be about him. She couldn't believe he'd said his life depended on getting his hands on the proceeds from the sale of the horses. *Such drama.* She wondered briefly what he planned to spend the money on. He apparently didn't remember why they had decided to sell off the stock.

She rubbed her hip, which still smarted from colliding with the coffee table. *That's going to make a bruise.*

Now, she just had to hope her father was having a good enough day so she might be able to spend the evening with Colton Garrett. Maybe it was Misty's turn to think of herself.

She went into the kitchen and made a list of basic groceries they were out of. Since Joe had taken the truck, there was no way to go into town to shop, but at least she would have a list. Worried about her father, she decided to make something to feed his sweet tooth. She found a can of peaches and put together a pie plate with the peaches on the bottom and a topping of oatmeal mixed with a little flour, butter, sugar, and cinnamon. She set this in the oven, wishing she had a carton of ice cream. This might keep a little weight on her dad.

"What are you making?" Mark asked. He had come into the kitchen with his headphones around his neck. "Whatever it is smells awesome."

"Sort of a peach cobbler. I hope it turns out to be edible," she said, ruffling his hair. "Are you feeling better about the horses being sold?"

Mark shrugged but managed a grin. "At least we know they will be taken care of over at the Garretts' place. And I can ride the school bus over there to see Sam. Colton said he would give me some chores to do and pay me for them too." He seemed proud of himself, which was an about-face from the sadness that had kept him so depressed.

"That's wonderful." Misty felt the ache of tears in her throat. "I'm sure you'll do a great job for him."

Mark nodded enthusiastically. "Colton said I could buy Sam back from him whenever I wanted." He blinked and gazed up at her solemnly. "But if you need the money, I'll give it to you instead."

Misty grabbed her little brother in a fierce hug. "You are the very best brother ever. I'm pretty sure we're going to be just fine."

Colton supervised the unloading of the horses into a temporary corral. He kept an eye on the big Appaloosa stallion. *Quite a handsome fellow, aren't you?* And somehow he would have the use of Sam until young Mark earned enough to buy him back. That would be fine. He was glad to give the boy a break. Colton thought the family could use the money, one way or another.

He eyed his brother Beau speculatively. "Thanks for getting Dad all riled up about Misty. What did you tell him, anyway?"

Beau shrugged. "I only passed along what you said… that you were going to marry her."

Colton heaved out a huge sigh. "Well, remind me to repay the favor, Little Bro. I owe you one."

"Aw, Colt." Beau fisted his hands on his hips. "It's just that I've never seen you go all ape-shit crazy over any girl before. I mean, you've dated some of the most smokin'-hot females known to mankind, and now you're acting like a fool over a girl who just isn't in your league. She's got no education. No class."

Colt felt a muscle twitch in his jaw. "I'm going to forget you said that, because if I think about it I might get angry." He huffed out a sigh. "And for your information, Misty earned a full-ride scholarship to Oklahoma State…she dropped out when her dad got sick."

"Sorry." Beau shook his head. "Okay, I'm shutting up. You do what you want, but I'm telling you, I think you're making a big mistake here."

"And you think I'm going to take dating advice from my baby brother? The one who still hides girly magazines under his bed? I think not." Colton stomped over to secure the corral after the last horse was unloaded.

Six horses were milling around in the enclosure. The big Appaloosa was clearly the leader, whinnying and nickering to show his uneasiness over the situation. He rushed around the makeshift corral with the females and the gelding following in his wake.

"It's okay, big fellow," Colton said. "I know how you feel, but don't you worry. Your friend is going to be here after school on Monday, and he'll help you adjust." He spoke in a soothing voice, hoping to calm the horse. "In the meantime, let's get to know each other."

Sam paused, arching his neck to gaze at Colton with intelligent eyes.

Oh, yeah. This horse is a proud one. He'll definitely be a good ride.

Colt let the new horses settle down within the confines of the temporary corral and got to his other customary chores. His thoughts were mulling over a wealth of new considerations.

He thought about the land his father had apportioned for his middle brother Tyler to build his new house and wondered where, on this sprawling ranch, *he* would choose to build. He was certain Big Jim would allow him the same courtesy. A home of his own within the compound.

Colt thought about a place where he had always liked to fish. A section of land where the creek curved around in an arc. Good to have close access to water. Good to have a handy place to fish. Yes, he could see building a cabin there…with a big deck. Maybe plant a few fruit trees.

He realized he was smiling, and he realized it was because he was picturing Misty there. He heaved a sigh. Not a good thing when he had known the girl such a short time. Maybe Beau was right. Maybe he was rushing things. Maybe he should just relax and let things play out a bit.

He went to feed the calves while giving himself a good, sensible talking-to.

———

When Misty called Colton, she could hardly draw a breath. She felt tongue-tied and shy.

"Hello." The voice on the other end of the line sounded big and busy and slightly out of breath.

"Oh…Colton?"

"Misty?" Suddenly the voice changed. She could hear the smile and picture his handsome face.

"Yes, it's me." She paused, a warm feeling spreading through her chest as though he was right there with her. "I, uh…my dad is feeling better, and the hospice lady said he should be fine tonight."

"Great! I was hoping you would be able to keep our date this evening."

"Date," she repeated, thinking of the lame boys she had dated in the past. This thing with Colton was nothing that she had experienced before. Since she had come home to care for her father, she had been dateless. She sucked in a breath and let it out. "Yes, I'll be able to go on a date. Rosa will be here with Dad and should be able to help him with anything he might need."

"That's great news. I'll pick you up at about six, if that's okay. We could take in a movie after dinner, if you want."

"That would be nice. I haven't seen a film in a theater in a long time."

"I have no idea what's showing at the movie theater." He paused for a few seconds. "I hope it will be something you like."

"I'm sure I'll like it." She couldn't tell him that she would enjoy anything as long as she was with him. "I—I wanted to tell you how much I appreciate you for being so kind to Mark. You know he's crazy about Sam."

"He's a great kid. He's going to be here after school to start his work with the horses."

Misty felt a tightness in her chest. "Oh, Colt. You have no idea how much that means to him...to me."

"It's no big deal. He can give me some real help. See you later."

When the call ended, she stood for a time, holding her phone with both hands. The warm feeling Colton engendered stayed with her for some time.

That evening, she fed her father and spent more than a little time getting ready. She didn't want to overdo it. Above all, she didn't want to appear as needy as, in fact, she was feeling.

By the time six o'clock rolled around, she was a basket case. She had changed clothes several times, had put her hair up and taken it back down, and was now peeking out the front drapes to see if the big silver truck was approaching the house.

As it happened, she stepped out back to see if Joe was going to be staying at the ranch that evening.

"So you're going on a date with one of the Garretts?" Joe said. "Well, don't let it go to your little head. You're nothing to him. Just a pretty piece of ass, so don't go thinking it means anything at all. You don't want to get knocked up and then think you got it made. You ain't near good enough for a Garrett." He turned away, angry. "We don't mean nothin' to folks like that."

Hurt, Misty went back inside. She supposed the

Garretts were a cut above the other ranchers in the area. There were a few other big ranches, and they were owned by families who had held them for generations. She glanced at herself in the mirror and straightened her shoulders. *I may not be from a wealthy family, but I am worth something.*

That was when Colton and Mark arrived.

"Hey, Misty," Mark called as he came through the door with Colton on his heels. "I had the best time at Colton's place. You should see it."

She gave a smile in return, but it faltered, Joe's words echoing in her head. Pressing her lips together, she sucked in a breath and started again. "Glad to hear it. Your dinner's on the stove, so help yourself when you're ready."

Colton was standing just inside the door, his Stetson in hand. He somehow seemed to dwarf everything in the room. "Hey, Misty. You sure do look pretty tonight." He looked so earnest she couldn't believe he was being untruthful.

"Thanks, Colton. I'm ready." She reached for her jacket and approached him.

"I'm really glad you could make it." His deep voice wrapped around her like an embrace.

Misty felt as though a feather pillow had exploded in her chest. "Me too."

He held the door open for her and walked her to his truck, handing her up before taking his place behind the wheel. "Are you still up for the steak house, or is there some other restaurant you prefer?"

"No, that's fine."

To tell the truth, she had never eaten at the steak house, so this would be a treat on more than one level.

Colton made small talk about Mark and the horses.

"It was really nice of you to give him a job to do. He was so miserable about Sam being sold. Thank you for saving Sam and being so kind to my little brother."

Colton shrugged. "Not a big deal. I was a boy once and just as horse crazy. I know how he feels."

"But no one ever sold your horse out from under you, did they?"

He shot a glance at her. "Uh, no. That didn't happen to me, but I can understand how he feels. Just glad for the help. He's a really good kid."

She watched the road ahead, thinking she had made the drive into Langston a zillion times yet this felt like the first time in so many ways.

Colton reached over to gather her hand in his. He lifted it to his lips and pressed a kiss to her fingers. It felt good.

She gazed at him, and he turned to meet her eyes. Swallowing hard, she tried to clear away the image of Joe telling her she wasn't good enough for a Garrett. *Maybe not, but Colton doesn't seem to think so.*

When they reached the steak house, she saw that quite a crowd had gathered. Colton tucked her hand in the crook of his arm and strolled right inside. There were people standing near the front door, waiting to be seated, but Colt led Misty to the hostess stand.

"Garrett," he said. "We have a reservation."

The hostess glanced at Misty and gathered two menus. "Right this way, Mr. Garrett. Your table is ready."

He indicated Misty was to follow the hostess, and he fell into step behind her.

Misty tried not to blush when heads turned to stare at them.

Colt raised his hand to wave to several people who greeted him. He didn't seem to be ashamed to be seen in the company of a girl from a poor family.

Colt held out the chair for her and seated himself next to her at the table. The waitress passed the menus and left.

"How do you like your steak, Misty?" Colt said.

She smiled. She had no idea how she liked her steak because most of her beef came in the form of hamburger or stewing beef. "Perfect."

A wide grin split his face. "Me too. How about a rib eye?"

She nodded. "Sure."

"A little salad? A baked potato?"

"Sure," she repeated.

He gathered her menu and laid it aside with his. "Glad that's settled."

When the waitress came with water, Colt placed their order.

Misty took a sip of water, glancing around the restaurant. There were a few people she knew, or recognized at least. There were people she had gone to church with and a couple of people she had known in school, but for the most part, they were strangers. She wondered why it felt as though everyone was staring at her and Colton.

"Is something wrong?" he asked.

"No, I just…" She took a deep breath and blew it out. "Why are people staring?"

He smiled and stroked her cheek. "Probably because you're so beautiful. I know I can't take my eyes off you."

She wasn't accustomed to receiving compliments or, for that matter, affection from a man, especially in public. But Colt seemed to feel comfortable expressing himself in front of friends and neighbors.

When their meal was served, Misty inhaled the aroma of the perfectly grilled steak. She watched Colton and took her dining cues from him.

After their meal, she pulled out her cell to call her home. She spoke with Rosa, who reported that her father had watched television and fallen asleep after she had given him his nightly medication. Mark was doing homework in his room. She hung up and returned the phone to her small handbag. "Everything is going well at home. My dad is asleep."

"Does that mean we can go to the show?" Colton asked.

She nodded. "I'd like that."

He took her to the only movie theater in town, and they watched a film, eating popcorn from the same container. Colton kept his arm around her shoulders. Somehow she felt as though there were only the two of them in the theater.

When they walked out, she was still feeling close to Colton. He helped her into the truck and drove out of town toward the Dalton ranch. Actually, in the direction of the Garrett ranch as well.

Colton drove, holding her hand. The moonlight spilled over the long, straight highway, lighting it up like an arrow in the darkness. The headlights were on bright because of the infrequency of oncoming traffic. Folks in these parts generally turned in early, even on a Saturday night.

Off to one side of the road, Misty saw something that drew her attention.

"What's that up ahead?" Colton asked. He pointed to a cluster of flashing lights to the left side of the highway.

He slowed the truck, easing up to the scene. "Accident," he pronounced, pulling to a stop. He lowered the window as a state trooper approached. "What happened, Officer?"

Misty sat up and leaned forward, peering through the windshield. "Oh no! That's Joe's truck!" Her chest tightened as though in a vise. She couldn't draw a breath.

Colt pulled the truck to the side of the road and shut off the motor. He opened the door and jumped from the vehicle. Turning around, he held out his arms to Misty and she leaped into them as he swung her to the ground. "C'mon," he said, grasping her hand. They ran toward the overturned truck.

Once they were closer, Colton stopped short. "Wait here. Let me see what's going on."

Misty's legs felt like jelly, but she managed to stay on her feet and watched as Colt ran toward the wrecked truck. She sucked in a shaky breath and slowly followed behind him.

He was talking to one of the troopers when she caught up to him. The trooper turned to Colton with a grimace. "He's gone."

"What? Where did he go?" Misty demanded. "Oh, my daddy is going to be so upset with him for wrecking the truck."

Colton caught her by the shoulder and pulled her close. He addressed the state trooper. "What is it you're saying?"

"The young man driving...you knew him?" the trooper asked.

"Yes, Joe Dalton. This is his sister."

The trooper's jaw twitched. "Miss Dalton, I'm sorry to inform you that your brother didn't make it. The ambulance took his remains to the county morgue."

Misty covered her mouth with both hands. *It couldn't be. Not Joe.* She felt her knees give way, but Colton was lifting her...carrying her in his arms.

Colt swallowed. "How did it happen? Was there another vehicle involved?"

The trooper settled his fists against his waist and frowned. "Yes and no. There was no impact, but it appears this driver was shot from another moving vehicle. It was a head wound. He died instantly, and the truck spun off the road through the fence over there and came to a rest on its side here." He pointed to the place the fence was broken and showed where the truck ended up. "We're treating this as a homicide."

Misty was shaking. "Oh no. Oh no. This will kill my father."

Chapter 5

COLTON HELD HER TIGHT. HE WAS AT A LOSS. THE LAST thing he expected when Joe Dalton went stomping out of the Eagles Hall the night before was that he would be killed, but that was apparently what had happened.

Misty wept against his chest, her arms around his neck. Her softness bespoke her vulnerability, and the sobs that racked her body, her heartbreak.

Colt tried to comfort her but felt totally inadequate. How does one deal with the loss of a brother? He thought about his disagreement with Beau that morning. How would he feel if one of his brothers had been killed? Beau and Tyler were every bit as precious to him as Misty's brothers were to her.

"I'm going to take her home," he said to the trooper.

"Wait! How can we get in touch with you?" The trooper took out a notebook and wrote down Misty's name and phone number as well as the number to the Garrett ranch.

Colton carried Misty in his arms back to his truck and carefully lifted her inside. He fastened the seat belt around her with a grim expression on his face.

They rode in silence to the Dalton ranch. When he pulled up in front of the house, it was dark. An outside light came on, but Misty sat beside Colt as though frozen in place.

"I don't know how I'm going to tell Dad," she said.

"I'll go in with you," Colt said as he opened the door

and got out. He turned to offer his hand, and she took it hesitantly.

She stepped out, and he kissed her hand. "I'm here with you."

Nodding, she took a few steps toward the house, but the screen opened and a small Hispanic couple was framed in the doorway.

"Miss Misty," the lady said. "Your brother..."

Misty pressed her lips together and nodded.

"Yes, we know," Colton said.

"And your father," the lady continued. "The ambulance come to take him to the hospital in Amarillo. He got very bad after the sheriff tell him about young Joe."

"Oh, my poor daddy." Misty's voice came out as a whisper. "I should be with him."

Colt reached out to stroke her hair. "I can take you to Amarillo, if that's what you want."

She gazed up at him with an expression that clutched at his heart. "You would do that for me?"

He shrugged, feeling uncomfortable. "Of course. That's what friends are for. Why don't you pack a bag in case you need to stay with him overnight?"

"Thank you. Thank you so much," she said. "You don't know how much this means to me. I'll be right back." She hurried inside.

Colt stared after her, wishing he was capable of alleviating her pain. The Hispanic couple stayed by the door, staring out at him.

In a few minutes, Misty returned, giving directions to the couple and telling them that if she didn't return before morning, Mark should call her cell phone when he woke up.

Colt helped her back into the truck and stowed her backpack on the back seat. He started up the truck again and headed for Amarillo.

———

Misty felt totally numb. She knew she should be feeling something, but as she rode along in Colton's truck, she felt as though someone had flipped a switch and turned her to the off position.

She couldn't think. She couldn't react. She couldn't cry. Joe was dead. *Killed.*

All she could remember was that he had told her he was in trouble and she had thought he was grandstanding. The last words he'd said to her reverberated through her head.

"You better find a way to get me that money. My life depends on it." And then Joe had walked away from her, angry.

Had there been some truth to his words? Had his life really depended on getting his hands on the money from the sale of the horses?

As the truck sliced through the darkness toward Amarillo, Misty felt as if she were wrapped in a cocoon of sorts. Not forced to deal with reality. Not fully alive.

But, all too soon, the flash of city lights jarred her from her trance.

Colton was pulling in at the emergency entrance to the hospital. He found a parking place and guided her from the truck. "Come on, Misty. Let's find out how your father is doing."

Once inside, there were a lot of people milling around. It was Saturday night in a fair-sized city, so the ER was busy.

At the information desk, Colton asked about her father, and they were told that Mr. Arnold Dalton was being seen by the doctors.

"Can she go back to see him? His son died tonight in an…accident. I'm sure it would mean a lot to him for his daughter to be with him."

The clerk said he would let them know if this would be allowed, and he picked up the telephone, punching in a sequence of numbers.

Colt slipped his arm around her.

"Oh, Colt, I don't know what I would have done without you. I can't even think what I should be doing."

"You've got to be in shock," he said. "This has been a lot for you to process."

Misty nodded, leaning against him. "It has, but I want you to know I appreciate what you're doing. I'm sure my father will want to thank you for your kindness too."

He shook his head, rocking her in his arms. "Not necessary." He looked up, and Misty followed his gaze.

A doctor came out through the automatic doors and strode purposefully toward them. He looped his stethoscope around his neck.

"Are you Miss Dalton?" the doctor asked.

Misty nodded.

"Come this way, please." He gestured to the doors he had just passed through.

Misty looked at Colton, who hung back as though waiting to be asked. She reached toward him, and he fell into step beside her.

The doctor walked rapidly, and she had to hurry to keep up. They were in a corridor that opened into a large, sterile-smelling room with a number of green-curtained cubicles. He pulled one curtain aside and gestured for them to enter.

Misty's heart contracted as she saw her father propped up on the narrow bed.

He seemed to have shrunk, and his color was ashen. "Misty," he croaked, reaching a hand toward her.

She rushed to his side. "Yes, Daddy. I'm here."

He pushed the oxygen mask aside. "Did you hear?" he asked, his voice thick. "Joe…"

She grabbed his hand and held it to her cheek. "Yes, Daddy. I know."

"There's so much to tell you…" His gaze strayed to where Colton was standing.

"It's okay," she said. "Colton is my friend."

Arnold Dalton's gaze returned to her. "The land… the banker said someone was willing to buy it…before we lose it to foreclosure. I think it might be a large holding company or maybe one of the big local ranchers. They're always trying to swallow up the small holdings." He was seized with a racking cough.

A nurse threw open the curtain and replaced the oxygen mask over his face. She adjusted some of the equipment, cast a sorrowful glance at Misty, and left.

"Daddy, hang on," Misty begged.

He patted her hand. "Honey, I'm done for. I'm sorry I let you and Mark down. I thought Joe would be there to take care of you, but now…"

She swallowed and attempted a bright smile. "We'll be okay. Don't you worry about us. Mark and I will be just fine."

"My sweet girl. Try to sell off the cattle and the

equipment fast. Only the land is mortgaged. Get that lawyer feller to help you. Ryan is pretty smart."

She nodded.

Just then some piece of equipment began to ding, and the nurse returned, followed by the doctor who had brought them here.

"I'm sorry," the doctor said. "But you two will have to step out."

Misty leaned over to place a gentle kiss on his cheek. "I love you, Daddy."

The doctor held the curtain for them to walk through and then closed it abruptly. Another nurse rushed in, and she could hear a flurry of activity going on behind the curtain.

Colton put his arm around her and pulled her against his chest. He leaned against the wall across from the cubicle where her father lay and comforted her by holding her with both arms when she felt she might have fallen to the floor in a heap.

After what seemed like an eternity, the machines went quiet, and activity ceased behind the curtain. One nurse stepped out, glanced at her, and then departed, followed by the second nurse.

Finally, the doctor came from behind the curtain. He looked tired. Looping his stethoscope around his neck, he walked toward the place where she stood with Colton.

"I regret to inform you that your father passed away a few minutes ago. His heart stopped, and since he was terminally ill, he had a 'do not resuscitate' order in place. Our hands were tied."

Tears poured from her eyes. She was shaking. How could this happen? How could she lose her older brother and her father on the same night?

—w—

Colton tried to console her. It was unthinkable that Misty and her younger brother had been dealt a double tragedy.

Now, she would be alone on the Dalton ranch with only the elderly couple and her twelve-year-old brother. *Unthinkable*.

The doctor escorted them back to the cubicle so Misty could have a moment to say goodbye to her father.

Colton stepped aside, trying to allow her some privacy.

Mr. Dalton looked as though he was sleeping and didn't appear to have been in distress when he passed, although he must have been.

Misty wept silently, her shoulders bowed and shaking. Her queenly posture was bent to her grief.

An attendant in scrubs, carrying a clipboard, entered the cubicle. "Pardon me, Miss. Have you made arrangements for your father?"

Misty raised her tear-ravaged face to stare at him.

"We'll take care of that." Colton stepped forward and offered his phone number. "I'll call when we have a decision."

He gathered Misty by the shoulders and led her out through the automatic doors, through the teeming ER waiting room and into the night. Once in the truck, he headed back toward their homes. "I'm going to take you to the Garrett ranch tonight. We can stop and pick up Mark. I don't want the two of you to be alone."

"Thank you." She raised her red-rimmed eyes to meet his gaze. "I—I don't know. I think there are some arrangements for my father. The—the hospice service knows."

He nodded, reaching to take her hand. "Don't worry. You need some rest. We'll figure this all out tomorrow."

When he pulled up to the Dalton house, the sky was growing lighter in the east. He left Misty sitting in the truck and went inside to gather Mark and a couple of changes of clothing. He didn't tell the boy the reason for the impromptu sleepover, but helped him into the truck beside his sister.

"What's going on?" Mark asked when he got a look at Misty's face.

"Oh, Mark. Daddy's dead…and so is Joe," she wailed.

Mark looked stunned, as though he had been dealt a hard physical blow. "Dead? You mean, like…dead?"

Colton started the truck and pulled out. "Joe was in an accident, and your father's heart gave out. I'm sorry."

Misty curled her arms around her younger brother. She pulled him against her shoulder and leaned her cheek atop his. "I'm so sorry. We have no one else. Just each other now."

Colton wanted to tell her she was wrong…that he was there for her and for Mark, but he knew he should just keep quiet. This was not the time for his declaration of love.

Mark raised his head, his expression stunned. "Don't worry. I'll get a job. I'll take care of you."

She stroked his cheek, but he continued to gaze at her in bewilderment.

Colton cleared his throat. "I want the two of you to stay at the Garrett ranch until we can get things sorted out."

He drove home as quickly as he could. They passed the scene where the Dalton truck had lain on its side, but it had apparently been hauled away. Only the place where Joe had ripped through the fence and his tire tracks were evidence to mark the site of his death.

Colton turned in at the big horseshoe-shaped gate, drove the circuitous drive, and pulled up to the Garrett ranch house. Shepherding Misty and Mark inside, he found his father had risen early. Big Jim was making coffee in the kitchen when Colton passed by. Their eyes met briefly, Big Jim's expression questioning and Colton's closed-up.

He deposited Misty in a guest room and showed Mark to another. "Get some rest," he said. "We'll figure things out when you wake up."

When he joined his father back in the kitchen, he could see Big Jim looked somewhat irritable. Colt held his hands up as though to ward off the oncoming storm. "Hold on, Dad. These two lost their father tonight as well as their older brother."

Big Jim's expression changed to one of concern. "Damnation! What happened?"

Colton shook his head. "I was taking Misty home, and we saw her brother's truck turned over, and the state troopers were there. I thought he must have had an accident, but the trooper said he'd been shot dead." He paused to let this sink in.

"Shot? Are you saying he was murdered?" Big Jim's brows drew together.

"Looks like it. And then when we got to the Dalton place, her father had been taken to Amarillo to the hospital. He was on hospice, and he couldn't take the news of Joe's death. Shortly after we reached the hospital, Mr. Dalton passed on." He blew out a deep breath. "At least she got to tell him goodbye."

Big Jim reached out a hand and gave Colton's shoulder a squeeze. "Tough situation, son. I can see why you brought the Dalton kids home with you. Do they have any other family who can take them in?"

"I have no idea. Let them rest, and we'll try to sort this out later."

"Speaking of rest…it looks like you could use some." Big Jim took a sip of his coffee. "Why don't you go catch some sleep? I'll wake you when the Dalton kids start stirring."

Colton stifled a yawn. "Good idea. I have to call the hospital back to let them know what to do with Mr. Dalton's body. Misty said some kind of arrangements had been made through the hospice service, but it's too early to call."

Colton headed to his room, treading as quietly as he could and unbuttoning his shirt as he went. Once inside, he walked out of his clothes and fell across his bed. Sleep overtook him in a matter of seconds.

———

Leah Garrett woke up without the alarm. She awakened her daughter, Gracie, and got her started getting dressed for church.

While Gracie pulled on the clothes that had been laid out for her the night before, Leah went to the kitchen and started breakfast. "Good Sunday morning, Mr. G," she sang out. "Looks like it will be a lovely day."

"Morning," he said. "But I don't think anything much is good about it."

She gave him a questioning look. "And why not? I was planning on having an excellent morning myself."

She flashed a big grin to try to coax her father-in-law out of his mood.

"We have houseguests," Big Jim stated flatly, his voice deep and morose.

"Oh? Well, that's good, I guess. Anyone I know?"

"Some people Colt knows. Their father and brother died last night, so Colton brought them home like a couple of stray puppies."

She glanced at him to see if he was kidding, and indeed he was not. Someone had died, and someone was here under Big Jim's roof, and he wasn't at all happy about it.

Her grandmother, Fern Davis, came into the kitchen. She was dressed for church and placed her handbag on the countertop. "Good morning, folks. What's this about puppies? I really love puppies." She hoisted herself onto a stool and looked at Leah expectantly. "I hope there's a cup of coffee left."

"Sure is, Gran." She placed a cup on the counter in front of her grandmother, filled it a little over half full, and nudged the coffee creamer close to her elbow. "I'll have breakfast ready in a bit. It seems Colton brought some people home last night."

"Here you go, Miz Fern." Big Jim offered the sugar bowl. "You may know the family...Dalton?"

Fern stirred her coffee thoughtfully. "Well, 'course I know old Arnold Dalton. Knew his wife too." She took a sip of coffee and set it back on the counter. "You say some Daltons is here?"

Big Jim nodded. "The two youngest Daltons are with us." His voice was grim.

"That girl is a real beauty, but the older boy is a piece of work."

"Gran! Don't say things like that." Leah frowned.

Fern turned to her granddaughter, a question on her face.

Leah folded her arms over her chest and leaned her hip against the counter. "Big Jim was just telling me that these young people sustained a tragedy last night."

Big Jim gripped his mug with both hands. "Yes, it seems that Arnold passed away last night. He was on hospice, according to Colton."

Fern looked stricken. "Oh, that's too bad. Oh my… those poor children."

"And the older son was killed on the highway." Big Jim's mouth thinned to a grim line as he regarded his coffee.

"And so Colton brought the two younger ones here?" Fern's brows rose as she peered at him through her glasses.

"Yes, ma'am. They're here."

"Well, that's mighty sweet of Colton. He's got a good heart."

Big Jim huffed out a sigh. "Yes, I suppose he does."

Fern's mouth formed an O as though something had dawned on her. "I can always go back to my little house if you need my room."

Big Jim raised his big paw to stave off her offer. "Don't even think of it. We have plenty of rooms here. My wife insisted we have enough for all our family to come visit." A sad look settled on his face.

Leah considered what she might be able to do to ease the situation and decided a good, hot breakfast would be her contribution. She laid strips of bacon on baking pans and set them in the oven to bake nice and slow.

She returned to Gracie's room and helped her with her hair and then brought her to the kitchen, where she made eggs and toast to serve with the bacon. She fed Gracie, Gran, Big Jim, Beau, and herself, but it didn't look as though anyone else was going to emerge right away.

Colton and his guests were sleeping in.

Leah helped Gracie wash her face and hands and then returned to the kitchen in time to hear Big Jim and Beau discussing the two Daltons who were sleeping under their roof.

"I can't believe Joe's dead," Beau said. "We saw him at the Eagles Hall on Friday night. He was being as big a horse's ass as ever." He shook his head. "And now he's dead?"

"Murdered," Big Jim pronounced. "And Colt brought the two Dalton kids here."

"It's a bad business," Beau said. "I hope Colt doesn't get too attached. The girl is gorgeous, but the whole family is bad news."

Leah went to collect the dishes she and Gracie had used. "I don't know these folks, but it seems that fate has dealt them a pretty rotten hand. It wasn't too long ago I was having a run of bad luck." She turned her attention to Big Jim. "I seem to have come under your roof like a whipped puppy myself…and yet…" She paused, sucking in a breath before going on. "You have survived my company this long." She fixed a dazzling smile on her face and looked from father to son.

"Oh, that was different," Big Jim hastened to say.

"Yeah, we thought Tyler was long gone." Beau spread his hands. "We were just glad he stuck around for you 'cause he sure was hell-bent on leaving the ranch."

Leah leaned back against the counter and folded her arms across her chest. "Let me get this straight. Ty bringing me home was okay, but Colt bringing his girl-friend home isn't?"

"Umm…" Big Jim seemed to be stuck on that one.

"Well, yes and no," Beau started and then ran out of steam.

"You gentlemen just think about this for a while. We'll have to go to the late church service today. Gracie and Gran are ready. I'm going to finish getting dressed and see what I can do to help these poor unfortunates who have been placed under our care." She gave a penetrating gaze to both men. "I'm not judging here, but you might want to think about your Christian charity before you get to the church."

She left the two Garrett men silently drinking their coffee.

When Misty woke up, her head hurt and her eyes were puffy. She had no more tears. She'd wept them all out and felt drained dry. The weight of the previous night's events hit her like a semi barreling down the highway.

Joe's dead. Daddy's dead.

Now she had to figure out what to do about get-ting them both buried and then see how she was going to find enough money to support Mark for at least another six years until he would, no doubt, graduate from high school.

It had been hard enough to try to prepare for her father's death due to his illness, but she had always thought her big brother would be there to hold the family together. Now, she was heartbroken and wondering if she was strong enough to keep a roof over her baby brother's head.

She heard a tentative knock at the door. "Yes?" she called out.

"Hello, I brought you some breakfast." It was a female voice.

"Oh, thanks." Misty struggled to get up, but the door opened and a very pretty blonde woman with large brown eyes swung in with a tray.

"I'm Leah," the woman said. "I heard about your loss. I'm so very sorry." She arranged the tray over Misty's lap and stepped back, smiling at her.

Misty sighed. *This young woman must be their housekeeper or maid.* "Thank you. I still haven't processed it all. I'm Misty Dalton."

"If there's anything I can do to help, just let me know." She turned to leave and then spun back around. "Your brother is eating in the kitchen. I think the smell of bacon got to him."

Misty managed a weak smile. "That boy! Keeping him in groceries is always a chore." She pressed her lips together. Too soon, she would have to be figuring that out for herself.

Leah smiled. "I have an eight-year-old daughter. The problem with her is trying to get her to eat enough to keep a bird alive." She shrugged. "Gracie is a picky eater."

Misty looked over the tray. "This looks delicious. I haven't had an omelet since my mother died."

"I hope you like it," Leah said.

Misty took a bite, and for a moment, the heavenly

taste was all she could focus on. "Delicious. Are you the Garretts' cook?"

Leah laughed. "Among other things. I'm married to Tyler Garrett. But I try to pitch in and do whatever is needed around here."

A fierce blush crept up Misty's cheeks. "Oh, I'm sorry. I didn't mean—"

"No problem," Leah said. "I love to cook, and being a part of the Garrett family ensures there are some hungry mouths to feed." She opened the door to the hallway. "There's a bathroom across the hall. I put fresh towels in there for you."

The thought of a shower made Misty smile. "I appreciate that so much. Thank you for your kindness."

"I'll be back to check on you in a bit. Let me know how I can help you." Leah slipped out before Misty could respond.

Misty made short work of downing the omelet. She got out of bed and gathered a change of clothing before opening the door and peering both ways up and down the hallway. She scampered across the hall to the bathroom and secured the door behind her.

The bathroom was large. Everything was shining white enamel or dark mahogany. There was an old-fashioned claw-foot bathtub, but there was a white-tiled shower enclosure as well.

She thought she would enjoy soaking in the tub but opted for the quick shower instead. When she emerged, she did feel somewhat better. At least the tear-streaked face had been cleaned and her eyes were less puffy.

She dressed hurriedly and carried the breakfast tray to the kitchen. The sound of voices led her to a large and cheery kitchen. Mark was sitting beside Colton at a long eating bar.

"Are you sure you don't want more eggs?" Leah asked. "I can whip up another batch in a jiffy."

"No, ma'am. Thanks anyway." Mark relinquished his plate to Leah, who rinsed it and slid it into the dishwasher.

Leah greeted Misty with a smile and took the tray from her.

"Thanks so much," Misty said. "Everything was delicious."

Colton caught Misty with his steady gaze. She raised her hand to give him a finger wave, but he held out his arms.

Misty glanced around to see who was watching, but Leah got busy clearing things away.

An older man sat at the other end of the counter, sipping coffee.

She exhaled and went to be enfolded in Colt's arms.

He kissed her forehead. "How did you sleep?"

Misty slipped her arms around his waist and spoke with her face pressed against his chest. "I slept well. I didn't think I would, but I just passed out."

"You were exhausted." Colton drew far enough back to be able to gaze into her eyes. "Today, we need to make arrangements for your father and for Joe."

She nodded, stepping away. "I...we have a plot. Mom's buried there." Straightening, she sighed. "I need to call the hospice. Dad had made some arrangements with them. I think they take care of some things."

"Whatever you need, we're here for you." Colton glanced around, meeting Leah's gaze and then that of the silver-haired man at the end of the counter. "Misty, that's my dad, Big Jim Garrett. He got to meet Mark earlier."

Misty nodded to Big Jim. "Nice to meet you, Mr. Garrett."

Big Jim Garrett raised a hand. "Sorry it had to be under these circumstances, young lady."

"Thank you, sir." Misty pressed her lips together. "I appreciate your kindness. I just didn't know what to do last night."

Leah stepped closer. "Losing two loved ones in the same night is too much for anyone. You're welcome to be here." She reached out and patted Misty's forearm. "I've got to take Gracie and my grandmother to church now. I hope you'll join us."

Misty covered her face with her hands. "Oh, I don't think I can face the congregation yet. I feel like everything I've ever known has crumbled away."

Colton cleared his throat. "Um, not a problem. I'm going to stay home with you today. We'll go to church together next Sunday."

Relief flooded her chest. "Thank you, Colt. But I don't want you to stay home because of us. Mark and I can just be here by ourselves."

Colton stroked her cheek with his fingertips. "That's not going to happen. I'll be here with you."

When she glanced at Colton's father, he didn't look happy.

Colton showed her to a phone in an office and stayed with her while she called the hospice group. They helped her make arrangements to transfer her father's remains to a local funeral home.

"How much do funerals cost?" she asked Colton. "I was in school when my mom died. Dad and Joe took care of everything."

"That depends. They can be simple or elaborate."

Misty nodded. "This will have to be as simple as possible. I'm glad you bought the horses. I guess that money will bury my dad and Joe."

Colton made a call to the hospital in Amarillo and found out that Joe's body was at the morgue. When he tracked it down, he was told it wouldn't be released until the medical examiner had performed a complete post mortem examination. He also learned that the wrecked truck was at the crime lab being tested—for what, they didn't tell him.

Misty sat close, watching him and listening to the information he relayed to her. Her head hurt, but at least the dull pain kept her focused.

"Do you want to have one funeral for your dad and Joe together or two separate ceremonies?" Colton held her hand and stroked the back gently.

"I think one might be less expensive. Right?"

He nodded. "The pastor can hold the ceremony at church. It would cost more to have it in the funeral home. Don't worry so much. You'll get through this just fine."

She heaved a sigh. "I'm sure I will, but it's Mark I'm worried about. He's so young to have lost both his parents and an older brother." She gazed up at Colton. "I'm not sure I can give him what he needs."

Colton's brow furrowed. "Do you have any other relatives who can help you?"

Misty shook her head. "My mother was an only child, and all of my dad's people are scattered. I would have no idea where to start looking, and even if I could find them, why would they care about us? We're strangers to them."

"I guess so." Frowning, Colt drew her to him.

Just being in his embrace made her feel stronger, as though she might be able to face the trials ahead and survive.

"And I can get a job. I'm not sure what there is in Langston, but I can learn."

"I'm sure you can. What are you interested in?" Colt gazed down at her.

"I wanted to be a librarian. I didn't get to finish my degree because I had to drop out after my sophomore year and come home when Dad got sick." She shrugged. "It really killed me to give up the scholarship. I knew there really would never be any extra money for my tuition, let alone living expenses." She offered a weak excuse for a smile.

A smile spread across Colt's face. "A librarian, huh? I can see you sorting all the books. Maybe reading to the little kids."

"I would be in heaven. There have never been enough books to feed my reading habit."

He stroked her cheek. "That's nice. Maybe you can go back to school."

"Maybe, but I can't see that happening for a long time." She shrugged. "I loved Oklahoma State University in Norman. It was just wonderful. I loved living in a dorm with a bunch of other girls. We had such fun."

"I'll bet you did. You might want to look at taking some classes online. There are a lot of programs that accept remote students. Check with your Okie friends to see if the librarian degree can be finished online."

"That sounds like a great idea. I'll contact them when things get a little calmer. Right now, I just need a way to support my little brother."

She figured she could be a waitress, if she were lucky enough to find a job in Langston. But still…the thought of finishing her degree in library science put a wistful smile on her face.

Chapter 6

TYLER GARRETT WAITED FOR HIS BRIDE TO ANSWER her phone. He figured she was busy preparing breakfast for Gracie and Gran plus his dad and brothers. He wondered if his male relatives would be able to cook for themselves when he moved his girls to the new house being built for them.

He leaned back against the headboard in his hotel room. He was about to climb aboard the tour bus heading for another city, but he hoped to have a chance to talk to both Leah and Gracie. As a newlywed, he was feeling especially lonesome for his bride and newly acquired family.

He pictured Leah's sweet face, her large Bambi-like brown eyes that ensnared his heart from the first day they met. "C'mon, darlin'…pick up the phone."

"Hey, Ty!" She sounded out of breath.

"Hey, Leah. What's going on? You've been running around the house?"

"Oh, so much is going on here. Do you remember a guy named Joe Dalton? He was supposed to be in Beau's class."

Ty frowned. "Yeah. Kind of a snarky asshole."

"Well, he's a dead snarky asshole. He was murdered last night. Someone shot him in the head, and then his father, who was terminally ill, passed away. He just gave up when he lost his oldest son."

Tyler pictured the cocky young man who had grown up with Beau. "That's terrible, but why does that have you out of breath?"

He heard her expel a long breath. "Because your big brother is in love with Misty Dalton. He brought her home with her twelve-year-old brother in the wee small hours of the morning…um…we're having a little chaos around here this morning."

"Whoa!" Ty sat up straight. "Did you say that Colton Garrett is in love?"

Leah giggled. "That's what I said."

"How did that happen? I was thinking Colt was going to be an old maid."

"No, seriously, Ty. Colt just needed to meet the right girl."

"Sounds like this girl is a hot mess."

"Well, your dad and Beau sure seem to think so. Big Jim is acting like Misty is a gold digger who has set her cap for a rich man's son."

Ty considered that for a moment. "They could be right."

"Oh no! Not you too."

He could hear the disapproval in her voice. Sensing he had hit a sore spot, he quickly backed up. "Um, I mean…" He heaved a deep sigh. "Let me start over. What did my dad base his feelings on? Usually he's pretty broad-minded."

His usually super-feminine bride let out a snort. "Oh, puh-leeze. Big Jim Garrett has a skull as thick as concrete, and once he makes up his mind, it's near impossible to change it. Misty is a very sweet young woman who has suffered a terrible loss. She's very nice. You should see her with Colt. They were made for each other."

"Oh, well...I can't wait to meet her." *Now shut up*, he ordered himself.

"I can't wait for you to come home. I miss you so much."

"I miss you more. I can't wait to hold you in my arms again." He acknowledged the hollow ache in his chest. "I'll be home before you know it."

She sighed audibly. "No, you won't. But I'm so very proud of you, Ty. Don't let me hold you back. We can get through this."

"Sure we can. How's Gracie doing? Is she all ready to go to church?"

"Yes, we're about to leave. I think it will be just Gracie, Gran, and me, though. Your dad is pouting over Misty, and Beau and Colt seem to be mad at each other. It's gonna be a really fun day."

"Poor baby. Hang in there, and take care of you for me."

"Love you," she said, her voice suddenly taking on a soft tone.

"I love you more."

When Leah disconnected, he sat on the side of the bed for a while, trying to sort out the things she had said. His brow furrowed as he considered his father's opinion of the woman his older brother was in love with. Big Jim was concerned that Colton might have latched onto someone who was after a piece of the Garrett property.

He picked up his bag and turned out the lights. He couldn't recall the name of the next town they were headed for, but he trusted that the driver would get them there. He grabbed his guitar and headed down to drop off his key and board the tour bus.

—◦◦◦—

Big Jim stomped out of the house. He didn't feel comfortable in his own home with strangers there. He was confused, and he didn't like to be confused...ever.

The Dalton kids—and they were kids—were at least polite.

Big Jim saddled his favorite horse, a sorrel gelding. He figured that whatever was eating at him could be worked out on a good ride.

He hefted himself into the saddle and headed north. There was a little rise, and he wanted to climb up on something to look out over his domain.

The Dalton boy had been quiet. *Sure. Losing his father and his brother would knock the stuffing out of a boy.* Big Jim shook his head. *Sad. Very sad.* But just because a couple of kids were orphaned, that didn't mean Colton had to drag them into the Garrett household. He would have to have a talk with Colt. Yes, he would.

He rode, thinking about his son. Yes, he was proud of him. Colt had a great and generous heart, but it was easy to see he was totally smitten with the Dalton girl.

She was a lovely little thing. Slender with long, straight dark hair. And her eyes were dark as onyx. Yes, a stunner...but looks alone weren't enough to base a relationship on.

Beau was right. Colton's face betrayed how he felt about the girl... What was her name? Missy...Misty.

He had heard the Dalton ranch was hanging on by a thread. Mortgaged to the hilt because of the father's drinking and, later, his illness. Now Arnold was gone, leaving his youngest children to pay the price for his foolishness. A real man would have sacrificed a lot for his kids. Big Jim was an expert in that arena.

Big Jim had worked his whole life to make sure his family would have something of value when he was gone. The land would only increase in value as time went on. Now Tyler had brought his bride, Leah, to live at the family ranch. Ty was building a home and putting down roots here for future generations to grow and prosper.

All Big Jim had to do was ensure that his other two sons were happily married and committed to the Garrett ranch as well. And part of his duty would be to ensure both sons married loving women who weren't just looking for financial security. *No gold diggers for my boys. No way!*

Colton made arrangements with the funeral home to hold the remains of Arnold Dalton until those of Joe Dalton could be released.

The medical examiner had made his decision. Joe's death had been ruled a homicide by person or persons unknown. The bullet had been recovered and was being compared to those used in other crimes.

Joe's body was to be delivered sometime in the next couple of days.

Mark climbed on the bus with Gracie and went off to school. Misty didn't want him to get behind in his schoolwork, and she thought he needed to get his mind off the loss of his father and brother.

Colton thought he would try to distract Misty by taking her for a ride. He saddled up his usual choice, Gremlin, a bay gelding, and a mare he knew to be gentle for Misty.

He'd intended to assist her up into the saddle but

was a little thrilled when she approached the horse and hoisted herself up in one easy move.

She gathered the reins and glanced at him.

Colt closed his mouth and mounted his own horse. He headed out across the pasture toward the place he had been thinking about. His favorite fishing place…and the site where he might want to build his future home.

They rode in silence at a good pace.

Misty's coloring improved, and she was smiling.

When he pulled up close to the bend in the creek, Misty looked happier than he had seen her since Joe's death. Her eyes were sparkling, and her cheeks had a tinge of pink.

"This is just beautiful," she enthused.

"I thought I would share one of my favorite places on the ranch with you. It's a great fishing spot too."

"Really? I love to fish." Her face clouded. "I haven't been in a long time. My daddy used to take us."

"That must have been great fun. I come here often," he said. "I'll take you anytime you like."

She glanced at him shyly from under her long, dark lashes. "Colton, you've been so nice to me…to us. Kind, actually." She gnawed her lower lip. "What I want to say is thank you. I don't know how we'll ever repay you." She held the reins grasped in her hands on top of the saddle horn.

"Don't be silly. I don't want your gratitude. I just want to help." He reached out to place his hand on top of hers. "I know this is a tough time for you, but it will pass. Things will be better. I promise."

She lifted her gaze to meet his, her expression clearly stating she didn't believe him. "I hope so."

"Is there something you're not telling me?"

She made a sound in the back of her throat. "Lots."

"For instance?" Colt asked encouragingly. "You can tell me anything."

"For instance, I don't know what was going on with the ranch. I know Dad borrowed some money against it, but I don't have any idea what's going on with that. Daddy and Joe wouldn't discuss it with me."

"I can take you to the bank, if you like. You have a right to know."

She heaved a sigh. "That would be great, if you have time. I don't want to take you away from your work."

"Not a problem." He squeezed her hand. "What else?"

She frowned, her finely arched brows drawing together. "The last thing Joe said to me." She swallowed hard. "I think I might have gotten him killed."

Colt sat up straighter. "What? How could that be?"

Misty shuddered. "I was afraid he was going to squander the money you paid for the horses. He had been drinking pretty hard the days before the sale. So I took the check and had Dad sign it over for deposit. I got to the bank early and made sure it was safely in the ranch account." She pressed her lips together and seemed to curl in on herself.

Colton stroked his hand over her hair. "That doesn't sound like a bad thing to do."

"Yes, but when Joe found out, he was very angry. He said he needed the money or he might be killed. I thought he was just being dramatic, but now—"

Colton frowned. That was worrisome. Could Joe have been involved in something shady that got him killed? "I think we should make a trip into town and talk to the sheriff."

—✑—

Misty enjoyed the ride with Colton. It had been a while since she had gotten on a horse just for the pure pleasure of it.

The more she got to know Colt, the more she liked him. He was kind and compassionate. He was great-looking. And he seemed to truly care for her.

At least she hoped so, because she was growing to care for him more and more each day.

She was still anxious about the fate of the Dalton ranch and about Mark's future. She hoped the upcoming trip into town with Colton would reveal that her fears were groundless.

Somehow, she had fallen into the habit of talking freely to him and enjoying the luxury of having someone respond with solid advice.

Misty pondered her current state. Suddenly, she was without a father and older brother. Her mom had died years before. There were no close relatives to help out, and she was pretty sure she couldn't run the ranch all by herself while waiting for Mark to grow up and take over, even if the bank did not foreclose.

All the while a question was screaming in her brain. *Who killed my brother Joe, and why?* A shiver snaked its way along her spine.

She shook it off and climbed into Colton's big silver diesel truck.

He gave her a smile as he started the motor and shifted into gear.

A warm feeling washed through her, leaving her with a tightness in her chest. Just being in his company was comforting…and more. The feelings that were growing were both thrilling and frightening.

As it stood, she was grateful to Colton for so many things, especially for the interest he was taking in Mark. Every day when the school bus delivered him and the little girl, Gracie, a routine was developing.

First there was a snack provided by Leah, and while Gracie did her homework, Mark headed out to the stable to begin his chores, most of which revolved around giving Sam some exercise and making sure the stable was clean. He saw to it the horses were fed and watered and that clean hay was in their stalls. He was thriving under Colton's wing.

She especially appreciated the way Colton took the time to recognize Mark's accomplishments and praise him for them. This was a boy who had been only six years old when he lost his mother, the parent who had been generous with affection and positive comments.

When they reached Langston, Colton pulled in at the bank and accompanied her inside. He asked to speak to the banker, Fred Hamilton.

"He'll be right with you, Mr. Garrett," the teller assured them. Misty didn't recall any time when the Daltons had been treated to such an immediate audience.

Colton took her hand and ushered her into Mr. Hamilton's private office.

The bank president was standing when they entered. He extended his hand to Colton, a wide grin in place. "What can I do for you today, Mr. Garrett?"

Colton gestured to Misty. "I believe the bank has had some dealings with Miss Dalton's father, and now that he has passed away, she would like to know what sort of debt you have against the ranch."

Hamilton's grin turned into a grimace. A muscle in his cheek twitched. His gaze flicked to Misty and settled again on Colton. "Let's sit down, shall we?" He gestured to the two burgundy-leather chairs situated in front of his desk. He blinked and finally looked at Misty. "Well… well, due to your father's terminal condition, we had held off on any procedures to collect the debt."

"What sort of procedures?" Misty asked.

Hamilton swallowed. "Calling in the loan. That's the next step."

Colton looked grim. "Mr. Hamilton, she would like to have a copy of the paperwork pertaining to this debt and what it would take to satisfy it."

"Oh, um…I can have that sent to her." Hamilton's face reddened.

"We can wait." Colton's voice was cool. He held Hamilton in place with a steady gaze.

"Well, yes…I can do that." He pushed a button on his intercom and asked someone on the other end to bring the file on the Dalton property.

Misty gripped her hands together. Her stomach was seized in a similar grip.

Shortly, a young woman entered the office with a file and slid it onto the desk in front of Hamilton. He leafed through the papers.

"Why don't you just copy the entire file for us?" Colton suggested.

Hamilton blinked and handed the file back to the young woman. "Certainly. Doris, make a copy of the file for Mr. Garrett."

"For Miss Dalton," Colton corrected.

"Um, yes. For Miss Dalton," Hamilton said. While they waited for the copies, he tried to make small talk, asking about Big Jim and Colton's brothers.

In a relatively short time, Doris returned with the copies. She handed both the original and the copy to Hamilton who heaved a sigh before passing it over to Colton, who handed it to Misty. He stood and extended a hand to Mr. Hamilton, who immediately stood and shook with him.

Misty left, feeling confused and not sure what had just happened, but she did understand the words "procedures" and "calling in the loan."

A kernel of rage simmered in Colton's gut. He didn't like Hamilton. At least, he didn't after the meeting they had just held. *Something shifty about the man. Something secretive that Hamilton doesn't want discovered.*

Colt helped Misty into the truck and started it up. He didn't want to share his misgivings just yet. "Are you hungry?"

Wordlessly, she shook her head.

"I suggest we have lunch and look over these papers. It won't do you any good to get run down." He drove to Tio's Mexican Restaurant and asked for a corner table in the back.

When they had ordered, he asked to see the paperwork the banker had so reluctantly given up. He noted that the ranch contained two sections of land at 640 acres each. It was a fair-sized ranch. Nothing to compare with the Garrett spread, but the Daltons should have been able to make a living on it. It appeared that the loan had been made only on the land and not on any of the livestock or equipment. He explained this to Misty, who nodded.

"I guess that was why Joe was trying to sell off the stock." She pressed her lips together.

"I'll see what can be done to stave off any further actions." He gave her hand a squeeze and returned the papers to her.

When their orders were served, Colton encouraged her to eat, although she only seemed to pick at the food.

At one point, she raised her eyes to meet his. "Thank you so much, Colt. Everything looks hopeless, but at least I know what's going on now. I really hated being kept in the dark."

He made a scoffing noise. "You can't get discouraged. You have to keep a positive attitude."

"I'll try." She nodded and took a bite.

Colt felt a warming sensation in his chest when he looked at her. He wanted to take her in his arms…he wanted to do so much more. At least he hoped to ensure that the surviving Dalton siblings were treated fairly.

He figured that Hamilton had planned to foreclose on the property as soon as Misty's father was in the ground.

After they had eaten, Colton took Misty to the sheriff's office. She appeared to be even more nervous. The sheriff came out to shake hands with Colton and to offer his condolences to Misty.

"Thank you," she said, her voice betraying her discomfort.

He escorted them back to his office, and when they were seated, Colton asked about Joe's death. "Do you have any suspects, Sheriff?"

The sheriff shook his head. "Early days yet. But don't you worry, little lady. I have every confidence that we'll be able to bring the perpetrator to justice."

"I brought Miss Dalton in today because she may have something worth following up on," Colton said.

The sheriff leaned forward, a look of concern on his face.

With a little prodding, Misty related the story of Joe telling her he needed the money from the sale of the horses and that not having it might cost his life.

The sheriff frowned. "We'll look into it. Right now, there hasn't been any indication of what might have led to the shooting. The coroner thinks the fatal shot was fired from the passenger side of a pickup truck, judging from the angle of entry. Not a pleasant subject to discuss, but there it is." He shrugged his massive shoulders. "Might be a case of road rage."

Colton scowled. "Almost everyone around here drives a pickup. There might be a second car for a family, but there's always at least one pickup."

The sheriff nodded. "Sounds about right. We'll be looking for anyone who might know of some reason young Dalton needed money."

Colton rose and shook the sheriff's hand. "Thank you, sir. We appreciate you keeping us in the loop."

"Am I to understand that Miss Dalton will be staying at the Garrett ranch?" the sheriff asked.

Colton glanced at Misty. "Yes, at least for now. With her brother being murdered, I don't want to put her in danger as well. When you've caught the killer, she will be able to return to her ranch."

He turned to leave, noting the strained expression on her

face. This was just too hard for her to contend with. *Maybe, after a little time has passed, things will be different. Maybe then she'll be able to see what we have between us.*

The funeral took place on Friday. The preacher said nice things about both men, and Glenda McAbee sang several moving hymns, hitting all the high notes with her clear, sweet tones.

Misty sat in the front pew, with Colton and Mark on either side of her. She held hands with both of them.

The entire town seemed to be crammed into the church. There was standing room only, with a group of her father's old cronies huddled together, leaning against the wall.

Most of Joe's classmates were there, including a girl who had dated him for a while, but she was there with her husband. It appeared she had moved on.

At the end of the service, when Colt escorted Misty from the church, she glanced up to notice that Joe's three running buddies were also in attendance. Eddie, Stan, and Ron were sitting together on the last pew. They stared at her solemnly. Surprisingly, they showed up at the cemetery as well.

A pop-up canopy had been erected at graveside with a few folding chairs underneath. Misty sat beside Rosa Hernandez, who wept quietly into a tissue, Paco standing behind her. Likewise, Colton had taken his place behind Misty, his hand resting lightly on her shoulder and Mark standing beside him. She thought it was a good sign that her little brother was taking his cues from Colton. At least he finally had a great role model to use as a pattern.

The pastor said a few more words as she sat beside Rosa on the stiff chairs. Although Rosa's tears continued to roll down her cheeks, it seemed that Misty was all cried out. Her eyes felt puffy and gritty. Maybe she had dried up. Perhaps worry had taken the place of grief, or at least nudged it out of the way for the moment.

When the caskets had been lowered into the ground, Colton gathered his charges and shuttled them back to their temporary haven.

All the church ladies brought food out to the Garrett ranch.

People came to pay their respects to the two surviving children, but Misty detected some kind of underlying energy. She thought it might have to do with the precarious financial status of their ranch.

She felt as though she was surrounded by scavengers and she was merely some piece of carrion. She didn't know what they expected to gain. The bank held the lien on the ranch. Nothing she could do about that. *No bones for the predators to pick.*

While the visitors were chatting among themselves, Misty sat in the kitchen, talking to Leah. She learned that before Leah married Tyler, she had held a job with the lawyer in Langston and that Leah was willing to take her in to talk to him. To Leah's knowledge, he hadn't replaced her yet, and she went in occasionally to help keep his filing in order.

"Monday I'll take you to see Mr. Ryan," Leah promised. "He's a very nice man, and he just needs someone with a few organizational skills and the ability to type."

"I—I can do that." She considered the two years of undergraduate work under her belt. She hoped it would lead to a degree in library science. "I would appreciate it if you can help me get hired."

If Misty could get a job quickly, she would be able to at least provide for her little brother. Maybe they could find an apartment to rent in town. She heaved a sigh. It seemed life would go on, just in greatly reduced circumstances. They couldn't continue to live off the charity of the Garretts, and it appeared their previous home was about to be jerked out from under the Dalton heirs.

She hoped the new owner would allow Rosa and Paco to stay on at the ranch. Surely their help would be needed, and Paco knew every blade of grass on the land.

A wave of sorrow racked her body. *It's just not fair.* She shook it off, consciously replacing her grief with fortitude. *I must be strong...for Mark...for me.*

She had always thought the land would be there, a part of her family, something to hand down to her future children. A mantle of sadness wrapped around her, heavy like a shroud.

Misty gazed out the sliding glass door opening onto an enclosed patio. A profusion of purple bougainvillea and yellow *esperanza* flourished in the space. Chairs were collected around a large table under a gazebo-type structure. She envisioned festive Garrett family gatherings held there.

Colton came up behind her. His big hands settled gently on her shoulders. "How are you holding up?"

She leaned back, and he pulled her against his chest. "I'm holding up."

"People are leaving. Come say goodbye, and it will soon be over."

She nodded and followed him to the front room.

Shaking hands with the guests, she tried to smile and accept their condolences without breaking into tears.

Mark stood beside her, looking grim. *How difficult this must be from his perspective.*

Colton took a stance beside her, his hand on her shoulder. He shook hands with the departing guests and managed to say the right words when hers failed.

When they had closed the door on the last guest, Colton pulled her close and brushed a kiss against her temple. "Well, that's done. Now you can start putting your life back together."

She gazed up at him. Something she saw in his eyes made her shiver. An intense hunger reached out to her.

"Are you cold?" he asked. "I can get you a jacket."

"I'm okay." She patted his hand before moving away. "I appreciate everything you've done for us, Colt. I just don't feel right imposing much longer. We'll try to get out of your way as soon as possible."

Big arms surrounded her. "Hush, now. You aren't imposing." He brushed her hair away from her face. "I love having you here." His voice grew husky.

"You're very kind, but I know we've overstayed our welcome." She turned to gaze up at him. "We could go back to the ranch until the foreclosure is final. I have to find a place for Paco and Rosa Hernandez. They've lived on the ranch since before I was born. I feel so bad for them."

"Honey, you worry too much," Colton said. "I have a feeling things are going to work out fine."

She rested her head against his chest. She couldn't imagine how anything at all could work out fine.

———~~~———

After the funeral was over and all the guests were gone, Big Jim tromped out to the horse barn. That was the one place he could get away and have a little time to himself.

Of course, he didn't mind if Colt or Beau joined him, but Colt seemed to have his mind on only one thing, and that was courting the lovely little Miss Dalton.

Big Jim had watched her all the way through the funeral. She was doing pretty good with that wounded act. And Colton was rising to the bait. He was all over her, holding her hand or putting his arm around her. He looked like he wanted to carry her away with him, and he probably did.

Now everyone in the county knew Colton was head over heels in love with this little opportunist.

Sure, Big Jim couldn't blame her. She probably didn't know where her next meal was coming from and Colt looked like a steak dinner.

He stepped inside the big steel building, at once on alert when he heard a scraping noise. As quietly as he could, he crept toward the source of the sound. He leaned around the corner and spied Mark Dalton cleaning out the horse stalls.

The kid's face was set in grim determination, but he worked steadily. Not what one would expect on the day he'd buried his father and older brother.

Big Jim stepped into the huge room lined with stalls. "Hey, young fellow. What are you doing out here?"

Mark jumped and turned toward him. "Hi, Mr. Garrett. I was just taking care of the horses." He swallowed hard. "It's my job."

Big Jim swiped his Stetson off his head and raked his fingers through his thick mane of silver hair. "Seems to me I heard about that arrangement. Well, I don't think anybody expected you to do your job on the same day you buried your father."

"Why not?" Mark asked. "The horses don't know any difference. Somebody still has to take care of them, no matter what." He resumed his cleaning.

Big Jim settled his hat back on his head. *Pretty smart kid*. Maybe somebody had raised him right. Big Jim leaned against the doorframe and crossed his arms over his chest. "So, how are you doing, son? I know it's been a rough week for you."

"I'm okay." His brow furrowed, and he kept his head down.

"And your sister. How is she doing?"

The kid blew out a breath and leaned on the shovel. "She's worried. She said she has to find a job so she can take care of me." He gazed at Big Jim earnestly. "But I don't need anybody to take care of me… I'm the man of the family now, so I should be taking care of her."

Big Jim's chest tightened. He found it difficult to speak. "That's a mighty admirable attitude, son…but you need to finish up your schooling first." He cleared his throat. "It's Mark, isn't it?"

"Yes, sir." He commenced shoveling again.

"Well, Mark, what kind of work is your sister looking for? What has she done in the past?"

Mark set the shovel aside again. "Nothin', I guess. She was in college in Oklahoma to be a librarian." He tightened his lips. "She loves books, but then when Daddy got sick, she came home to take care of him." He shrugged. "Maybe there's some sick people who need somebody to be nice to them. She's real good at that."

Big Jim swallowed hard. "Maybe." He continued to

watch young Mark work in the stable. He cleaned out the stalls of the horses Colton had purchased and then set about doling out feed and water.

Big Jim thought about the girl, Misty. He hadn't realized she had any education at all. He blew out a breath. *Librarian, huh?* And she had dropped out to care for her terminally sick father. Maybe she wasn't just a scheming little gold digger after all. At least, he had to give her the benefit of the doubt.

Big Jim huffed out a deep breath. He hoped there was more to her than just her beauty.

Chapter 7

LEAH FOUND MISTY SITTING ON THE LITTLE PATIO off the dining room. She had a faraway expression on her face and her hands folded in her lap. Leah almost hated to disturb her, but she had good news.

"I called Breck, and he said he would meet with us Monday at ten." Leah grinned at Misty. The hope that sprang to life in Misty's eyes was heartrending.

"Really? You mean he might hire me, even though I have no experience doing anything in the legal field?"

"Relax, Misty. It's not like he has a large talent pool to choose from. You'll do fine. And I promise to train you." Leah sat down on the bench beside her.

Tears formed in Misty's eyes. "Oh, that would be wonderful." She sighed and glanced down. "I don't want to get my hopes up."

Leah slipped her arm around Misty's shoulder. "I have a feeling you're going to find just the exact right fit. There's no hurry. You can stay here until you do."

Misty's large dark eyes opened wide. "Oh, no! We can't do that. We've imposed too much already."

"Don't be ridiculous. We have plenty of room, and I know Colton is enjoying having you here." Leah sobered. "And besides, Colt said it was dangerous for you and Mark to stay at your ranch. There's a murderer out there on the loose. Better to be safe than sorry."

Misty nodded doubtfully. "Yes, I suppose. But we

won't be alone. We have Paco and Rosa living with us. They've been with us forever."

Leah heaved a deep sigh. "I'm sure they have, but aren't they pretty old? Seriously, how much help would they really be in an emergency?" She shook her head. "I mean, a twelve-year-old boy and an elderly couple would not be much help if you were in danger. I'm sure the person who murdered Joe will be caught eventually, but in the meantime, you owe it to Mark to stay alive."

Misty grimaced. "I—I know, you're right. But if I can get a job, I'll need to find us a place in town. The truck was wrecked, and it looks like the bank is going to take the ranch. I don't know what's going to happen to Rosa and Paco." Her brow furrowed as she shook her head. "There's just so much."

Leah patted her on the shoulder. "Yes, there is. That's why you need to stay here and let things get sorted out one by one and not try to make everything happen like magic. I don't know about you, but my magic wand is fresh out of bullets."

Misty raised her head and laughed. "Thanks for everything, Leah."

Leah rose and gave Misty an encouraging smile. "Let's see if the guys left us any coffee. If not, I'll make a fresh pot."

Tyler's tour bus made its way across the country. He sat with his head against the window and a pillow behind his neck. He hoped to get some rest, but his brain was crawling with the difficulties going on back at the Garrett ranch.

Beau and Big Jim were not fans of Colton's new girl-friend, but Leah and Gracie thought she was wonderful. He had to be careful what he said when he was talking to his girls.

The main problem was that the surviving Daltons were in the process of losing their family home and land. For a ranching family, that was the ultimate disaster.

But when he talked to Colt, he had nothing but admiration for this Misty. He had never heard his big brother go on and on about any female. He knew Colton had completely lost his heart to her...maybe his head too.

Ty sighed and took out his cell phone. He pushed Leah's number and waited for her to answer.

"Hi, Ty." It was Gracie who answered.

"Hi, sweetie. How are you?"

"I'm good. Mark is tutoring me in math, and I got a ninety-five on my test this week."

"That's awesome. I'm so proud of you."

"Mommy said to tell you she's coming and I'm supposed to entertain you."

"I see." A broad grin split his face. "Well, you're doing a great job. Tell me about this Mark guy. He's Misty's brother?"

"Yes, and he's my friend. He rides on the bus with me, and nobody bothers me when he's sitting beside me."

Ty recalled too vividly when Gracie had been bullied on the bus. "That's a good thing, honey. I'm glad you have a friend."

"Here I am," Leah said. "I was just finishing up in the kitchen."

"Not a problem. I always enjoy getting to talk to my Gracie girl. It sounds like Mark is being a good friend."

"He is," Leah said. "He's such a serious little boy, and he's been through so much lately. He takes care of some of the horses after school too."

Ty adjusted his pillow. "Must be a nice kid."

"He is. I think Misty has done a good job helping to raise him. He's pretty horse crazy, but Colt and your dad have both taken him under their wings."

Ty huffed out a breath. "So, how is Big Jim feeling about Colt's girlfriend, Misty, now? Has he warmed up a bit?"

It was Leah's turn to hesitate. "Maybe. I think he'll come around eventually. You know he hates to admit he's ever wrong."

Ty laughed out loud, gaining the attention of some of his bandmates. "I don't ever recall Big Jim Garrett admitting he was wrong."

--~~--

Two identical vehicles traveled from the Garrett ranch to the church. Big Jim drove his big silver diesel truck with the Garrett ranch emblem on the sides. Gran sat up front with him, while Leah, Gracie, and Beau rode in the back seat. Colton drove Misty and Mark in his truck that was identical to his father's.

Going back to the church so soon after the funeral made Misty's stomach tense up. When Colt pulled into the pea-gravel parking area, she realized her jaw was so tight she had to consciously unclench it.

"Here we are," Colt announced. He parked right beside his father's truck, but it was already empty. "Let me get that door for you." He jumped out on the driver's side and made his way around to open her door. He looked so sweet standing with his hand held out to assist her that she wanted to cry. But it seemed everything was making her cry these days. *Better stop being such a baby and gut up, girl.*

Mark scrambled out of the back seat as she placed her hand in Colton's. She loved the way he tucked her hand in the crook of his arm. He was so strong. He made her feel safe for the first time in a long time.

When they entered the church, she sucked in a deep breath and steeled herself for the pity and the scorn she figured the churchgoers would have for the Daltons who were still lingering on with the Garretts.

Thankfully, Mark was oblivious to any negativity. He was just glad to be able to work with Sam.

She looked around, wondering where they would sit, but Colton went straight to the pew where the Garretts always gathered.

Big Jim was sitting on the outside, with Gracie, Fern, and Leah next to him and Beau on the opposite end. When Big Jim saw Colton coming his way, he scooted over to make room. With no fear, Mark slid in next to the Garrett patriarch, and darned if Big Jim didn't smile and slide his arm along the back of the pew where Mark was sitting. Not actually touching him, but it looked friendly anyway.

Misty swallowed, glancing at Big Jim, who looked friendlier than he ever had in the past. She had always thought he had some kind of problem with her, but he appeared to be downright human at this moment. She wondered what he'd had in his coffee that morning.

She sat down beside Mark, surreptitiously glancing at Colton's father. Yes, he had the same big, strong physique as Colt and the same intense blue eyes ringed with dark lashes, but where Colt's eyes reflected kindness and humor, Big Jim's looked steely and critical.

Reaching for a hymnal, she glanced over the songs listed on the handout. She knew them all by heart—had known them since she was a young girl listening to her mother's sweet soprano.

The pastor entered from the side door and took his place behind the pulpit. He looked out at those gathered together and led them in an opening prayer. He prayed for the local men and women serving in the armed forces and for the ill and infirm. He prayed for the souls of the departed, and he prayed for the welfare of his flock.

His words gave a bit of comfort to Misty. Life would go on...hopefully...

Colton slipped his arm behind her on the back of the pew, much as Big Jim had his arm behind Mark. It was as though the two big men were surrounding them with their strength.

Misty took a deep breath and let it out slowly. She smiled at Colton and felt for the first time that maybe—just maybe—things might work out okay.

~~~

After church, Big Jim always took his family out for lunch. Today, his "family" was a little larger.

Colton had sensed his father had some reservations about Misty. He couldn't for the life of him see any reason Big Jim wouldn't be as crazy about her as he was. He blamed Beau for Big Jim's negative take in the first place.

He was certain that, in time, his dad would come to appreciate her finer qualities. At least he hoped so. He knew Big Jim could be stubborn, and once he'd set his mind to something, it was tough to change his opinion.

Today, the Garrett party was seated at a long table at Tio's. There were only three restaurants in town, and this was a favorite. Big Jim was holding court at one end of the table, with Colt at the other. Gracie, Fern, and Leah sat on one side, and Beau, Mark, and Misty on the other. Of course, Colton had seated Misty next to him.

He thought this was a good arrangement, because Misty and Leah sat across from each other and were chatting about Breck Ryan, the attorney. And the two kids were across from each other, flanking Big Jim.

Colton was glad Mark seemed to have gotten acquainted with Big Jim. They appeared to have bonded over their mutual love of horses.

Big Jim ordered fiesta platters all around, even though Leah protested that it was much more food than she or Gracie could eat.

Colton figured it was too much for Misty as well, but she kept mum about it. He suspected she was terrified of his father, and he wasn't sure how to bridge that gap.

When the platters were served, everyone dug in with gusto. Flour and corn tortillas were passed around, along with little bowls of both red and green salsa.

"How's your food, little lady?" Big Jim called down to Misty.

She looked startled but responded, "It's delicious, Mr. Garrett. Thank you for asking."

Big Jim blotted his mouth on his napkin and set it aside. "Now looky here, young lady. You're gonna have to start calling me Big Jim. Otherwise you're gonna hurt my feelings."

Misty set her napkin aside and gazed at him coolly. "And you're going to have to start calling me Misty instead of young lady. Is that a deal?"

There was a long stretch of silence.

Big Jim cleared his throat. "I'm pretty sure I can manage that, Misty. It's a deal." He glanced at Colton and gave him a nod.

"Thank you, Big Jim," Misty responded with a smile.

Colton saw her hand was trembling as she reached for her napkin again. He was proud of her for holding her own with his dad. He hoped they could come to appreciate each other in time.

"Well, my food is just great," Beau piped up. He reached for another flour tortilla to demonstrate the point.

When the main meal had been eaten and everyone was stuffed, Big Jim ordered a serving of flan all around. There were groans of protest, but when the delicious caramel custard was served, everyone picked up their spoons to dig in.

Beau nodded to a trio of men just entering the restaurant. Colton recalled that Beau had gone to high school with those three.

The trio approached the table, but Beau got up and stood a little ways away to chat with them. Quickly, he returned to the table with the three in tow.

"Misty and Mark, you know Eddie Simmons, Ron Diaz, and Stan Lynch. They were friends of Joe's."

Although she had always thought these three had been a bad influence on Joe, she managed a nod of greeting. "Yes, I know Joe's friends."

The three stood, looking ill at ease and shuffling their

feet until Eddie spoke up. "We just wanted to tell you how sorry we are about Joe's accident. If there's anything we can do, just let us know."

The other two muttered "sorry" as a chorus.

Misty sucked in a deep breath and let it out. "Thanks. Mark and I appreciate it. I'm glad Joe had such good friends."

Eddie leaned close and whispered something in her ear. She nodded and replied in a voice so low Colton couldn't hear it.

"Let me know," Eddie said, and the three friends went to a table across the restaurant but kept casting glances back at the Garrett table.

"You know those guys?" Colton asked Beau when the Garrett party was leaving.

"Yeah. They hung with Joe. They were in my graduating class, but I really don't know them very well." Beau shrugged. "Ron was in band, but he dropped out. Stan was a nice enough guy, but Eddie's always been a jerk...at least in my humble opinion."

Colton glanced back at the three huddled around a table. Something about them made him uneasy. He slipped a protective arm around Misty and Mark as they walked out of the restaurant.

When he had Misty safely in his truck and Mark was climbing into the back, he asked her what Eddie Simmons had said to her.

Misty shrugged. "He just asked about the ranch. He asked if we knew how much longer we would be able to keep it before the bank took over." She pressed her lips together. "I guess it's no secret. Everyone must know we're losing the ranch."

Colton gazed at her, wondering if everyone could be wrong.

On Monday, Leah drove into Langston, with Misty in the passenger seat. She was driving Tyler's red Ford pickup because her husband hated her driving her old beater of a car. She always felt empowered when she was driving the truck. Sitting up so high gave her an entirely new perspective.

When they reached Langston, she pulled in at the office of Breckenridge T. Ryan, attorney at law. The lawyer was in, as evidenced by his truck parked right in front.

Leah gazed through the windshield at the law office, housed in a storefront. The entry door was inset with an oval beveled-glass panel. A cardboard sign hanging inside the glass declared the place to be OPEN.

She gave Misty an encouraging smile, and they climbed out of the truck. Striding up to the front door, Leah gave it a few taps before going inside. The outer office was empty, but the door to Breck's inner sanctum was open. She heard his deep voice droning on, so she presumed he was on the phone.

Peeking around the corner, she gave him a wave to announce herself and then led Misty to a desk in the front office that she had used when she was working here. "Sit down," she ordered. "I'll show you where everything is."

Misty perched on the edge of the swivel chair while Leah opened the drawers, pointing to the contents.

"This is the extra key to the front door, and those open all the filing cabinets. Be sure to lock up the files when you leave because there are people's important private papers in there. Wills and deeds and such."

Misty looked properly impressed.

"I had a devil of a time getting all the files in order, but I made a database here in this computer to show what was filed where. Just type in the name of the individual, and everywhere they have something on file will pop up."

"I think I can do that," Misty said. "But I'm not sure I would know where to file something in the first place."

"I'll teach you. No worries."

Breck came out of his office, grinning broadly. "Angels. Come to straighten out my mess." He was referred to by the old-timers as "that young lawyer feller," but he thought of himself as a rancher most of the time.

"Hi, Breck," Leah said. "I've brought my replacement. I'm sure she'll be a lot more reliable than I've been lately."

Breck came to the desk where Misty was seated. "I must say, young lady, you look right at home there." He reached out a hand to her.

"Breckenridge T. Ryan, meet Misty Dalton, your new secretary and receptionist."

"I'm happy to meet you, Misty. Leah has been saying good things about you."

Misty blushed and shook hands with him. "Pleased to meet you, Mr. Ryan."

"Please, call me Breck," he said.

Leah let out a little chuckle. "She probably won't be nearly as much trouble as I was."

"Nonsense," he said. "You didn't cause the problems that befell you. I'm just glad you're settled now."

"Me too. Ty's building us our own home on the

Garrett ranch. I have to stick around to see what's going on, since Ty is on the road right now. He told me to be sure to oversee the project." She let out a little giggle. "As if I would know what to look for."

"I understand," Breck said. "But you got me all spoiled. Now I expect my papers to be filed and new papers to be typed up. I appreciate you bringing Misty to me." He stood beaming down at them.

"I'm going to train her in everything I did, so this is her first day, right?"

He nodded. "Right. Welcome to the firm, Misty. I'll offer you the same salary I've been paying Leah." He raised his brows, gazing at her for confirmation. When Misty gave a hesitant nod, he went on. "I hope this will be a long-term position."

"Yes, sir. Thank you, sir."

"By the way, I was going to contact you concerning the reading of your father's will." He cleared his throat. "With the recent demise of your brother Joe, that just leaves you and your younger brother as the surviving heirs. As far as I know, Joe died intestate, so the terms of your father's will remain sovereign as to the disbursal of his estate."

"Oh." Misty sucked in a breath and let it out. "There's a loan against the ranch, Mr. Ryan. The bank is about to take it away from us, so it hardly matters what my daddy wanted to pass on to us."

Breck's brow puckered. "It always matters. Your younger brother needs to be present as well. Let me know as soon as possible when you can bring him to the office. Maybe after school?"

"Yes, sir."

"And welcome to the law firm. You're now in charge of everything clerical." He made a sweeping hand gesture. "This is your domain." He turned and went back into his office, closing the door behind him.

Misty covered her mouth with both hands.

"That's all settled then." Leah leaned down to give her a hug.

"Just like that? I have a job?" Misty's hands were shaking.

"Just like that."

"But—he's going to pay me the same as he's been paying you? But I'm just starting out. That doesn't seem right."

"He pays every Friday. I'm sure he'll get his money's worth. Most of the time, you will just be sitting here waiting for the phone to ring. Breck spends a lot of time at his ranch, and he relies on his secretary to make sure his clients are taken care of here in the office. That means contacting him if it's something important. Take messages. Type up the papers he needs, and keep everything filed away. Easy as pie."

"For you, maybe. For me, not so much."

"You're going to do great." Leah started with teaching her how to answer the phone and where to keep messages for Breck. By the time noon rolled around, she was going over some of the standard will forms and how to fill them in.

Breck emerged from his office again, Stetson in hand. "Ladies, I'm going to take my wife, Cami, to lunch. Then I'll be going to the county seat for a bail hearing, and I'm probably not coming back. I'll be at the ranch after that if you need me."

"Don't worry," Leah said. "We'll lock up."

Misty was smiling as she watched Breck's departure. "I can't believe I'm employed. I thought I would be lucky to get a waitress job." Heaving a sigh, she spun around, gesturing to the interior of the office. "I mean, this is a really nice place to work."

"Breck needs someone steady and you fit the bill. Don't you worry about a thing. I'll train you. You'll probably be much more organized than I've been. Everything happens for a reason."

Misty nodded, pressing her lips together. "Afraid so."

"Oh, I didn't mean that was why your father and brother died." Leah felt a surge of guilt. "I'm so sorry. I didn't mean that…just that you came to the ranch at the time I was trying to figure out how to let go of this job. I've only been coming in a couple of days a week, just to file and type for him. Now he'll have you here five days a week."

Leah saw a frown pucker Misty's brow. "What's wrong?"

Misty heaved a huge sigh. "I just realized there is another problem. It's great to have a job, but how am I going to get here?" She grimaced. "Mark and I can go back to our ranch until the bank takes it away from us, but the truck Joe was driving when he—when he wrecked was our only transportation."

Leah frowned too. "Hadn't thought of that. How about my old car? It's not pretty, but Ty got it to run pretty well. Gracie and I made it all the way here from Oklahoma. You're welcome to use it."

"Really?" Misty brightened.

"Sure. It's just sitting there." The flash of hope in

Misty's eyes gave Leah a warm feeling. "Let's go to lunch, and this afternoon you can learn how to create a will. Breck does a lot of wills and trusts."

Misty stood uncertainly. "I didn't bring any money to eat out."

Leah grinned at her. "We're eating in." She gathered her bag and headed for the door. "When you leave for lunch, turn this sign around so it shows in the front, and lock up." She adjusted the hands on the clockface sign and hung it so it was visible in the beveled-glass door panel.

"Where are we going?" Misty asked.

"Not far." She led the way past a couple of other storefronts to the shop belonging to her friend, Sara Beth Jessup. She pushed inside and held the door open for Misty to enter. Looking around, Leah tried to visualize the store as Misty must have been seeing it. An array of hand-stitched quilts lined one wall, and various pieces of used furniture were arranged artfully around the space. Some items were on consignment, while others had been acquired at estate sales. There were glass cases containing smaller items such as a collection of art glass and some costume jewelry. "Hey, Sara Beth," she called.

"Hey, Leah," Sara Beth greeted her from behind the back counter. She had her daughter in an infant seat and was spooning baby food from a jar into her mouth. "Come on back here. Cami Lynn is having her first experience with carrots. Looks like a winner."

Leah got close enough to see that the baby was covered with orange splotches of pureed carrot. "Quite a fashion statement."

Sara Beth laughed. "She's just an enthusiastic eater."

She turned her attention to Misty. "And who is this? I haven't seen you around town."

"Sara Beth Jessup, this is Misty Dalton. She's been caring for her father, who was ill for several years. Before that she was in college."

Misty gave a little finger wave and a smile. "Hi."

"Good to meet you," Sara Beth said. "And this is my daughter, Cami Lynn." She gestured to the wide-eyed baby.

"She's beautiful," Misty said. "Cami? Isn't that Mr. Ryan's wife's name?"

"Absolutely right." Sara Beth tickled her baby's cheek, eliciting a smile. "I named my daughter after the wonderful doctor who delivered her. Doctor Cami came all the way out to my ranch to deliver my baby girl. I don't know if either one of us would have made it without her."

"That's nice," Misty said.

"Her full name is Camryn Lynn Jessup." Sarah Beth wiped a bubble of drool from the baby's chin.

"Well, I think the doctor should be extremely honored to have this lovely little girl named after her." Misty reached out, shyly, to stroke her forefinger over the baby's arm.

"Misty is a local girl," Leah said. "I think she's been out of pocket the entire time since you arrived here in Langston."

"But now you're back in the pocket," Sara Beth said. "Welcome to my store."

"Misty is going to be working for Breck now, so I wanted to be sure you two got to meet." Leah took a seat on one of the stools in front of the counter and indicated that Misty should be seated on the other. She reached for her bag and pulled out an insulated container. "I brought fruit salad and lemon bread."

A big grin split Sara Beth's face. "It must be a salad kind of day, because I made chicken salad and brought some wheat bread for sandwiches. And tea. I made iced tea."

"A feast," Leah proclaimed. She hoped Sara Beth and Misty would hit it off and become friends. With her sunny, upbeat personality, Sara Beth would be a good influence on Misty.

After Sara Beth mopped the pureed carrots off her daughter's face, the three women shared the food and chatted. Misty told about the events that had happened to her since she left college after her sophomore year, and Sara Beth explained how she had married a local man and relocated to Langston and then immediately become pregnant. Once the baby was delivered, her husband became involved in a trucking company running illegal loads and had been murdered. The two women gazed at each other, each perhaps feeling the other's sorrows.

"Well," Sara Beth pronounced, "this just means we're all survivors." She raised her glass of tea in a toast. "Here's to good times to come."

They all clinked their glasses together.

"Amen," Misty said, taking a gulp of tea.

~~~

Colton wasn't too sure how he felt about Misty getting a job, but she seemed to be thrilled over it. He was even less happy about her using Leah's old beater of a car.

At supper, the new job and the use of the car were

all Leah and Misty could talk about. They were both happily chattering, oblivious to the glances shared by Big Jim, Beau, and himself.

When the meal was over and the leftovers put away, Colton drew Misty aside. He took her into the formal parlor that his mother had loved so much but was rarely used now.

"Misty, honey…that car is a piece of crap. It could break down any minute."

She swallowed hard, gnawed her lower lip, and then smiled. "Maybe it won't. Maybe it will take me to work and I can make enough money to take care of my brother."

He gazed at her, not wanting to discourage her but also not wanting to put her at risk. "It won't do you or Mark any good if you have a breakdown on the road. I mean, anything could happen to you."

She nodded, lips tight.

"Look, how about if you get into any trouble, just give me a call. You have a cell phone. That way you could just call me if you needed help."

"I promise to call you if the car breaks down, but I need to stand on my own two feet."

Colton gave an eye roll. "Okay, Miss I'm-So-Independent, if you feel that way about it, why don't you just give me a call anytime you want to and especially if your piece-of-crap car breaks down?"

She glanced down and then back up at him. "I guess that would be okay."

He stuck out his hand, and she shook with him. "Just until you get a better vehicle."

She gazed up at him, a flicker of fire in her dark eyes.

"I really don't need to have you hovering over me like a nervous parent. I'm a grown woman, and I'll be okay," she said, her voice sounding a little shaky.

"I'm pretty sure you will," he said.

Chapter 8

THE NEXT DAY, MISTY RODE INTO LANGSTON AGAIN with Leah, who spent the day training her. Leah brought another lunch to share with Sara Beth, and the three of them had an enjoyable hour to talk.

Breck had not come into the office at all but called in for his messages and to say he would return to the office at 4 p.m. if Misty could arrange to bring her younger brother in for the reading of Arnold Dalton's last will and testament.

"Um..." Misty glanced at Leah. "I suppose we can pick him up from school before he can get on the bus."

Leah nodded her head furiously. "Yes," she whispered.

"Then I'll see you all at four." Breck disconnected.

"Is it always like this?" Misty asked.

"Pretty much. Breck takes care of just about everything legal around the Langston area. If someone gets in trouble, he's the first one they call."

"So, he's a good attorney?" Misty felt a moment of tension in the pit of her stomach. She wasn't sure why this was important, but she had to know.

Leah quirked a smile at her. "Breck is the very best. He was awesome when I got arrested for murder." Leah's eyes opened wide, and her mouth formed a perfect O shape. She threw both hands over her mouth and blushed prettily. "Well, I never meant to share that little tidbit with you. The whole thing was a mistake, and I was cleared right away, but it scared me. I assure you that Breck was right there to demand they let me go."

Misty tried to hide her surprise. She couldn't imagine someone as sweet and gentle as Leah ever being accused of murder, but she was glad to know Breck had taken care of Leah's troubles. She remembered her father's deathbed instructions that she contact Breckenridge T. Ryan to help her sell off the cattle and equipment quickly before the ranch was foreclosed on. "Good to know," she said.

Leah drove Misty to pick up Mark and Gracie after school. Catching them before they got on the bus proved to be challenging, but they were able to intercede in time.

Mark was grinning. "So we get to go back to your office? I was wondering what it looked like."

"For us, it's business," Misty said. "Mr. Ryan is going to read Daddy's will." She gave Mark an encouraging smile. "It's just a formality. We know the ranch isn't free and clear, but this will spell out everything for us."

It wasn't yet four o'clock when they returned to the office, but Breck's truck was already there. When they had trooped inside, Breck waved Misty into his office.

"Bring your brother along," Breck directed. "I have your father's will right here." He formally shook hands with Mark and gestured for them both to be seated.

Leah gently closed the door behind them.

Misty glanced at Mark, giving him a smile of encouragement. Tall for his age and lean, he appeared to be dwarfed by the big leather chair.

Breck's voice took on a sonorous tone as he began the official reading of Arnold Dalton's will. The document detailed the property being passed to the surviving Dalton progeny.

Misty cringed when she heard Joe's name followed by hers and Mark's.

When Breck concluded the reading, he folded the document and placed it in a folder. "I'll file this at the county courthouse tomorrow."

"Mr. Ryan, could I ask you something?" Misty clasped and unclasped her damp hands. At his nod, she continued. "When my daddy was dying, he told me the land was mortgaged and way behind. He said the livestock and equipment were not included in the loan, and he told me to get your help in selling off these things before the property was foreclosed on."

"I would be happy to assist you, Misty. Why don't you get Colton to help you with an inventory of the equipment and a head count on the cattle? We can put an ad in the local paper and online. I'm sure there will be someone to grab them up." He stroked his chin thoughtfully. "Maybe post a list at the Agricultural Extension office and a few other places."

Misty heaved a sigh of relief. "Thanks so much, Mr. Ryan. We really appreciate this."

"You were going to call me Breck, remember?"

She nodded. "Breck."

With that, he showed Misty and Mark out and bade them all goodbye.

While Mark and Gracie busied themselves at the back table with their homework, Leah and Misty worked until it was time to close for the day.

Then Leah handed Misty the key. "You're on your own. Show me what you need to do to close up."

Misty found the sign with the clockface on it. She turned it to the side that said CLOSED, adjusted the hands to nine o'clock, and then hung it in the beveled glass of the door. They stepped outside, and Misty locked the door behind them. She started to hand the key to Leah, but Leah held up her hands.

"Nope. That's your key now and your job. Tomorrow you can drive yourself in and start working on your own."

Misty grinned but felt her stomach twist in fear. "Are you sure I'm ready? Do I know everything?"

"Hey, I probably don't know everything, but Breck is always just a phone call away. All you have to do is come in to work five days a week, open the doors, answer the phone, and do whatever typing and filing needs done. You'll be great."

Misty exhaled, trying to let the tension go. "Thanks for everything, Leah. Thanks for helping me get the job, and thanks for training me."

Leah climbed in the big red truck and shut the door while Misty scrambled in on the passenger side and the kids in the back seat. "I'm so glad to hand this job over to you. I loved working for Breck, but now I need to stay on the ranch during the day while our house is under construction. I'm so excited to finally have a home of our own."

Misty buckled her seat belt and stole a glance at her friend. Her face always seemed to radiate her happiness. Misty wondered if she would ever be able to shine like that. She wondered if she deserved to be that happy.

Leah backed out and headed for the highway. "I mean, I'm very happy to have a home with Big Jim right now, but it's time Ty and I break away to make a home for Gracie…and…" She dropped her voice to a whisper. "And for any future children we may have."

Misty sucked in a breath. How would it feel to be

planning future children? With Colton? She quickly dismissed the thought. She wasn't even certain he was thinking about a long-term relationship.

That evening, she helped Leah prepare dinner. She set the table, and when the males had assembled, she helped carry the containers of food to the table.

Mark was sitting next to Colton. She loved that Colt had taken her little brother under his big, powerful wing.

For his part, Mark seemed to be coming out of his shell, recovering from the loss of his father and big brother.

She set a napkin-lined basket of hot rolls on the table, and Colton pulled out the chair on the other side of him. She grinned and slid onto the seat.

"How are you doing?" he asked in a low voice.

"Great," she said. "I'm on my own at work tomorrow. Leah said she's taught me everything."

His brow furrowed for a moment and then cleared. "Yeah, that's great. I'm planning on coming into town tomorrow. Maybe I can take you to lunch."

She felt the color rising in her cheeks. "You don't have to do that," she protested.

He shrugged. "No big deal. I want to take you to lunch. I enjoy your company."

She was aware that others were watching, surreptitiously. "Well, I...um, I would love to have lunch with you tomorrow." She picked up the basket of rolls, offered it to Colt, and then took one for herself and passed it on.

She glanced around the table. She felt remarkably comfortable here. Considering her tenuous relationship with the Garretts, she wasn't sure she should feel so comfortable. She knew she would have to be leaving soon. When she received a paycheck, maybe she could

check around Langston to see if there were any apart-
ments available that she could afford. Then she could
provide for Mark and maybe be able to keep them afloat.

She still needed to sell the cattle and the equipment
from the ranch, certain that Colton would help her with
the inventory.

She helped herself to a pork chop, then a couple
spoonfuls of creamy mashed potatoes, and finally peas
with crumbled bacon.

Glancing across the table at Mark, she was delighted to
see him digging in with a great appetite. This was the way
a twelve-year-old boy should be eating. She hoped she
would be able to provide for him this well in the future.

All through the meal, the Garretts tossed conversation back and forth across the table.

Big Jim was in a good humor, talking to Leah about
Ty's tour and the construction of their new house.
He asked Gracie about her school and then turned to
Mark. "How about you, Mark? Is everything going
well at school?"

"Yes, sir," he replied.

"What's your favorite subject?" Big Jim asked.

"Math and PE," Mark said.

Beau chuckled. "My favorite subject was recess."
Everyone laughed.

Leah looked at Misty. "Tomorrow is Misty's first day
on her own working for Breck. I'm out of a job now.
She's a fast learner."

Misty blushed when everyone turned to gaze at her.

Beau started clapping, and the others joined in.

She shrugged. "It's a pretty easy job, and Leah is a
great teacher."

Only Colton frowned. "So that means you'll be driving to town in...in..."

"In my car, Colt," Leah finished. "I know it's a piece of junk, but Ty worked on it, and it's running great."

"If you say so," Colt said, but he still looked doubtful.

Colton got up early the next morning.

Leah had assured him her piece-of-crap car was in good running order, but the thing about old cars is anything could happen. After a certain number of years and a certain number of miles, they were bound to break down. He didn't want Misty out on the road when that happened.

Trouble was, Misty was proud. He knew she was reluctant to accept his help.

Well, today he was going to help her, whether she liked it or not. He kept the conversation light while Misty gobbled a piece of toast and a cup of cocoa for breakfast.

She was nervous but excited.

He wanted to be supportive, but he wanted to protect her as well. He walked her out to Leah's old beater and held the door open for her.

She flashed him a grin and slid inside. Sticking the key in the ignition, she started it up. The car grumbled a bit but growled to life.

At least it started. He heaved a sigh of relief. Maybe Tyler had done a good job of patching it together. Maybe it would hold up for a few more trips to and from Langston.

She rolled the window down. "See? This car runs just fine."

"I'm relieved." He stuck his head inside and planted a kiss on her lips.

Misty kissed him back, her lips soft and pliant against his. "Don't worry. I'll be okay."

He gazed at her intently. "You better be." He sucked in a breath and gave the door panel a thump. "See you at noon."

She nodded and put the car in gear, driving out of the compound and onto the drive leading to the interstate.

Colton gave her a fifteen-minute head start, then climbed in his big silver truck and headed for Langston, determined to straighten out some things on his own. And if the old car had broken down by the side of the road, he would be on hand to offer assistance. *Good enough.*

He was relieved not to find the car sitting on the road-side. When he rolled into Langston and spotted Leah's car in front of Breck Ryan's office, he released a pent-up breath. *Yeah, she's okay.*

Colt proceeded to the bank and got out. He had some questions for the banker, and he wanted answers.

Inside, he asked to speak to Mr. Hamilton and was shown to his office.

Fred Hamilton rose to his feet and leaned across his desk to shake Colton's hand. "Good to see you again, Mr. Garrett. How's your father?"

Colton pumped his hand. "Thanks, Mr. Hamilton. My dad is just fine."

Hamilton gestured to the cushy chairs across from his desk. "Please, sit down. Would you like some coffee?"

Colton declined. "I have a transaction I'd like to discuss with you." He gazed at Hamilton steadily.

"Of course. What can I do for you?" Hamilton spread his hands.

"What would it take to bring the loan on the Dalton ranch up to date?"

Hamilton swallowed, sat up straight, and rearranged a couple of items on his desk. "Um, I'm afraid that's impossible. The foreclosure paperwork has already been initiated."

Colton stared at him without blinking. "Mr. Hamilton, it's been my experience that nothing's impossible. What will it take to bring the loan up to date?"

Hamilton cleared his throat. "Well, let me check on that for you." Reluctantly, he tapped on his keyboard and sighed. "To bring the loan up to date would be quite expensive. There is the overdue amount, plus some serious late fees have been applied."

Colt leaned forward. "What are we talking about? Give me a figure."

Hamilton turned the monitor around, and Colton tried not to react when he saw the number. *A hefty amount indeed*.

"I'll be back this afternoon, and we'll work this out." He stood and held his hand out to Hamilton, who slowly came to his feet to shake his hand.

"You know," Hamilton said, "you're not the only one interested in the Dalton ranch."

Colton's back teeth locked together, and he felt the urge to punch Hamilton's smarmy face. He exhaled and eased his jaw. "No? Well, I'll bet I'm the only one who is interested in preserving the ranch for the current owners."

Colt left the bank, still feeling there was something

else going on, some reason Hamilton had an interest in the Dalton ranch that went beyond simple bank business.

He hung out for a while and then went to Breck's office early. When he entered, a bell tinkled against the glass. He found Misty sitting behind a large, old mahogany desk, typing on a computer keyboard.

She looked up and smiled when she saw him. "Hey, Colt. You're early."

"Yeah," he said. "I thought maybe I could sit here and bother you for a while."

Misty laughed. "I only need to fill out this form. I should be finished by lunchtime, but you can keep me company while I'm typing."

"Go ahead," Colt said. "I'll just watch you while you work." He pulled up a chair beside her desk. He liked the way she looked, so prim and pretty, sitting ramrod straight with her fingers on the keyboard.

She continued with her typing but kept glancing at him. After a short time, she sent the document to the printer. Misty smiled at Colton then pushed her chair back and took the printed pages off the printer. Letting herself into Breck's office, she placed the papers on his desk.

She saved the work she had done and turned to Colton. "I'm ready for that lunch now."

He got to his feet and gestured toward the door. "After you, Miss Dalton."

Colton drove her to the steak house on the edge of town and asked for a table in the back.

"This is nice, Colt," she said when she was seated.

He chose the seat next to her and took her hand after the waitress had doled out the menus and water. "You're nice."

She looked pleased when he kissed her fingertips.

"I was going to suggest we take a ride out to your ranch after you get off work. You should keep an eye on things."

She pressed her lips together for a moment. "I suppose you're right. It will seem so odd to be there without Daddy or Joe."

"I'm sure it will be, but you're the owner…you and Mark." He rubbed his thumb across the back of her hand. "You're in charge now."

She shrugged. "Until the bank takes it away from us."

"Maybe that won't happen." He kissed her hand and released it when the waitress approached.

She took their order and went to turn it in.

Misty clasped her hands together on the edge of the table. "Colton, I know you're trying to make me feel better, but I don't think there's any way to save the ranch. I just need to do what my daddy told me to. Sell off the cattle and the equipment. He said Breck could help with that. I asked Mr. Ryan, and he told me to give him a list of the equipment and a head count of the cattle and he will try to help me find a buyer."

"You need cattle and equipment to run a ranch," he said.

She sighed. "Colton, I can't save the ranch. The bank will take it. I'll be doing good to make enough money to support Mark and myself."

"How about if I save the ranch? Would you like that?"

She swallowed hard. "It's a huge amount of money. Why would you do that?"

"I'm thinking of it as an investment. You have a ranch, and you don't have the money to bail it out, and you don't know how to run it. I was thinking we could become partners. My investment. My knowledge and expertise. Your property. Your cattle and equipment."

Misty stared at him, her mouth slightly agape. She blinked a couple of times.

"It's a simple business proposition. Breck can draw up the paperwork." He gazed at her encouragingly.

Suddenly, tears filled her beautiful dark eyes and spilled down her cheeks.

"Aw." Colt used his napkin to dab at her tears. "No need to cry. We can make this work."

Misty swallowed hard. She glanced around the restaurant and then turned back to Colton. "Why would you do this?"

He smiled, brushing a strand of hair away from her cheek. "You know that I care about you. I don't want to see you lose everything. That ranch is your birthright."

Her lips trembled, and she looked as though another bout of tears was imminent. "I—I don't know what to say." She sucked in a deep breath and let it out. "Of course I want to save the ranch. It's all I've ever known...but I don't know if it's fair to you. I don't want to burden you with my problems. According to Joe, the ranch hasn't been profitable for some time."

He leaned back, fixing her with his gaze. "Ranching is all I've ever known. My dad steeped it into me from the time I was a toddler. I'm the oldest, so I always knew the responsibility for the ranch would one day fall to me. I have a lot of knowledge to share with you and Mark and a lot of resources at my disposal." He flashed a grin at her. "I'm a good deal. You should snatch me up."

Misty giggled. The sound of her laughter was like music to his ears. She looked so pretty, her dark eyes dancing with mirth and her dimples flashing. "That almost sounded like a proposal, Colt."

He reached out and touched her cheek. "It was."

Misty almost fell out of her chair.

A proposal from Colton?

He was smiling, and his little gestures of tenderness would have made her fall in love with him...if she hadn't already fallen.

Colton's expression was enough to start a fire. Indeed, it felt as though flames were licking at her insides right now.

She swallowed and took a sip of her water. *Get a grip!* She realized he was talking about a business proposal and not marriage. But if it had been the latter, she would have jumped on it.

"I accept." Misty extended her hand, and Colton clasped it in his, giving it two firm pumps.

"So, we're partners?"

She nodded, feeling her heartbeat pulse through her entire body.

"I'll go to the bank this afternoon."

Their food arrived, and they concentrated on the meal and much lighter conversation.

Colton expressed his doubts about the car again, and she assured him she had no trouble with it on the drive in to Langston.

Misty realized it had been a long time since anyone had actually cared this much about her and about her well-being. *Maybe when Mama was alive.* That was the last time she had felt so safe and confident that she was important to someone.

And now there was Colton. She couldn't let that go. She had to hope his caring would become real love. That he would return her feelings just as strongly as she felt them.

She managed to eat the delicious food although her stomach was tense and all she wanted to do was beg for more of Colton's kisses and tenderness.

He's going to save the ranch. That's what I should be thinking about. He's going to save us.

She thought about Mark and what it would mean to him. He too would be a partner with Colton. He already idolized the man. This would cinch their bond even tighter. *Yes, this partnership is definitely a good thing.*

After lunch, Colton returned her to Breck's office, gave her a kiss, and took off for the bank.

"Remember," he said before he departed. "When you get home, I'll take you to your ranch so you can check things out."

Chapter 9

COLTON WALKED OUT OF THE LAW OFFICE WITH THE taste of Misty's sweet kiss on his lips. He was still smiling when he climbed into his truck.

All of Misty's reactions were so real, so genuine. In that instant when she had giggled and said his proposition sounded like a proposal, he realized that was exactly what he wanted. *She's the one. I want to spend my life with this girl.*

Now, all he had to do was figure out a way to make her fall in love with him. He hoped that by spending more time together, they might grow closer.

He hadn't discussed his proposed partnership with his dad, and he knew that would cause a huge uproar. Big Jim would expect to be consulted and to weigh in with his advice. Given more time, that was exactly what Colt would have done, but that was not an option. Time was of the essence.

Colton knew there was still some kind of barrier to his father's acceptance of Misty, and he didn't know what it was. She was beautiful and sweet. Colt could only think there was some kind of issue with the Daltons as a whole. He didn't know if it was the father's drinking, the whole failure of the ranch, or perhaps some problem with Joe, but there was something standing in the way of Big Jim's approval. And Colton didn't have time to work this out and also save the ranch. He had to act fast if he was going to keep it from forfeiture.

He drove straight to the bank, only to learn that Fred Hamilton had gone for the day.

Colton drove back to the Garrett ranch, frustrated and angry. He had told Hamilton he would be returning that afternoon, so this felt like a deliberate evasion.

He blew out a breath and loosened his grip on the steering wheel when he realized he had it white-knuckled.

There was definitely something going on. Colt intended to find out what it was and put a stop to it. He was determined to protect the rights of Misty Dalton, the woman he loved…his partner.

Colton pulled off the interstate and drove through the gate of the Garrett ranch. He tried to release his anger as he wound along the drive leading to the house.

The school bus would deliver Gracie and Mark before Misty got home. He didn't want to spill anything to Mark. That was Misty's job, but he thought she might want him to come along.

If she chose to make the trip with Colton and not include her little brother, the whole evening would have a different focus. He would have to wait and see.

He parked in front of the ranch house, next to Big Jim's truck. That meant his dad was nearby and he would have to be careful not to let anything slip. He didn't want to stir up a hornets' nest until he had everything locked in.

He strolled into the house and found Leah in the kitchen. "Hey, Leah. Where is everyone?"

She turned from whatever she was stirring on the stove. "Well, I'm someone. But if you're talking about your dad and brother, they're out in one of the barns. I don't remember what they said they would be doing, but it had something to do with animals." She flashed an enigmatic grin and turned back to stirring.

"Thanks." Well, he would just have to avoid the barns for a while. "It was very nice of you to help Misty get a job and train her on how to do it. She seems to really like it."

"I enjoyed the job, but now, with so much going on, I'm just glad to pass it along to Misty. Breck is great to work for, so she should do well. I hope she feels comfortable there."

Colton slid onto a stool, leaning his forearms on the granite breakfast bar. "She does." He grinned, remembering how cute she looked typing away at the computer.

Leah turned around, giving him a calculating look. "You went into Langston today, didn't you? You had to check up on Misty."

Colton frowned. "Well, I went to Langston, and I thought I would take her to lunch. I wasn't checking up on her."

"Yes, you were." She chuckled. "You've got it bad, Colt."

He expelled a lungful of air. "Yeah, you're right."

"I like her. The two of you make a great couple." She leaned on the other side of the bar. "Don't worry. Everything will play out as it should."

He heaved a huge sigh. "I hope you're right."

"Misty has been through a lot. She's been taking care of her father and her brothers for years. Now, she's lost everyone except Mark, and her whole situation has changed. Give her a chance to find some balance. Everything's still topsy-turvy."

He nodded, not willing to share with her what he had planned.

Just then, Leah's phone rang. It was a special ringtone Ty had created of him singing a song he had written just for her. Her face reflected her feelings as she answered. "Hi, Ty. What's going on? Where are you?" She put it on speaker.

"Hi, baby. I miss you something fierce. We're on our way to Kansas City. We're opening for Brad Paisley at the Sprint Center. I hear it's a sold-out performance."

Leah's eyes teared up. "Oh, that sounds wonderful. I'm so proud of you...and yes, I miss you too."

"What are you up to right now?" he said.

"I'm waiting for Gracie to come home and hanging out with your big brother." She giggled. "We're discussing his love life."

"What? My big bro has a love life? Since when?"

She let out a derisive snort. "You know I've told you about the Daltons coming to stay with us. Misty is just the loveliest person, and Colt is completely smitten. I think they're perfect together."

"Really? Well, let me talk to that rascal."

Leah laughed and held the cell toward Colton.

"Hey, Little Bro. Sounds like your tour is doing well."

"It is. There are promo people who sell my T-shirts and music before the shows. That's been amazing. I may be able to put Gracie through college." He paused for a moment. "Now, what's all this love stuff I've been hearing about?"

Colton sighed. "Yeah, the love bug got me too. I'm a goner."

"About time, big fella. When you find the right girl, you gotta grab her right up, like I did."

Colt glanced at Leah. "You got a good one, all right."

"Listen, I'm sorry your girlfriend has gone through so much lately, but I'm sure things will work out. I remember when Beau hung out with Joe Dalton. He was an okay kid for the most part…but he started hanging with some other kids. Eddie Simmons was the ringleader. Joe just sort of went off course."

"So it seems. But Misty and her little brother, Mark, are great. I'm glad to have them here…although Big Jim seems to have some reservations."

There was a long silence on the other end.

Finally Colt heard Ty expel a long breath. "That's too bad. I'm glad Dad fell in love with Leah and Gracie right away. I know they're safe there at the ranch under his watchful eyes."

Colton nudged the phone back toward Leah and went to the refrigerator to help himself to a glass of iced tea while she finished her conversation.

He hung out with Leah until Gracie and Mark walked in the door. Then he sat with the kids while Leah fed them a snack.

"Okay, let's get started on your homework now," Leah announced.

Gracie opened her backpack and started pulling out her books and worksheets.

Mark, however, left the table. "I need to work with Sam and the horses. I'll do my homework when I get done."

Leah frowned, staring after him, but pressed her lips together.

Colton met her gaze and nodded. He followed the

boy out to the stables, catching up to him as he put a hand on Mark's shoulder. "You could finish your home-work first, you know?"

Mark's brow furrowed. "I can do homework when it's dark. Now I need to do my job. Sam expects me to come after I get home from school."

Colton could see his reasoning. "I see. Well, let me know if you have trouble with any of your subjects. I can help."

Mark gazed up at him. "Really? I've never had anyone help me before, except Misty."

Colton shrugged. "Well, I'm here if you need me."

"Thanks." A grin spread across Mark's face as he opened Sam's stall. The horse neighed and tossed his head in greeting.

Colton saw the friendship between the boy and the animal, smiling when he recalled his past experiences. This young one definitely had a natural affinity for horses.

He watched the boy set to work and then walked back to the house.

"Hey, Colton," Big Jim called. "Where have you been all day? I was looking for you to help inoculate the calves."

Colt stopped in his tracks. It was inevitable he would have to answer for his absence, but he would have put it off a bit longer. He turned to see his dad and youngest brother advancing toward him from the direction of the barns. "I went into town. Had some things to take care of."

Big Jim's eyes narrowed. "What kind of things?"

Colton let out a snort. "My kind of things. That's what." He fell into step with Big Jim and Beau. "All you had to do was call me if you needed my help. Or you could have told me last night."

"Whoa!" Beau slapped him on the shoulder. "I think my big bro is keeping secrets."

"Appears so," Big Jim said. "Now, I wonder what could have my son sneaking off to Langston in the middle of the day." He stroked his chin and pantomimed thinking. "Could her name be Misty Dalton?"

"Colton's in love!" Beau singsonged.

Colton heaved a sigh. "She's a nice girl."

"She's very pretty," Big Jim said, but his inflection indicated there was an unspoken "but" attached to his sentence.

Colt felt a muscle in his jaw twitch. "She's more than pretty."

Big Jim made a noise in the back of his throat. "Just be careful, Son. Take it slow and easy. You don't want to rush into anything."

Colton gave his father a sideways glance. "What makes you think I'm rushing into something?"

"Damnation, Colt!" Big Jim erupted. "You've brought the Daltons home like a couple of stray puppies, and now you feel responsible for them. You bought their horses. Leah got Misty a job and lent out her car. Next thing I know you'll be booking the church."

An uncomfortable silence followed.

Colton knew his father wanted him to deny the accusation, but he couldn't. He figured anything he said would just add fuel to the flame. Without commenting, he stormed into the house.

<center>~~~</center>

Big Jim was stunned. His normally coolheaded oldest son had just stalked off in a snit over some girl.

He expected his sons to bring girls home, but not the Dalton girl. Her father had been a drunk, and her older brother was a thug. He just couldn't stand by and let Colt make a huge mistake with his life.

He stood stock-still, staring at the door Colton had just stomped through.

Beau cleared his throat. "Dad, maybe you shouldn't make it such a big deal. The more you attack Misty, the more Colton's going to think he has to defend her."

Big Jim swallowed hard. "You think?"

"Yes, I do. Just reel it back, and let him get over it."

"Perhaps you're right." Big Jim felt his shoulders sag. "Why couldn't he fall for some nice girl he met in college?"

"Well, he didn't." Beau removed his Stetson and raked his fingers through his hair. "Is that what you expected me to do too?"

Big Jim shrugged. "Well, it wouldn't have hurt you none."

"Let me tell you, Dad. Most of the girls I met in college weren't interested in living in the middle of nowhere and being a rancher's wife. They had their sights set on having careers. Being professionals."

Big Jim snorted.

"The ones who came to college to get married were looking for husbands in the professions that pay big bucks...doctors, lawyers, football players." Beau flashed a grin, as though trying to lighten his father's mood.

"Is that so?" Big Jim wasn't happy with either Beau or Colton at the moment. It seemed they had ideas about

what would make up a suitable bride...ideas that dif-
fered from his.

Beau chuckled deep in his throat. "I'm afraid so. I'll
probably find my wife at a dance at the Eagles Hall."

Big Jim snorted. "It sounds like you're on Colton's
side."

Beau set his hat back on his head. "Not really. I think
Misty is a sweet young woman, but from that family,
how could she turn out any different?"

"Exactly."

———— ∿ ————

Misty pulled into the driveway about five thirty.

Colton had been watching for her. He went out to
meet her, and when she climbed out of the car, he gave
her a hug that lifted her off her feet. "Do you want to
take Mark with us to the ranch or not?"

"Maybe not this time. I don't want to get his hopes
up until I'm sure everything is set. He's had too many
disappointments for a boy his age."

"Then let's go while it's still light. We can drive
around and make sure everything is in order."

She nodded, and he gestured to his truck. He helped
her up on the passenger side and went around.

"Are they expecting us for dinner?" she asked when
he had climbed in.

"I told Leah we were going to run over to your place
for a while. She said she would save us some food."

Misty grinned. "I'm getting so spoiled. Leah is a
great cook, and she's a whiz in the kitchen."

He pulled out of the drive and headed back to the
interstate. "You don't like to cook?"

"I guess so," she said. "The last six years since my mother died I've cooked for my dad and brothers. And the last three years, since Daddy got sick, I've just tried to make something he could eat. I never thought about doing the fancy recipes Leah tries."

Colton turned onto the interstate and headed for the Dalton ranch. He was still upset over his father's words, but he wasn't going to allow them to destroy the time he had with Misty. "How did your afternoon go? Did Breck come in to the office?"

"Not today, but he plans to be there tomorrow. He has some client coming in."

"Good. Maybe I need to call for an appointment."

She giggled. "Or you could just tell me. That will work too."

He ruffled her hair. "Okay, Madame Secretary. Can you fix me up with an appointment with Breck tomorrow?"

"Sure thing. I'll call you when he gets there and tell you what he says."

"That will work." He turned off at the entrance to the Dalton ranch. The farm had a windmill turning close to the house and a couple of barns and outbuildings.

"Okay, tell me where to go."

"Just keep driving down this road. This cuts through the middle of our property. It's actually two sections of land. My grandparents owned one section to begin with, and Daddy inherited the land from them. Then my father bought the rest when he was able. A couple of years before my mother died."

"So part of this land has been in your family for some time."

She nodded. "I know that we have a total of 1,280 acres."

He winked at her. "Yeah, that equals two sections of land."

An old rusted truck was pulled close to the house when they passed it.

"That's Paco's truck," she said, as though reading his mind.

"He's the one who helps out around here?" Colton said.

"Well, he's getting pretty old now. He does what he can, and his wife helped me with my dad. They've lived here since before I was born. I know that for certain."

He reached over and gave her hand a squeeze. "That's nice."

They rode for a while in silence. Misty held his hand in both of hers. This made him very happy. He tried to overlook the run-in with Big Jim earlier.

"Do you know how many head of cattle you have?" he asked as they passed a pretty decent herd for the size of the ranch.

"I have no idea. Mark might be able to tell you."

He glanced at her. "You don't know?"

She shrugged. "Mostly, the guys talked when I was fixing dinner, and then when I put everything on the table, they were stuffing their faces. Seriously, Mark probably knows. He was a part of the male bonding thing."

Colton felt a little rancor on her behalf, but Misty didn't seem to take the slight too seriously. "Well, from now on, you and I will share everything."

She gave him a sharp look.

"Everything we know about the ranch," he added. "No secrets."

She breathed out a sigh. "That will be a totally different situation for me."

"What's that up ahead?" he asked, gesturing toward a ramshackle house and outbuildings. He slowed the truck and inched along, surveying the damaged structures.

"Oh, it's abandoned. It was the farmhouse on the second section of land. My father rented it out for a time, but it's almost falling down now. Nobody's lived there the past few years."

"I hate to see an abandoned farmhouse. That means a farming family didn't make it."

"I guess you're right. This place was owned by the Simmons family. You probably know Eddie. He was in the same class as Beau and my brother Joe."

Colton frowned as he glanced at Misty. "This was Eddie Simmons's place?"

She shrugged. "Sort of. This was the house where he grew up. Then when he was about twelve, his parents lost the ranch and moved away. Eddie went to live with his uncle, Levi Blair. He was the same age as Mr. Blair's son, Nate."

"The boy who disappeared? I remember the whole county searched for that young man, but they never found any trace of him."

"I remember. Mama was still alive then, and she organized prayer vigils. It was so sad. The house looks sad."

"It looks as though the farmhouse and outbuildings are in pretty bad shape." Colton weighed the pros and cons of pulling it all down and hauling it off. It was probably a haven for varmints. Rats, mice, snakes. *Yeah, demolish it and haul it off. No sense in keeping it there.*

It was getting dark by the time they had made a

complete tour of the land and headed back to the Dalton
house. There was an outside security light spilling
brightness in the area from the house to the largest outbuilding. And one light shone inside the house. The little
cottage where he had made love to Misty was dark and
looked closed up.

Colton pulled up in front of the ranch house. Almost
immediately he saw a face peering out the window
beside the door. "Your hand is checking us out."

"Yes," she said. "That's Paco." She opened the
passenger-side door before Colton could react and slid
to the ground. "Paco, here I am."

The door opened, and the elderly Hispanic man
stepped out. He grinned when he recognized Misty, and
immediately Rosa came out to join him. The woman
held out her arms, and Misty rushed to embrace her.
"Rosa," she cried.

"*Mijita*." The woman held Misty tight, rocking her
in her arms. "We didn't know you were coming, *mi
preciosa*."

"I'm sorry. I should have called, but I wasn't certain
that we would stop by." She gave Rosa another hug.
"We just took a drive around the property, but now it's
getting dark."

Colton swung out of the truck, suddenly seeing Misty
as a little girl instead of the woman he loved. He was
glad she had this couple to provide some comfort.

Paco eyed him warily as he approached. The old man
offered his hand. Colt shook it somberly.

"Welcome, Mr. Garrett." Rosa looked shy, but she
managed to get that much out. "Come inside, both of
you."

When they had all trooped into the house, Rosa turned to Misty. "I cleaned your father's room and folded his things. I thought you might want to go through them to see what you want to save. There are some good clothes to give to the poor."

Misty sighed. "Thank you, Rosa. I'll come this weekend and go through everything."

Rosa invited them to the kitchen, where she offered them hot chocolate.

"Oh, Rosa makes the best hot cocoa. She puts cinnamon in it, and it's so good."

Colton smiled, catching some of her enthusiasm. "I'll try a cup."

Misty pulled him to a round table in one corner of the kitchen. She sat down, and he took a chair beside her.

"Paco," he said, "do you have any idea how many head of cattle are on the ranch?"

The old man blinked. "Of course."

Misty's eyes grew wide. "Really? How many?"

Paco glanced at Colton and leaned over to whisper in Misty's ear.

Colton managed to refrain from laughing. *No trust there.*

Misty smiled and said the number aloud for Colton's benefit.

"That's a good-sized herd for this ranch." Colton nodded at Paco.

The old man frowned, exchanging a glance with his wife.

"It's okay, Paco," Misty said. "Colton is my very good friend." She reached out to take his hand. "We have no secrets."

Paco nodded, but his gaze remained guarded.

After they had enjoyed the hot chocolate, Misty went to her room and gathered a few of her things in a small bag, and they took their leave. Misty promised to come back on the weekend to decide how to deal with her father's and Joe's personal property.

Colton drove her back to the Garrett ranch, knowing she would be getting up early to go to her new job the next morning. He stole a sideways glance at her.

She looked pensive, staring out the window without seeing the passing landscape.

"What's on your mind?" he asked.

She gave a slight shake of her head. "It's just everything. I can't stop thinking about Joe. I mean, why would someone murder my brother?"

"I have no idea," Colton said. "But I'm sure the sheriff will figure it all out soon."

She looked at him doubtfully. "I hope you're right. The anxiety is eating me alive."

He had thought maybe she was recovering from the loss, but apparently she had been keeping it inside.

"And I will be sorting through their things and getting rid of them. Giving away my dad's clothing seems so final. I know it's just stuff, but there's so little of him left."

"I understand. How do you feel about Joe's things?"

"The sheriff's men went through everything, but I haven't gone in there since he was murdered. I dread even going into his room. He always kept it off limits to Mark and me. It will seem like an invasion."

"I can help if you want," Colton offered.

"Thanks, but I think this is something I need to do by myself. A final chapter of sorts."

He didn't want to tell her that the banker had flaked out on him. He thought he would discuss it with Breck tomorrow and get his take on it. Maybe if Breckenridge T. Ryan were to accompany him to the bank, they could force Hamilton to cooperate.

The next day, Colton set off for Langston, determined to get things straightened out with Fred Hamilton. Misty had called to tell him Breck was in his office and that he would meet with him at eleven. Colton was early, but he thought he could visit with Misty before meeting with Breck and then take her to lunch afterward.

He was still pissed off that the banker had ditched him the day before. Hamilton had to know Colton would come back with a vengeance. That he would have his attorney in tow would just be bringing in the heavy artillery.

He stopped at the florist to pick up a small offering before heading to Breck's.

Colton arrived at the law office a little after ten, relieved when he saw Leah's crap car safely parked next to Breck's big diesel truck. When he went inside, he grinned as he saw Misty working at her desk.

She looked up and returned his grin. "Breck's got someone in his office right now."

"I'll just wait." He took a seat beside her desk. "What are you working on?"

She smiled prettily. "I'm typing up some things Breck asked me to work on. I'm not a fast typist, but Breck was really nice about it. He said he would prefer I was slow and precise rather than fast and careless."

Colton leaned over and placed the pink roses he had picked up at the local florist on her desk.

Her brow puckered. "Oh, Colt. I don't know what to say."

He reached for her hand. "I just thought you deserved something pretty today. Pretty like you are."

Her luminous eyes opened wide. "You think I'm pretty?"

"No, I think you're beautiful." He flashed a grin. "But I didn't want you to get a big head."

She sucked in a deep breath and released it, a smile breaking on her face. "Thanks, Colton. This is so sweet." She held the bouquet close to her face and took a deep breath. "Lovely. Thanks for making me feel good."

"I'm glad the roses cheered you up, but don't forget what happened to your brother. I want you to keep those big eyes open. You may be in danger too."

Pressing her lips tight together, she nodded.

They sat chatting while Misty worked through the document. In due time, the door to Breck's office opened and Breck appeared in the doorway, apparently in the midst of showing his client out.

Colton stood, and Breck nodded at him.

"Colt Garrett, do you know Levi Blair?" He indicated the grizzled man beside him.

Colton nodded. "I know the name." He reached out a hand to the man. "I've never had the pleasure. Good to meet you, Mr. Blair."

Levi Blair flicked his gaze over Colton and offered his hand in return, albeit reluctantly. "I knew yer pa," Blair said. "You look a lot like he did when we was young."

"I've heard that before," Colton said.

The old man cast a shrewd glance back at him and then made his way out the door.

"Whoa! What was all that about?" Colton asked.

"Old Levi might not be Big Jim's biggest fan." Breck rubbed his chin thoughtfully. "I think it has something to do with property and boundary lines. They disagreed over the exact property line, so your dad paid for a new survey, and it was determined that Big Jim's claim was valid. Levi went around telling anyone who would listen that Big Jim paid off the surveyor to come up with his determination."

Colton frowned. "My dad wouldn't do that. He's not a cheat."

"You and I know that, but Levi's ranch abuts a part of yours. He was pretty much a sore loser about the outcome." Breck turned to Misty. "Levi and your father knew each other too, Misty. Actually, the Blair property touches on the north part of the Dalton spread too."

"I think I knew that," Colton said. "Mr. Blair's spread lies between our ranch and Misty's place."

Misty looked up from her keyboard. She shrugged. "I wouldn't know. I'm sure Joe was aware of anything having to do with the ranch, but they never told me anything about it."

Breck's brow furrowed momentarily and then cleared. He glanced at Colton. "Now, what did you want to talk to me about?" He gestured to his office.

Colt went into the office and took a seat as Breck closed the door behind them. "I want to do something to help a friend."

Breck eased into his chair and turned to a blank page on the yellow legal pad. He reached for his pen. "What's going on?"

"You may or may not be aware that the Dalton property is about to go into foreclosure. It's comprised of two sections of good land for tillage and pasture. I want to go into partnership with the heirs and bring the loan up to date."

Breck nodded. "Seems to be a sound investment. How much is the loan behind?"

Colton told him and watched Breck write the figure on the pad and draw an ornate box around it. "I met with the president of the bank yesterday morning and just got a bad feeling. It was like he was trying to hide something." He shrugged. "I told Mr. Hamilton I would be back in the afternoon to pay the loan up to date. I wanted to take Misty to lunch and make sure she was on board with my plan, but when I went back to the bank, Hamilton had taken off for the day."

Breck loosened his tie. "That was rude but doesn't necessarily prove anything. What else do you have?"

Colton heaved a sigh. "Just a feeling. He was evasive. He was shocked I was there to try to save the Daltons' ranch. He did say there was other interest in the property."

Breck grinned. "So you thought maybe the two of us could double-team Hamilton and make sure the ranch gets paid up to date?"

Colton gave him a grin in return. "Something like that."

"That bastard Hamilton has probably got the vultures lined up to snatch the Dalton property and line his own pockets in the deal. Not my favorite person."

Colton gave him a nod. "I was thinking along those lines. He was just too upset and edgy when I told him I wanted to pay off the loan."

Breck abruptly stood up. "I like it. Let's get it done." He straightened his tie and reached for his Stetson.

Colt pushed back his chair and got to his feet. "Thanks, Breck. I appreciate it, and I know Misty will too."

Breck led the way from his office. He stopped by Misty's desk to tell her he was going out and would return shortly.

Misty glanced from Breck to Colton, obviously wondering what was going on, but he was reluctant to inform her in case their mission failed. He gave her a wink and followed Breck out the front door.

Once outside, they climbed into Breck's truck and headed for the bank. It was only two blocks away, and they made it there in a few minutes.

Colton was surprised to find his stomach was tied in a knot. This should have been a simple matter, but for some reason, Hamilton was making it difficult. He hoped that Breck could get to the bottom of whatever was going on.

The two men got out of the truck and entered the bank. Breck went straight to Hamilton's office and rapped on the frosted glass inset in the door. He knocked a second time.

"Oh, Mr. Hamilton didn't come in today," a pleasant-looking middle-aged woman said. She had been passing by but stopped when she saw them outside Hamilton's door.

Breck frowned. "Why not? Where is Hamilton today?"

The woman's eyes opened wide. "No one knows. He didn't call in or anything. He must be sick. Poor man."

Breck and Colton glanced at each other, and then Breck turned to the woman. "Who is available to conduct business?"

She smiled. "We all are."

"I mean, is there a banker who is able to help us?"

Breck stood with his hands fisted at his waist. "We want to discuss a loan."

"Well, I'm pretty sure I can help you," she said. "I'm Abigail Parsons. I'm the vice president of the bank. Let's go to my office." When the two men had followed her to her office, much smaller and less pretentious than Hamilton's, she asked, "What do you need?"

Breck gazed at her earnestly. "We want to bring a loan up to date. It's in default."

She took the information and typed into her computer.

"Can you stop the foreclosure?" Colton asked.

She looked up from her screen, a puzzled expression on her face. "The property is not in foreclosure."

Colton exchanged a glance with Breck. "It's not?"

Ms. Parsons shook her head. "The loan is way over-due, and there are late fees applied, but no foreclosure procedures have been initiated." She told them how much it would take to reconcile the past due amount as well as pay the late fees. This was significantly less than the figure Hamilton had quoted.

"Can I write you a check?" Colton asked.

The woman looked at him, mild surprise registering on her face.

"I have an account here," he assured her.

When she made sure he had sufficient funds to cover the check, she followed through with the transaction and gave Colton a receipt.

He reached for it, realizing what a big chunk of his savings had gone into rescuing the Dalton land. Heaving a sigh, he tucked the paperwork under his arm. *It's worth it. Misty is worth it. At the very least, this is an investment.*

When the two men stood to go, Breck leaned forward
to offer his hand. "Thank you, Ms. Parsons. We appreciate doing business with you."

She smiled and shook hands with both Breck and
Colton. "I assure you, gentlemen, we appreciate your
business."

When Colton and Breck left the bank, Colt felt as
though he could breathe. "We did it. You did it."

"No," Breck said. "You did it. Now we need to draw
up a partnership agreement between you and the Dalton
heirs." He drove Colton back to his office and had him
wait while he drew up the paperwork to make the partnership legal.

While Breck was in his office, Colt went to stand in
front of Misty's desk. "We did it. The loan is paid up
to date."

She gazed up at him, her mouth falling open and her
eyes wide. "Really? You got the bank to stop the foreclosure? How did you do that?" She stood and came
around her desk to stand close to Colton, placing her
hands on his chest.

"I paid the past due amount. Simple as that."

"Oh, Colton, that was a huge amount. I can't believe
you were able to make that kind of payment."

He pulled her close. "I did what needed to be done.
Breck is preparing a partnership agreement, just to make
it official. Everything is going to work out okay. Have
a little faith."

She gazed up at him. "I have faith in you."

Breck called them into his office and told them to take
a seat. "Misty, since Mark is underage, he can't sign a
legal contract, but as his guardian, you can sign for him."

She nodded, tight-lipped. "I understand."

"We're here to draft a simple partnership agreement between the Dalton heirs and Colton Garrett in the venture known as the Dalton ranch." Breck went through the particulars and made note of anything Colton or Misty added. When he had read the last of it, he had Misty type up the agreement, using a legal form, with the specifics and details of the partnership; then Colton signed, and Misty signed for herself and as guardian for Mark.

When Misty returned to her desk, Colton asked Breck what he owed for his legal services.

Breck gave him a figure that seemed low to Colton, but considering the amount he had paid out that day, he was relieved. He drew up a check and handed it across the desk. "Thanks for everything, Breck."

Breck shook his hand and chuckled. "At least we didn't have to beat up old Fred Hamilton."

Chapter 10

MISTY WAS EUPHORIC. SHE TRIED TO CARRY ON LIKE A normal person for the rest of the day without dancing around in glee. Fortunately for her, Breck left the office, and she was on her own with her silly grin.

He did it. Colt said he would save the ranch, and he did it.

She was used to empty promises. Her alcoholic father's vows of sobriety; promises broken time after time, until it didn't matter anymore. So, for Misty, finding a man she could depend on was a great big deal. At the end of the day, she locked up the office and drove to her transitory home in a state of elation. When she caught sight of her face in the mirror, she let out a giggle. It seemed her entire being was elated. She felt as though she had wings.

Turning in under the gate to the Garrett ranch felt like coming home, but she jerked herself up short. *This is not our home. Mark and I have a home.*

She exhaled heavily. Now they needed to go there and stop mooching off the Garretts. She thought Big Jim Garrett would be glad to see them go. No, he appeared to have some affinity for Mark, but he would definitely be glad to see her leave his domain.

She pulled up in front of the house, parking in the space where Leah had always kept her vehicle before. Perhaps she could use the car for a while longer, just until she could make some other arrangements. Maybe there was a used car in Langston she could purchase. Maybe she could make payments. Maybe her paycheck would be enough to cover the cost and allow her to buy food for the inhabitants of the Dalton ranch.

Swallowing hard, Misty removed the keys and swung out of the car. She wondered if Leah would consider selling her the car. Not that she had any money right now, but tomorrow was Friday, and that was supposed to be payday. A bubble of anticipation welled in her stomach. She could go to the grocery store and bring fresh supplies to Paco and Rosa.

"How's it going, Misty?"

Her reverie was jarred by Beau, who strode toward her.

"Oh, good, I guess." She felt her cheeks flame. "I was just going to look for Mark."

Beau cocked his head to one side, grinning. "He's in the stables. That sure is one horse-crazy kid."

"I have to agree. He's always been that way." She turned toward the stables, intent upon sharing her news with her brother privately.

"Leah's going to have dinner on the table in about a half hour," Beau said. "You might want to tell Mark."

"Thanks. I will." She took a few steps in that direction, thinking Beau had something else he wanted to say and she wasn't sure she wanted to hear it.

He looked indecisive and then seemed to make up his mind, falling into step beside her. "I'll keep you company."

Great! Just great. She nodded acquiescence, hoping she had done so graciously.

"I just wanted to say…I hope you know Colton likes you."

"Yes, and I like him too," she said evenly.

"No, I mean he really likes you."

Before they reached the stables, she turned. "Beau, I know you mean well, but...seriously, do you think this is a conversation you should be having with me?"

He stopped, staring down at her with a slight frown on his face. "Well, no, but, I mean..."

"I'm not going to discuss it with you. My relationship with Colton is between the two of us. If you have something to say, take it to him." She lifted her chin, facing him in what she hoped was a calm and determined manner.

He blew out a breath. "Well, that's clear enough. I'll just butt out, then."

"Thank you." She turned and continued on to the stables. Once inside, she closed the door, leaned against it, and heaved a huge sigh. *What is it with Beau and Big Jim? Don't they think Colton is capable of acting for himself?*

She smiled. *Yes, he is.*

The sound of something scraping reached her ears. Venturing deeper into the outbuilding, she turned a corner and found her little brother hard at work. He was so intent on what he was doing he didn't appear to notice her approach.

"Hey, Mark," she called.

He looked up from his task, which was cleaning Sam's stall. Sam was tied to a nearby post, apparently waiting to be ridden as he wore a bridle but no saddle yet.

"Hey, Sis." He turned back to his shoveling.

"I have some incredible news." She wanted to hug him and dance around.

"Whut?" He raised his head to glower at her with one dark brow lifted.

"Well, put the shovel down, and I'll tell you."

He bleated out a snort and leaned the shovel, and then himself, against the stall. "Whut?" he repeated, crossing his arms across his chest.

She sighed. *Brothers!* "I just wanted to let you know we're not going to lose the ranch. Does that interest you?"

He pushed away from the stall. "Yeah," he said.

"Let's take a walk," she suggested. "I need some fresh air."

Mark fell into step beside her. "I don't understand. You said the bank was going to take the ranch." They walked outside the stables, strolling toward the barns.

"They were. The banker was just waiting for Daddy to pass away from his illness. Apparently he didn't want to throw a dying man off his property. Probably bad for his public image in a small community where everyone knows everything."

Mark frowned. "So, what changed?"

"Colton Garrett." She checked to see how Mark had reacted to that. "You like him, don't you?"

Mark shrugged. "Sure. He's been great."

"Well, he's our new partner in the ranch."

Mark's face morphed into a frown. "Partner? But it's the Dalton ranch. It always has been."

Misty heaved a huge sigh. "Well, the Daltons haven't done such a great job of running it lately. If it weren't for Colton, we wouldn't be able to keep it."

"So, what does this mean?"

"It means he is going to help us get the ranch back to being profitable, and he will share in the profits."

Mark's lips tightened, and he huffed out a sigh. "I suppose that's fair."

She hung an arm around his shoulders. "It's more than fair. Colton knows what he's doing. So we can have one hundred percent of nothing or fifty percent of something."

"How did you get him to do this?" Mark's eyes skewered her like daggers.

Misty shrugged. "He just did it. I didn't even ask." They walked a bit more in silence. "I wouldn't have even thought to ask him to bail us out...to pay such a huge amount of money just so we could hang on to our home." She shook her head. "He did it all on his own."

"I guess Colton's a pretty nice guy. He likes you a lot, doesn't he?"

She considered. "I think so. I like him too."

Misty hung out with Mark while he finished his chores and then they went into the Garrett home. Mark went to wash up, and Misty looked in on Leah in the kitchen.

"Hey, Misty," Leah called. "I was getting worried about you. I was beginning to think my car had made a liar out of me and left you by the side of the road."

Misty laughed. "Thankfully, no. I just needed to talk to Mark. There were some things he needed to know."

Leah gave her a speculative look but didn't comment.

"What can I do to help with dinner?" Misty asked.

"Easy dinner tonight," Leah said. "I put a beef roast in the Crock-Pot this morning, so we're having that with the veggies I cooked with it and a salad on the side."

"Lovely," Misty said. "You always come up with such great food."

Leah flashed a smile. "It took me a while to learn to cook for this bunch, but I enjoy it. Before I married Ty, I only cooked for Gracie and myself, so there was much less cooking involved. Now the guys really scarf up everything I put in front of them."

"I'm sure they appreciate it." Misty picked out enough plates and eating utensils to set the long table.

Leah shook her head. "The guys know this is only temporary. After our home is ready, Gracie, Gran, and I will be moving there. So when Ty is home, it will just be the four of us."

Misty hesitated and then asked, "He doesn't mind your grandmother living with you?"

Leah smiled. "No, he was the one who insisted she come here with us. There was some trouble when he and I were living at her little ranch. So we really didn't feel good about leaving her there. Of course, she put up a fuss about staying here, but we convinced her it was just temporary. Now she's okay with it. She loves to go with me to see the progress on our new home." Her smile went wall to wall. "I can't wait to move my family into our brand new home."

Misty felt a clutch of something she was surprised to recognize as envy. *It must be wonderful to share a life with the man you love*. "That will be great."

She made her way around the table, setting plates and utensils in place. She added napkins and then placed a large tossed salad on the table, all the while thinking about what she would need to do the next day. *Friday*.

Tomorrow she would be paid. She needed to open her own bank account. Or maybe just cash the check. Misty bit her lip in thought. She was a cosigner on her deceased father's ranch account. What about that money? At least there was the deposit from the sale of the horses to Colton. Maybe she should draw that out too? She decided to go to the bank on her lunch break tomorrow and see what needed to be done.

Colton had been feeling a little guilty. He normally didn't keep secrets from Big Jim, or Beau, for that matter. But, somehow, he dreaded divulging his partnership with the Daltons and how much he had paid for the privilege. Some things were best left unsaid.

Instead, he had thrown himself into working alongside them and hoped he didn't drop anything to make them suspicious. He just wanted things to go smoothly. He wanted Misty and Mark to get on their feet without a huge uproar from Big Jim. He figured Beau wouldn't say much, but he probably wouldn't be able to get a word in edgewise, what with Big Jim being on a rant.

Now the three men entered the ranch house, intending to clean up for supper. The aromas coming from the kitchen assured them of a tasty repast.

Big Jim led the way. He walked in the house and disappeared down the hall, unbuttoning his shirtsleeves, ready to shed his work clothes and step into the shower.

Beau and Colton followed more slowly.

Beau lifted his nose in the air. "Something smells great."

"Sure does," Colton agreed.

Just then Mark came around the corner and threw his arms around Colton's middle.

"Thanks for saving our ranch, Colton. Misty told me what you did." He stepped back, gazing up at Colton, his dark eyes shining like it was Christmas. "I'm really glad we're partners."

Well, the cat's out of the bag now. Colton didn't want

to squelch Mark's enthusiasm, so he offered his hand to shake and then tousled the boy's hair. "Me too, buddy."

When Mark had returned to the kitchen, Colt ventured a look at Beau. "Go ahead and say it." He grabbed his little brother by the shirtfront and dragged him outside again. The two men stood staring at each other under the portico.

Beau, for his part, looked stunned. He shook his head. "Did I just hear correctly? You saved the Dalton ranch from foreclosure? Tell me you didn't."

Colton blew out a lungful of air. "I did. And I'm sure you're going to beat a path to tell Dad." He fixed his brother with a stern glare.

"Why do you say that?" Beau's voice took on a defensive note as he folded his arms across his chest.

"Because it's what you do. You've always been a tattletale." Colt crossed his arms across his own chest.

"Am not."

Colton rolled his eyes. "Oh, come on. It's what you're known for. Don't make me call Ty for back up."

"Okay, I'll admit I have gone to Dad when I've had some concerns…"

"The thing is, Little Brother, this is my business and not any of yours. I will tell Dad when the time is right."

Beau's lower jaw jutted out. "And when will that be? When that little gold digger has drained you dry?"

It felt as though an explosion went off in Colton's chest. Without hesitation, his hands fisted, and he barely stopped himself from punching Beau into the next county.

"And now you're going to beat me up for telling the truth?" Beau took a step back, but his hands were fisted too.

"Don't push your luck," Colton growled. "She's not

a gold digger, and I would advise you never to say that again. This wasn't her idea. It was mine."

Beau huffed out a snort. "I'll bet. You're so crazy about her, you don't even know when you're being tooled around."

"You better shut up," Colt warned. "I have a legal partnership with the Daltons. Breck Ryan drew up the paperwork, so back off."

It was Beau's turn to roll his eyes. "Legal partnership, huh? What does that mean?"

"I'm in partnership with Misty and her brother. The Dalton ranch is good land. It's just been neglected. There's a decent-sized herd. It's an investment."

Beau nodded, his mouth tight. "I can see you're not going to listen to anything I have to say." He half turned toward the house. "I'm not going to say anything to Dad. You just blew a whole lot of money, and I sincerely hope your 'investment' pays off for you." He stomped inside the house, his face darker than a thunderstorm.

Colton heaved a sigh. This wasn't the way he had envisioned breaking the news to his family. He hoped Beau would keep his mouth shut. It was more likely that Mark would spill something. Maybe he could talk to Misty and ask her to keep a lid on her little brother.

Maybe he would be able to keep a lid on his own.

~~~

When Misty got to the law firm the next morning, she found an envelope with her name on it sitting right in the middle of her desk. She opened it and gazed in rapture at her name neatly printed on her first paycheck. Quickly, she stowed it in the bottom desk drawer along with her purse.

She had made a peanut butter sandwich and tucked it inside a plastic bag. That would serve as lunch, since she had personal business to conduct during her lunch hour.

When the noon hour approached, Misty put the sign in the door and opted to walk the two blocks to the bank building. She passed Sara Beth's store, waving as she went by.

Sara Beth rushed out onto the sidewalk. "Wait a minute. Where are you going in such a danged hurry? I brought a pasta salad for us to share."

Misty turned back to her. "That sounds incredible, but I have to go to the bank. I got paid." She flashed a grin.

"Woo-hoo! That's a reason to celebrate. Stop in on your way back, and I'll fix you a plate."

"Thanks, Sara Beth. I'll try to hurry." Misty trotted off toward the bank.

She felt a rush of joy. Everything in her life had turned around. For the first time in years, she was happy. She had two female friends she could count on, Leah and Sara Beth. Her ranch hadn't been jerked out from under her. True, she had lost her father and older brother, but she still had Mark. She stifled a grin. And she had Colton. She wasn't sure what he was. It would be great if he was her boyfriend, but at least he was a great friend, and now he was in partnership with her and Mark, so maybe the ranch would prosper as it had in her youth.

She sighed, a picture in her mind of her parents and brothers as they had been when the ranch was flourishing.

When she reached the bank, she pushed inside, using the polished brass handle to gain entrance. Pausing for a moment, she glanced around the lobby.

It wasn't too busy. There were two tellers attending customers from behind the half walls with glassed-in dividers. Only a couple of people were in line.

She turned toward the offices, reading the names imprinted in gold lettering.

FRED HAMILTON, PRESIDENT. Yes, he was the one who hadn't been particularly helpful. Well, she supposed he had come around when Colton paid the loan up to date. She peeked inside, but the office was empty, the chair pushed up close to the large desk. *Old Fred must have gone to lunch.*

There was another office farther toward the back of the building. Stepping forward, she saw an older woman behind the desk.

The woman looked up and smiled warmly. "Yes, may I help you?"

"I—I need some help with my check." Misty groped for her purse, but the woman waved her inside.

"Come right on in. Take a seat." She gestured to one of the chairs in front of her desk. "What can I do for you?"

Misty sat down and sucked in a breath. "I just got my first paycheck." She took it out of the envelope. "But I don't know what to do with it."

The woman cocked her head to one side. "Well, let me see if I can help you figure it out. I'm Abigail Parsons, the vice president of the bank." She held out her hand.

At first Misty started to hand her the check, but she realized it was an offered handshake instead. She shook the banker's hand. "I'm Misty Dalton." She heaved out a sigh. "My name is on an account already, but I think I need to open another account just for me."

"What is the account you're on?"

"The Dalton ranch account. But my father just passed away, and my older brother, Joe, was killed, so my name is the only one left." She had to press her lips together to keep from tearing up.

The woman's eyes lit up. "Ah, the Dalton ranch. I just dealt with two gentlemen who brought the loan up to date. I suppose you know about that?"

Misty nodded. "Yes, ma'am."

Ms. Parsons turned to her computer and tapped her keyboard, bringing up the account. "Let me see…" She made a few more keystrokes. "The account is set up as a survivorship account. It appears you are the only surviving signatory."

Misty swallowed. "Well, I have a partner in the ranch, and my little brother is my only other surviving relative. Mr. Ryan said Mark was too young to sign a legal document, but I would like his name to be added to the ranch account in case—in case something happens to me."

The woman gave her a pitying look. "Actually, very young children can have accounts, but usually there is a legal guardian who looks after their finances."

"Good to know. Mark is only twelve, but he's very responsible."

By the time Misty left the bank, she had a signature card for Mark on the Dalton ranch account, a brand-new checking account she could deposit her paychecks into, a few blank checks, and an ATM debit card. *Keep things nice and tidy.*

She returned to Sara Beth's store and spent the last twenty minutes of her lunch hour gobbling a delicious serving of pasta salad and drinking peach iced tea.

"Thanks so much, Sara Beth. This was really good. I'll try to bring something to share with you next week."

Sara Beth walked with her to the door. "I must say, you're looking a lot happier than you were at the first of the week. This past Monday you looked like a scared little girl. Now you're absolutely blooming. What happened to lift your spirits?"

Misty wrapped her in a fierce hug. "So many things. I'll tell you all about them when I've got more time. Have a great weekend, and I'll see you Monday." She rushed out of the store and hustled back to the law office before her hour was up.

It was Friday, and Colton wanted to spend time alone with Misty. There was a live band at the Eagles Hall, and he thought about asking her if she would go with him, but he supposed it wouldn't be appropriate for a young woman who had just lost her dad and her older brother to be out enjoying herself at a dance.

His little set-to with Beau the previous day still had both brothers dodging each other. Even when they were working side by side they avoided eye contact and only spoke out of necessity.

Now, he noticed that Beau was all cleaned up and headed for town. Probably going to grab a steak for dinner and then go to the Eagles Hall. Colton watched as Beau climbed into his truck and revved the engine before tearing out.

Colt turned toward the kitchen, puzzled when he realized he didn't smell anything cooking. In fact, only one small light was turned on.

He heard voices in the hallway coming from the bedroom wing. When he followed the sound, he found Leah with Gracie and Mark. She was fussing with Gracie's hair, and Mark was cleaned up too.

"What's going on?" Colton asked.

Mark turned to him eagerly. "Big Jim is taking all of us to dinner and then to the Eagles Hall. I've never been before."

Leah gazed up at him expectantly. "Didn't your dad tell you? We're all going out tonight." She turned around. "Hurry up, Gran. We don't want to be late."

"I'm a-comin'," Fern called out.

"Um, no. I guess I didn't get the memo."

"Well, now you got it." Big Jim came into the hallway. He wore a freshly starched Western shirt, and his Wranglers were pressed as well. "Come on. Get a move on." He flashed a big grin. "I've got a date."

"I better wait for Misty," Colton said.

Big Jim hesitated just a second and then nodded. "Well, you two hustle it up. We'll be at the steak house, and then we're going to get a table at the Eagles. I'm planning on dancing with Celia Diaz tonight. She's going to meet us for dinner."

Colton grinned. He was glad his father was seeing someone, even someone much younger. He didn't want Big Jim to spend the rest of his life alone. "Have a good time. We'll be there as soon as possible."

Fern Davis, Leah's grandmother, bustled into the room, tucking a handkerchief into her handbag. "You'd best hurry up, young feller. I'm a-savin' a dance for you."

"Yes, ma'am. I'll be right along." He followed them

to the doorway, watching as Big Jim herded Leah, her grandmother, and the younger two into his big truck.

Colton heaved a sigh and stepped back through the door as the truck roared off. He was glad his father was taking an interest in Mark. The boy certainly needed to be appreciated. He just wished some of his father's benevolence could spill over onto Misty.

For that matter, he couldn't understand why Beau held such a negative opinion of her.

It wasn't dark yet, but it was much later than Misty usually got home from the law office. Colton was just about to go look for her when Leah's old clunker pulled into the driveway. He felt as if a tight band around his chest broke loose when he saw her bounce out of the car with a grin on her face. Sucking in a deep breath, he returned her grin. "About time you got home. I was going to send out a search party."

She flew into his arms, and he swung her around. He had never seen her so happy. "What's going on?"

"Oh, Colton. This has just been the best day ever." She gave him a hug. "First off, I got paid, and when I went to the bank, a very nice lady helped me open my very own checking account. Then she straightened out the ranch account, and I have my own debit card and checks." She gave a little squeal at the end of her sentence.

"That sounds like a great day, all right."

"But right after work, I went to the grocery store and got food for Paco and Rosa. I took it by the ranch, and they were so happy." Her eyes were shining, and she was talking rapidly. "I love them both so much. They've been like another set of parents to Mark and me."

He planted kisses on her upturned face, skimming her

forehead and her nose and settling on her lips. "I'm glad you're able to provide for them, but you know I would have sprung for groceries."

"Oh, Colton, I'm so happy. I feel as though things might actually turn out well."

"Of course they will." He gave her another kiss. "Now, go toss on your jeans, 'cause we're late."

She looked up at him, brows raised in question.

"Everyone has gone into town. Dinner first and then the Eagles Hall. Are you up for that?" He stopped abruptly. "I don't know if you feel okay about dancing so soon after losing your father and Joe…but we can come home after dinner…"

"Everyone's going?"

"Your little brother is safely tucked under Big Jim's wing. He's really taken a liking to Mark."

She smiled, a little sadly, he thought. "That's great."

He wanted to assure her Big Jim would love her when he got to know her, but he thought better of it. "If you're up for it, hustle into your dancing boots, and let's go."

Misty grinned. "That sounds like fun." She headed down the hall, unbuttoning her shirt as she went.

Colt's libido surged into overdrive, and he followed her. "Let me help you with all those clothes."

She turned, laughing. "Why, Colton Garrett. I do think you have something on your mind."

"You bet I do." He slipped the blouse from her shoulders and traced a line of kisses down her neck and bare shoulder.

A look crossed her face that set fire to something in his chest. Without another word, he scooped her up in his arms and carried her to his bedroom.

He set her on her feet, but she clung to his neck, smiling so sweetly he had to feast on her lips not once but twice.

Her hands roamed over his chest, tugging at the top snap on his shirt. The snaps opened all the way down to his belt buckle, but the rest of his shirt was firmly trapped inside his Wranglers.

It pleased him that she wanted him out of his clothes. *It's not that easy to undress a working cowboy.*

He thought he would give her a little help, so he unbuckled his large belt buckle and stripped the belt from the loops on his Wranglers. Letting it fall to the floor, he moved her closer to the bed.

"You're making this easy for me." Her voice had dropped to a lower register.

Spreading his arms wide, he grinned. "Knock yourself out. I'm always easy for you."

A pretty blush of color stained her cheeks, but determinedly, she set about removing his shirt. She had to unsnap his cuffs and walk around him to slide the shirt off.

He took the shirt from her and arranged it on the back of a chair to keep it from getting wrinkled. He considered that he would need to put it back on to save face with his father, whose sharp eyes would immediately pick up the fact that something had transpired if he showed up wearing a different shirt.

When he turned, she had slipped out of her clothes, down to her bra and panties. He swallowed hard. "Well, all right."

"I—I just thought we better hurry…you know—if you want to meet up with your dad."

"Yes, ma'am." He slid the bootjack out from under his bed, eased out of his boots, and then slid off his

Wranglers. "May I assist you to my bed and ravish you thoroughly?" He gestured toward his king-size bed.

She giggled, covering her mouth with both hands. "Thoroughly?"

"Yes, ma'am," he drawled. "That's how I roll." He swept her up into his arms and did a fancy turn that landed her on the bed and him beside her.

They were both laughing, and then suddenly they weren't. There erupted a tangle of arms and legs as they struggled to get closer to each other.

Colton grazed his fingers over her warm skin, stirring a rage of desire in his core.

Misty arched closer to him, pressing against his skin as though to meld the two of them together.

He fingered the lacy material of her bra before slipping one strap down and pressing a kiss against her shoulder.

A soft moan escaped Misty's lips. "Oh, Colt…hurry."

"Yes, ma'am," he whispered. He quickly removed her bra and panties before divesting himself of his underwear.

She inhaled sharply. "Let's—let's do this. I mean, I don't want them to know."

"Well, let's don't tell them." He rolled her onto her back and trailed kisses down her body, taking a detour to pay homage to her breasts. He circled her nipples with his tongue, leaving each standing at attention and a grin on her face.

Colton's hand swept over her rib cage and down her flat stomach to cup her mound. Her legs spread apart, and he gently probed her wetness with his finger.

She expelled a sharp breath, writhing in pleasure.

He slipped on a condom. "Now we're dressed for success." Then he set about making sure she had no unfulfilled desires. When they were both satisfied, he reluctantly drew away. They lay together, damp and breathing hard.

"I guess we better get dressed and meet the others."

She let out a snort of laughter. "Y'think?"

He grinned, glad they'd had the house to themselves for a change. Now he wished he had his own place to share with her all the time.

Chapter 11

"WELL, ABOUT DAMNED TIME," BIG JIM MUTTERED when he glanced out the plate-glass window and saw Colton's truck pull up outside the steak house.

Leah gave him a grin and whispered, "Give them a break. They're in love. Can't you see that?"

He snorted and gave her a sideways glance. "Is that what it is? I thought maybe Colt just had the flu."

She smacked him on the arm. "Honestly! When did you get to be such an old curmudgeon?"

"Me? I'm being a realist," Big Jim protested.

Colton went around to open the passenger door and lifted Misty down. He managed to give her a kiss on the way. She was a pretty girl, Big Jim admitted, and she was looking happier than she had at first.

Leah gave him a knowing look. "I'm just glad you didn't treat me like this when I was first getting to know Tyler. I might have turned tail and run back to Oklahoma."

He put his hand on her shoulder. "Nah. You're made of sterner stuff. Besides, you brought my rebellious middle son back to me. I thought he was a lost cause for sure."

"My Tyler is the best man on earth. I love him so much it hurts." She nodded toward the door Colton and Misty had just come through, arm in arm. "Now, stop being an old grouch, and leave those two alone. They both deserve some happiness."

Big Jim drew back in mock indignation. "That's the

second time you've called me 'old' tonight. I have a date with a lovely young woman, so I'll thank you to keep that opinion to yourself."

Leah winked at him before turning to wave at the newcomers.

Colt pulled out a chair for Misty at the other end of the table and seated himself beside her.

There were greetings and good-natured teasing, but Big Jim noted that Beau seemed to be ignoring his brother as well as the woman who had Colt so enraptured. He wondered what was going on between his two sons. It wasn't the first time they'd had a difference of opinion, and he was sure it wouldn't be the last. Still, Big Jim kept an eye on both sons as they studiously ignored each other.

The waitress placed menus in front of Colt and Misty and then brought out plates to those who had arrived earlier.

Big Jim stood when he caught sight of Celia Diaz crossing the parking lot. His heart always took a leap when she made herself available. It was early days yet, but they weren't in any hurry. Well, she didn't seem to be, anyway. Their relationship was developing just fine.

Celia breezed into the restaurant, spied the Garrett party, and gave a little wave. "Hello, everyone. Sorry I'm late. I had to meet with a parent after school." She rolled her eyes but leaned close to Big Jim for a kiss on the cheek. "Occupational hazard."

Big Jim pulled out the chair beside him, the one he had been saving for her, and when she was seated, he leaned forward, inhaling the scent that seemed to be a part of her. "I'm glad you could make it," he whispered close to her ear.

She flashed a smile and picked up the menu. "Let me see…what do I want?"

Big Jim chuckled. "I took the liberty of ordering for you." He watched her wide-set eyes light up as she turned to stare at him.

"You did? Well, what am I dining on tonight?"

"Just a nice little steak, a baked potato, and a salad. Some kind of vegetable on the side. Is that okay?"

A wide grin split her face. "Perfect."

Yes, it's going to be a good night. He hailed the waitress and asked her to hustle up the food he had ordered for Celia. He didn't want to start without her, though she insisted he do so. He cut a bite of his steak and offered it to her on his fork.

Her perfect white teeth pulled the meat from the fork, and she released a soft moan. "Yes, you always know what I like."

When Big Jim looked up, he saw that Colton was staring at him, a little smile lifting the corners of his mouth. Colt reached for Misty's hand and laced his fingers with hers.

It suddenly occurred to Big Jim that Colton must feel about Misty the same way he felt about Celia.

Big Jim released a huge sigh. He wanted his sons to be happy. Tyler had found his perfect woman. Big Jim glanced at Leah, who was taking part in an animated conversation with Gracie and Mark. As a father, he was proud Ty had brought such a wonderful female into his family. She was lovely and had a generous, giving spirit.

Big Jim shifted his attention to the young woman who had captivated his oldest son's attention. Misty gazed at Colton, apparently reflecting the same loving expression as when Leah looked at Tyler.

Okay, I'll give her the benefit of the doubt. Let's just see how this plays out.

———∿∿∿———

In the morning, Colton stretched, taking up his entire king-size bed.

He had enjoyed a great evening at the Eagles Hall with Misty in his arms. He was pretty sure she'd had a good time too.

Of course, she started out the evening feeling pretty good due to her first paycheck and getting to visit with the couple living on her ranch. She appeared to be more hopeful and positive. He thought the rest of her happiness might have had something to do with him.

Making love to Misty was a luxury in that it didn't happen nearly often enough to suit him. He hoped she felt the same way.

It was Saturday, and Colt had a plan. He wanted to take a drive over to the Dalton ranch and talk to Paco. At least this man had some experience with the crops and the herd. Maybe he could get through the man's resistance to find out what had been done in the past and make a plan for the future.

He got out of bed, took a shower, and then headed for the kitchen. When he got there, he saw that Leah and Misty had beaten him to the table. He helped himself to a cup of coffee and checked out the breakfast fare.

"Hello, sleepyhead," Leah called. "Your dad and brother have already taken off. They got up early to take a drive to the county seat. They took Mark with them."

Colton gave himself a head smack. "I forgot. Dad

wanted to take a look at some old deeds archived in the county records."

Leah chuckled. "Not to worry. I think they can handle it without you."

"Mark was all excited to be taking a trip with Big Jim," Misty said. "You should have seen him. He thinks your dad hung the moon and the stars."

"I'll bet." Colton heaved a sigh and sat on the stool beside Misty. "On the other hand, I was hoping we could drive to your ranch today."

"I'd love that." She turned to Leah. "Would you like to come with us?"

Leah cocked her head to one side. "Sure. That would be great. I'd love to see your place." Her smile faded. "But aren't you in danger of losing the ranch?"

Misty glanced at Colton and then turned her attention back to Leah. "Not anymore. I've entered into a partnership to save the ranch and hope to make it a thriving place again."

Colton tried not to react. He hadn't wanted anyone else to be in on his actions before he had a chance to spring it on Big Jim...but it was too late now. He took a plate and scooped scrambled eggs and bacon onto it and snagged a couple slices of toast.

"A partner?" Leah's expression changed in a flash. She appeared to be concerned. "That sounds ominous. Is it someone you can work with? Someone you can trust?"

Colton shrugged. "I sure as hell hope so." He opened the jar of salsa and spooned some onto his eggs.

Misty laughed and leaned her head against his shoulder. "I trust you."

"Wait a minute!" Leah's gaze flicked back and

forth between him and Misty. "The two of you are in a partnership?"

"Yes," Misty crowed. "Isn't it wonderful? Colton saved our property, and he's going to make it profitable for all of us."

Leah held out her hands, palm up. "How come this is the first I've heard of it?"

Colton released the breath he'd been holding. "I haven't told Dad either. I just didn't want to hear any of his disapproval."

Misty turned to him, her brows drawn together. "Oh, Colt. I didn't know he wouldn't approve."

"You don't know my dad. He disapproves of anything that isn't his idea."

Leah leaned across the table to put her hand on top of Misty's. "I can attest to that. My husband, Tyler, had a huge blowup with Big Jim over Ty's singing career. It's a miracle they came back together. Now, Big Jim's proud of Ty's accomplishments, but it took him a while to come around."

Colton nodded in agreement. "Bad times."

"Don't worry, Colt." Leah leaned toward them in a conspiratorial manner. "I won't say a word."

"Thanks. I just want to get a plan in place before he has a chance to bash it."

Leah raised her glass of orange juice in a toast. "Sounds like a great idea."

He hurriedly finished his breakfast and set his plate in the sink. "Let's take a drive, ladies."

He loaded Misty and Leah into his truck and drove to the Dalton ranch. The sun was shining, and the whole place seemed to look better, or perhaps it just seemed less forlorn. He drove around the property first, pointing out the herd, mostly Hereford, Charolais, and Black Angus.

"I'm not an expert," Leah said, "but that looks like a pretty good-sized herd." She pointed out the window. "And there seem to be a lot of calves. That's good, isn't it?"

Misty shrugged. "I think they thrived on neglect. Joe sure wasn't paying much attention the past few years, and my dad was so sick he couldn't get out to deal with them. Paco did the best he could, but he's pretty old for all the responsibility."

"Well, we can take some of the load off him." Colton was certain he could turn the place around, and he wanted Misty to have confidence that he could do so.

"I love the faces of the baby calves," Leah said. "They're so sweet."

Misty nodded. "They are." Her voice sounded a little ragged. "It's really easy to fall in love with those big brown eyes. I fell in love with a newborn Hereford calf when I was a young girl."

"That sounds lovely," Leah said. "I wasn't raised on a farm, but that's the kind of childhood I envision for Gracie and any future children Tyler and I may have." She looked at Misty, and her brows drew together. "What's wrong, Misty?"

"It's nothing really…but something happened that made me stop falling in love with baby calves. It wasn't a big deal…" She gnawed her lower lip. "I just don't like to think about the eventual outcome for our beef cattle. Steak…hamburger…"

Leah sighed. "I can understand that. If I pondered the origin of the protein on my plate, I would probably be a vegetarian. I guess I better never check out any baby pigs, 'cause I really love my bacon."

"Well, you're a rancher now." Colton gave Misty's hand a squeeze. "Farming and ranching are essential businesses. My dad instilled that fact in all his sons when we were really little. It's our job to produce food for all Americans. Dad considers this his sacred duty."

"I know, you're right. I'll try to get my head on straight." She heaved a sigh.

Colton drove back to the Dalton house and parked between the house and the outbuildings. He wanted to check on the structures to make sure they were sound, and he wanted to see if there was anything worthwhile stored inside.

Misty and Leah fell into step beside him as he went to check out the machinery. There was a decent-size tractor with various attachments to serve multiple needs. It looked as though the equipment had been kept in reasonably good condition. *Good for Paco.*

There was an open shed with a small store of baled hay, but they would need more to last through until spring. He would need to see what could be baled, and perhaps another grain crop could be planted and harvested for winterfeed.

One of the doors to the barn stood ajar. He opened them both wide and stepped inside. There was a nasty smell that worked his gag reflex. *Something rotting.* A single bare lightbulb with a pull cord hung in the middle. There were small tools arranged along one wall above a workbench. More hay was stacked against the back wall.

A ladder led to the second story, and Colton decided to check it out. As he climbed, the stench grew worse.

He recognized the smell of decomposing flesh, thinking perhaps an animal had come up here to die.

Stepping out on the upper decking, he turned to give Misty his hand and then Leah. "I didn't figure you two would venture up here."

"Well, you were wrong," Misty said. "We're partners, remember?"

"What is that disgusting smell?" Leah put her hand over her nose. "Ugh!"

"Something's dead," Colton said. "Could be a possum or a raccoon. Be careful."

He opened a door at the front that could be used to load hay into the top of the barn. Using a conveyor belt made it easy. With a little more light, he saw there was nothing useful stored up there.

Misty let out a little yelp, and Leah gasped.

Colton turned to see both were staring wide-eyed at a dimly lit section of the loft.

Misty was pointing. "Who is that?"

Colton followed her gaze and saw a body slumped against the partition. He swallowed hard. Colton recognized the man as Fred Hamilton. There was a pitchfork stabbed through his gut, impaling him against the wall.

—⁓—

Colton called 911 and herded the women into the house. He paced outside, trying to piece together the fragments of the puzzle. The last time he'd seen the banker, he'd thought Hamilton was being evasive. Then Hamilton had left the bank abruptly to avoid dealing with Colton when he returned to reconcile the past due loan. Something shady was definitely going on. Now Hamilton was dead.

The sheriff himself came out to the Dalton ranch along with two of his deputies and an ambulance. The EMTs spent very little time in the barn and departed without removing Fred Hamilton from the hayloft.

The next vehicle to arrive was a van from the county medical examiner's office. The ME and one of his assistants climbed out and went to work. The men wore coveralls and donned gloves and masks to examine the remains of Fred Hamilton.

The sheriff questioned Colton as well as Misty and Leah. Then he questioned Paco and Rosa, who said they hadn't seen or heard anything out of the ordinary but that neither had ventured into the barn.

Misty looked so sad, it tore at Colton's heart. She had seen way too much death for one so young.

He sat at the Dalton kitchen table with Misty and Leah. They were drinking iced tea but not saying much.

Colton figured this was not a good time to talk to Paco about the ranch, the herd, or the crops, so he nursed his tea and waited.

In due time, the sheriff returned to tell them the body was being removed and that the medical examiner would make an official ruling but was calling it a homicide for the time being.

Colton nodded tersely. "I didn't think a man would trespass on someone's property, climb into the hayloft, and stab himself with a pitchfork."

"Highly unlikely," the sheriff agreed. "We'll wait for the ruling, but in the meantime, we're treating Hamilton's death as a murder."

Colton nodded. "Why would Fred Hamilton be out here, Sheriff? That's what I can't understand."

The sheriff raised an eyebrow. "And who the hell ran a pitchfork through him?"

Misty cringed at the sheriff's words. She sat between Colton and Leah, her hands gripped together on the table.

Colton covered her hands with one of his. He was so glad Mark had not been with them. For certain, he didn't need to be exposed to a scene like this.

The memory of Hamilton's swollen and discolored corpse, rotting in the barn, would live with him forever.

The sheriff departed, and Colton rose from the table. "Let's go home. We've done all we can do here today."

Misty's lips trembled. "This is my home." Her voice wavered. "And I was planning on moving back here with my little brother."

Colton frowned down at her. "Well, I don't think that's such a good idea at the moment. Someone else has been murdered here. Someone who had a connection to the ranch."

She pressed her lips together and nodded.

Colton put his hand on her shoulder, giving it a gentle squeeze. "Misty, I'm sure you don't want to put Mark in danger, do you?"

She looked as though the breath had been knocked from her lungs. "No, of course not."

"Then let me take you back to the Garrett ranch until the sheriff sorts this all out."

Leah slipped an arm around her as well. "Come on, honey. Let's go. It's too big a risk for you to stay here."

Misty's eyes teared up. "I—I need to sort through my daddy's things…and Joe's things. The church ladies can give them to people who need them."

"That's a great idea," Leah said. "Tomorrow, after church, I'll drive out with you and help you go through their belongings. We can bring some boxes and do it up right."

Colton thought a lot of his sister-in-law, but at the moment, he held her in even higher esteem. Her words seemed to be calming Misty and helping her to cope with yet another tragedy.

Misty turned to Colton. "Do you think Rosa and Paco will be okay here?"

"Is there a weapon in the house?" Colton asked.

Misty nodded. "Yes, several. There are rifles and shotguns. I think Joe had a handgun."

Colton called Paco over and told him to make sure the weapons were loaded and not to open the door to strangers. He said they would return the next day after church to reassess the situation.

When Colton had both Misty and Leah in the truck, he turned around, casting one last glance at the barn, with its doors still standing open. It looked ominous, as though it harbored a dark secret. He climbed into the driver's seat and started the truck, anxious to put some distance between his small party and the vivid image carved in his memory of Fred Hamilton impaled in the barn.

When they reached the Garrett ranch he found that the others had returned home before them.

Colton pulled his dad and Beau aside to have a private conversation with them.

"What's going on?" Beau asked.

Colton shepherded them into the office and shut the door firmly behind them. "What do you know about Fred Hamilton, the banker?" he asked his father.

Big Jim shrugged. "I dunno. Kind of a pompous ass. Full of himself. Why do you ask?"

"Because he's dead," Colton said. "I took Misty and Leah for a drive out to the Dalton ranch, and we found his body in the barn."

Beau took a wide stance, his hands fisted on his hips. "What the hell?"

"That's what I say." Colton shook his head. "I have no idea what happened to him, but the sheriff is calling it a homicide."

Beau turned away, taking a few paces and then spinning around abruptly. "You stay away from that place, Colt. It's got bad juju going on. That makes three deaths associated with the Dalton ranch."

"Aw, come on," Colton said. "Misty's father was terminally ill."

Big Jim stopped him by laying his big hand on Colton's shoulder. "But there have been two murders. Beau's right. You should stay far away."

"I told Misty and Leah I would take them back after church. She wants to go through her father's and Joe's personal belongings and give them away to the needy."

Big Jim expelled a breath. "I can understand that it has to be done, but it can wait until these crimes have been solved. No sense in you getting involved."

Beau flicked a glance at Colton and then looked away.

"I am involved, Dad. I think you know how I feel about Misty. I told her I would help her, and I will."

A muscle in Big Jim's jaw twitched. "Well, if you're going, we're all going. After church, we'll have lunch and then go to the Dalton ranch. There's strength in numbers, and I don't think anyone's going to mess with all of us."

Colton felt strangely relieved. "Thanks, Dad. I'm sure Misty will appreciate it too." He knew having his father and brother in tow greatly increased the chances of someone letting it slip that he had paid up the Dalton loan, but just having his family behind him felt pretty damned good.

The next day, Misty was feeling a little better. Somehow, the Garretts came together like a wall around her and her little brother. When they all trooped into the church, she felt as though she had been accepted.

Although she had not been attending church for the previous several years, due first to spending two years away at college in Norman, Oklahoma, and then to the ensuing years of caring for her father, she realized how much she had missed it. Sitting next to Colton, with his arm draped on the back of the pew, gave her a new sense of belonging.

Her little brother looked happy too. Between Colton and Big Jim, Mark was surrounded by excellent male role models. Even Beau seemed to be coming around.

She listened to the pastor's sermon. Somehow it seemed the message was aimed directly at her. It was about rejoicing in the things you had been given and not envying your neighbor who might have more in the way of worldly goods.

Well, we Daltons don't have much, but I'm very grateful for what we have. She glanced at Breckenridge T. Ryan, sitting a few rows in front of them with his wife, the town doctor. Misty was very thankful to be working for him and for having an ATM card in her purse and some money in the bank.

Her friendship with Leah and Sara Beth gave her the female companionship she had always needed as the lone woman in her male-dominated family.

Most of all, she was gratified to have been taken into the Garrett household at the time when she and Mark were so vulnerable.

And then there was Colton. She lifted her chin to gaze up at him. Colton was the very best thing she could imagine happening to her. She was in love with him, and whether he loved her or not wasn't important. What was important was that he had become the best friend she could ever imagine. Whatever the future had in store, she would guard that friendship and not let anything destroy it, even if it meant she kept her mouth shut about her feelings for him.

She knew he liked her, but was it love or just his kindness and friendship? They certainly had passion between them. Colton was so hot he smoldered. Surely if he loved her he would tell her. Wasn't that the way it was supposed to happen? Or maybe it just seemed that way in the movies?

After the church services, the Garrett entourage stopped at Tiny's Diner for lunch.

Big Jim explained to Misty, in detail, how Tiny served the very best chicken-fried steak in all of Texas and insisted she try it. They were all served a small dinner salad first, followed by an immense platter featuring a chicken-fried steak as big as a baseball glove. There were also mashed potatoes and a side of seasoned green beans.

Misty sucked in a breath. It was more food than she could eat, but she had to smile when she saw Mark digging in. Big Jim was watching Mark too and had an amused grin on his face. She figured he was thinking about his three sons at the same age.

She picked up her knife and fork, attacking the food with relish. "This is really delicious, Big Jim."

He smiled benevolently. Maybe he was warming up to her a little; at least she hoped so.

After the meal, they climbed into the two trucks and caravanned out to the Dalton ranch. As they approached, her stomach grew more and more tense. Big Jim had Leah and Gracie with him. Beau and Mark rode in the seat behind Colton. The conversation was sparse on the way to the ranch.

When they turned off the interstate onto the road to the ranch, the food she had eaten seemed to be twisting in her gut. The Dalton ranch had been such a happy place during her own childhood. Losing her mother had been the turning point. After that, a cloud of sadness and misfortune seemed to have settled over the property. Everything was lost in a downward spiral. Her father...Joe...

What would it take to turn it all around?

Colton pulled in behind his dad and parked.

When they had all piled out, Leah gestured to the back of Big Jim's truck. "I brought a few boxes to put the clothes and other things in."

Colton hefted the boxes out, and Leah grabbed some before heading into the house.

"Do you need some help with the sorting?" Colton asked.

"I'm sure Leah and I can get it done. We have Rosa to help too. Why don't you see if Paco needs anything? I still have a little money on my bank card."

Colton grinned at her as she took the rest of the boxes into the house.

Chapter 12

"So, where was the body?" Beau asked.

Colton heaved a sigh. "In the barn." He pointed to the structure. "Hamilton was up in the hayloft. Someone had speared him through the middle with a pitchfork." He felt Big Jim's and Beau's eyes on him. "Yeah, it was horrible. And he had been there several days, so he was plenty ripe."

"Ugh! I hate that smell." Big Jim made a face.

The three Garretts took off on a slow stroll around the area.

"That's a good John Deere tractor," Big Jim commented. "And the rest of the equipment is in decent shape. I wonder why they couldn't make a go of it."

Colton heaved a sigh. "Probably because her dad became a drunk after her mom died...and he was terminally ill." He shrugged. "And her brother Joe was a dumbass."

Beau nodded in agreement. "That he was. Joe sort of took a wrong turn somewhere along the way. He was never really interested in ranching. Spent most of his time partying with his friends." He looked thoughtful for a minute. "He always ran with Eddie Simmons and that bunch. Remember Eddie's cousin, Nate Blair? There were five of them who ran together before Nate disappeared."

"Yeah, I remember," Colton said. "Wonder what happened to Nate? Never saw him again after that summer he went missing."

Beau shook his head. "That's when Joe and the others really went off course."

"Shame," Big Jim commented. "This is a nice little ranch. How many head of cattle?"

Colton told him.

"Nice herd. With some tending, this place could shape right up. Maybe I should think about buying it from the Dalton kids. I'd hate to see them lose everything."

It's now or never. "Too late, Dad." Colton hooked his thumbs in his belt loops and took a wide stance.

"What? It's already been foreclosed on?" Big Jim turned to face him.

"No, Dad. I invested in this ranch. I'm a legal partner with Misty and her brother."

Big Jim's eyes narrowed for a moment. Then he gave a slight nod. "Good business decision. Just see that you turn this place around. It's a good acquisition."

Colton shook his head. "I didn't acquire it. I bought into it. I went to the bank with Breck Ryan and paid the loan up to date. And I have a legal partnership agreement with Misty." He shrugged. "Now, all I have to do is figure out how to make it productive again."

"Shoot, Son. That's the easy part. Put a crop in the ground, keep the herd fed, and start planning for the next season. We Garretts have been doing that forever. It's our way of life." He slapped Colton on the shoulder and turned back to his stroll.

Beau gave him a grin, shook his head, and then fell into step alongside his dad.

Colt took a second to come to grips with his father's easy acceptance of his expenditure. He had thought there would be a huge uproar. He breathed out a sigh of relief and caught up with Big Jim and Beau as they drew even with the barn.

Big Jim stopped, staring up at the open door to the hayloft. "I can't understand what Fred Hamilton was doing out here on the Dalton property."

"Neither can I, Dad," Colton said. "But the sheriff is looking into it."

Misty started on her father's room. She knew that was in fairly good shape because she had always been the one to make sure her dad's clothes were washed and put away carefully.

When she opened the door, a feeling of desolation washed over her, like a riptide pulling her under. She fought the urge to sink to her knees and weep her heart out.

The sight of the empty bed tore at her heart. Her loss felt enormous, but she sucked in a breath and stepped into the room, leaving the door open wide for Leah to follow.

With Leah to help, they sorted and folded her father's clothing before packing it in the boxes. Concentrating on this task helped to focus her energy on a positive project and avoid thinking of her father, at least for the moment.

She discarded the unused medications and cleared off the bedside table. The hospice company had arranged to come and remove the electric bed, but her parents' cherry bed and mattress were stored in the attic. Maybe Colton would help bring them down.

Rosa swept the floor, promising to mop and wax it before returning the area rug to the room. The hospice company had suggested removing it lest her dad stumble when he had still been able to walk.

Now the room looked forlorn, as though stripped of its dignity. Rosa said she would take down the curtains and wash them as well.

Nothing more to do in here. Sadly, Misty closed the door.

She tried to squelch the feeling of dread when she twisted the knob on Joe's door. She'd rarely even caught a glimpse of the interior. Joe had long ago threatened her with bodily harm when she had chanced to venture inside. Now, she definitely felt as though she was trespassing.

The room smelled like Joe. It probably smelled the way the boy's locker room did at the high school.

She sighed and opened the windows to air it out.

Leah came bustling into the room. "Okay, I took those boxes to the truck. We can drop them by church tomorrow." She raised her nose in the air. "Smells funky in here."

"Unwashed male," Misty said.

Rosa came in with an empty laundry basket and started picking up clothes off the floor. She stripped the bed and removed all the bedding from the room. Before she left, she sprayed a fabric freshener on the mattress and pillows.

"Much better," Leah said.

Since the clothes stuffed into Joe's dresser had taken on the musty odor, Rosa said she would wash and fold the contents and have them ready to donate in the next couple of days.

Misty started opening the drawers, one by one, dumping the contents of each into a wash basket.

Leah carried the first filled basket to the laundry room, leaving Misty alone to open the bottom drawer, but it seemed to be stuck. She could only open it halfway.

Misty sat cross-legged on the floor and tried removing the articles of clothing, mostly threadbare jeans and faded T-shirts.

She pulled out something hard from the back corner and gazed at it in disbelief. It was a revolver partially wrapped in a torn T-shirt. She didn't unwrap the shirt, but sat staring at it for a few minutes. A huge dose of anxiety grabbed her gut, and she put the gun in her large handbag. She was aware that Joe owned a handgun but didn't think it was a revolver. And this one looked old.

She sat back down to finish emptying out the drawer, and her hand brushed against something that had been keeping the drawer from opening all the way. Something firmly affixed to the bottom edge of the drawer. Misty gritted her teeth and forced the drawer out of its groove.

Groping along the underside of the drawer, she found it was a packet that was taped all around. She was finally able to pry it loose and examine it. Whatever was inside, Joe had kept it hidden but secure. Now that she had discovered his hiding place, she was reluctant to open it. That he had kept it concealed made her feel as though she was invading his privacy all over again.

When Leah returned, she found Misty still contemplating the carefully wrapped bundle. "Whatcha got there?"

Misty started guiltily. "Oh, um—I'm not sure. It was taped under one of the drawers."

Leah cocked her head. "Well, take it with you. Colton said we should get started for home."

Misty shoved the drawer in and scrambled to her feet, still clutching the packet. She saw that it was an envelope like one that might contain a greeting card. Large and square. Heaving out a sigh, she stuffed it in her purse as well. Whatever was inside, Joe had cared enough to hide it.

She glanced around the room. It looked better and smelled better than it had earlier. Some things remained to be sorted, but they had done a good job for one day. Crossing to the windows, she closed and latched them. That someone had been murdered in their barn was worrisome enough. The least she could do was make sure the house was secure.

—⁓—

When Misty had driven off to Langston the next day, Colton decided to take a look at the Dalton ranch without the Daltons. He figured if he were going to get into a head-to-head with the old man, he might as well get it over with. Paco had been working the ranch for years. No wonder he felt proprietary.

He drove straight to the property and knocked on the door. When Rosa answered, she smiled shyly when he asked if he might speak to her husband.

"He go to check on the cows. He be back later."

Colton nodded and told her he would return. He wandered around the outbuildings for a while and then decided to check on the herd himself.

He drove to the field where he had seen cattle pastured and soon spied the old ranch truck Paco drove. Pulling up behind the truck, Colton parked on the side of the road. Paco had climbed through the barbed-wire fence and stood eyeing Colton with suspicion.

Oh, boy!

Colt climbed through the fence and approached the old man with a smile. "Hey, Paco. How ya doin' today?"

Paco nodded at him warily but accepted the hand Colton offered.

"I wanted to get some of your insights about the ranch." Colton saw this register, but the old man stonewalled him. "I figured you were the best person to ask."

Paco stood a little straighter but nodded again.

"Mostly, I wanted to know what you think it will take to turn this place around. I know it was a productive ranch at one time."

"You bet this was a good ranch," Paco said, his voice gravelly. "It still is." He picked up a small rock at his feet and hurled it back toward the road. "All it needs is for someone to care about it. Mr. Dalton, he loved this ranch...but when the wife died, he just stopped caring about everything."

Colton gave a grunt of agreement. "Joe didn't care? I thought he had been working on the ranch."

Paco made a scoffing noise back in his throat. "That boy Joe, he only cared about Joe. He didn't care about the ranch. He didn't care about his family. He only cared about himself and his little pack of friends. They were like young wolves, always coming around to rip off the place."

Colton frowned. "Who were Joe's friends?" Though he knew the answer, he wanted to get the old man's take on the relationships.

Paco waved his hand, as though this was a trivial matter. "The youngest Diaz boy, the Lynch boy, and Levi Blair's nephew, Eddie Simmons. The four of them were like blood relations. Always together. Always sneaking around." He cleared his throat noisily and spat on the ground.

"Levi Blair, huh?" Colton recalled the frosty look the

old gentleman had given him when they had encoun-
tered each other in Breck's office. Something about
a history of a land dispute with Big Jim. *Well, that's
reason enough for Blair to dislike me.*

Paco spat again. "That man would cut your heart out
for a nickel."

A cold sensation twisted Colton's gut. "And Joe was
running with Blair's nephew?"

"He was running with Levi's son too before that boy
ran away."

"Seems like I heard something about that," Colton
said thoughtfully. "Nate Blair, right?"

Paco nodded.

"It's been a while back."

Paco's face contorted in concentration, his forehead
folding into lines. "It's been about eight years ago. The
boys were probably just fifteen or sixteen years old."
He shrugged. "Everyone thought Nate would come back
eventually. Never did."

Colton thought about the set-to between Big Jim and
Tyler. It could have gone the same way. "It's tough
when there are big disagreements between family members and neither one wants to give in."

Paco removed his hat, raked his fingers through his
thick head of mostly gray hair, and then set the hat back
on his head. "If I remember, Levi claimed there was no
reason his son would have left home. He thought the boy
had been kidnapped."

"Maybe he did meet with foul play," Colton suggested.

"Most likely," Paco agreed. He folded his arms over
his chest. "So, what's going on with you and Misty? Do
I need to get out my shotgun?"

Colton cleared his throat. "No, sir. I don't expect you do." Then he chuckled. "But maybe that wouldn't be such a bad idea."

Humorless dark eyes assessed him. "So you're serious?"

Colt lifted his shoulders and spread his hands in a "who knows" gesture. "I am. I'm not sure if Misty is yet."

Paco narrowed his gaze. "You better not break her heart."

"More than likely she's going to break mine."

As Colton was driving home, he felt pretty satisfied with himself. He thought he had won the old man over. They had retired to the house and chatted over coffee, finally getting around to discussing the management of the land and the stock.

The plan was to get a grain crop in the ground as soon as possible to harvest for feed, and rye grass in another field for winter forage. Colton would arrange for seed to be paid for at Moore's Feed and Seed, and Paco would pick it up the next day.

He felt somewhat elated that they were really making a start. He was certain that his partnership with Misty and Mark would work out to be financially rewarding for all of them. He just hoped that their personal relationship would work out as well.

Colton realized Misty had no idea how Joe had been spending his time. She thought he had been working to keep the ranch going. He wasn't sure he wanted to disabuse her of that fact. After all, Joe was her brother. *Her dead brother.* Colton would just keep Paco's revelations to himself.

Misty was having a pretty decent day. When she'd gotten to the law office, she'd discovered some typing on her desk that needed to be done. Apparently, Breck had come in on the weekend and made a nice pile of tasks for her.

I can do this. She prioritized her work and started right in on it first thing. By the time she took her lunch break, the pile was significantly smaller.

Lunching with Sara Beth was a treat. The shared meal was always interesting, but the shared conversation was even better.

Misty realized she was getting very attached to Cami Lynn, Sara Beth's baby daughter. She was such an adorable little thing. And Misty was growing very fond of Sara Beth as well. Having two close female friends was a luxury she had never known before. Between Leah and Sara Beth, Misty felt she was developing a support system she would need to get through the tough times ahead…especially in the event that Colton didn't reciprocate her feelings.

Misty knew Colton liked her, but he seemed to feel the same way about everyone. Like a big, lovable puppy. She considered her options.

Maybe she had been too subtle. Maybe she needed to do something to catch his attention. She shivered. *Maybe I should just forget about it.*

She had loathed the girls in school who appeared to be constantly flirting, even throwing themselves at the various popular boys.

And where are those girls today?

Misty let out a huff of air. *Happily married, that's where they are.*

She turned to the next project in her pile, quickly

scanned through it, and then heaved a sigh. Although she hadn't particularly respected the girls who had been so blatant, she had to admit their ploys had worked.

While she'd gone off to college and then come home to take care of her dad, her female classmates had been getting married and having kids.

She felt a pang, and the image of Cami Lynn sprang to mind. She wouldn't mind having a sweet little baby of her own.

Dropping the note back in the pile, she leaned against her fists.

Of course, her baby would look different. He or she would have dark hair, but it would be incredible if it had Colton's striking blue eyes. The blue eyes seemed to be a strong Garrett gene.

Misty snapped out of her trance. She had been a million miles away, fantasizing about Colton's eyes and having his baby.

Get back to work, girl. Breck isn't paying you to sit around and daydream.

She picked up the note again, and her eyes widened. It was about updating a will for Levi Blair. The new will was to name Edward Eugene Simmons, Mr. Blair's nephew, as the sole heir to Blair's considerable estate.

Something clicked in her brain. This was the Eddie who had been one of Joe's best friends. One of the guys he was always running around with. She pictured him in her mind. Tall, lanky Eddie with his ruddy complexion and a pinched look to his face. His hair was reddish-blond and curly. She had always thought it looked like it needed to be washed. He was probably twenty-five now. *Same age as Joe…as Joe would have been.*

Well, Mr. Edward Eugene Simmons. You are going to be a very lucky nephew when your uncle croaks.

Misty typed up the new will and sent it to the printer. She stood up and stretched. *Time for a break.* She pulled the copies of the will from the printer and carefully placed them in Breck's inbox.

She had made quite a dent in the pile of projects. Walking to the water cooler, she filled the tiny paper cup with water three times and drained it each time. She crushed the cup, tossed it in the wastebasket, and then returned to her desk.

She reached in the bottom drawer and opened her oversized purse. She knew she had a pack of gum in there, but it must have sunk to the bottom. Pawing through the collection of necessities and junk, she heaved a sigh and dumped the contents of her bag on top of the desk.

There was a clunk, and Joe's handgun lay on top of the pile. It was still peeking out of the ragged T-shirt in which it was wrapped. She didn't know why Joe had kept it like this, but she was reluctant to touch it.

Misty swallowed hard. Every time she looked at it, she cringed. She wasn't afraid of guns. Her daddy had made sure she knew how to use one. *But this thing just looks dangerous.*

She picked it up and deposited it in her now-empty purse.

Blowing out a breath, she tried not to think of the gun. What was it she'd been looking for? *Oh, yes. Gum. There it is.* She took a piece and removed the wrapper, folding the gum into her mouth. The pleasing mint flavor refreshed her taste buds immediately.

Misty focused on the mess she had just poured on her tidy desktop. She tossed a few things in the trash, and then her hand lit on the packet she had pulled from underneath the drawer in Joe's room.

Compared to the gun, this wasn't scary at all. She took a long, pointy letter opener out of the desk and carefully opened the envelope. Spilling the contents onto the desk, she saw they were mostly photos. Her eyes teared up as she recognized Joe in a few of them. It was his gang. Ron Diaz, Stan Lynch, Nate Blair, and Eddie Simmons...when they were all much younger. Joe's face was so innocent. No snarky superiority then.

Oh, yeah. The five of them were inseparable. Like a pack of feral animals.

She remembered how mad her dad would get when Joe snuck out of the house at night to go off with his posse. Or when he shirked his work around the ranch. She shook her head, but she had to smile.

The top photo showed four of them standing with their arms hung around each other's shoulders.

She recalled when Joe had received the camera for a birthday present. At the time, he hadn't been particularly thrilled with the gift, but over time, he had used it a lot.

She flipped to the next image.

Sucking in a breath, she experienced a choking sensation. Two of the boys were fighting. She couldn't tell who they were. It was quite a scuffle. She tried to eliminate the nonparticipants and finally decided the two involved were Eddie Simmons and his cousin, Nate Blair. The two combatants looked serious. The last image was just of Eddie holding a handgun. His shirt was filthy, and he looked scared.

She wondered why Joe would keep these photos and especially why he would keep them hidden all these years. Carefully, she slid the images in the envelope and slipped it back into her purse. She replaced the items she was going to keep and tossed the junk before stashing her purse back in the bottom drawer.

She felt a little anxious. Probably just seeing Joe's face again. *Yeah, that must be it.* Heaving a huge sigh, she reached for the next note in the stack Breck had left for her.

Big Jim Garrett had been amazed to learn that his oldest son bailed out the Dalton ranch. Perhaps he shouldn't have been so surprised, considering how Colton felt about the girl. It must have taken a big chunk out of his savings, and Colt wasn't one to fritter away his money.

He watched as Colt saddled the Appaloosa stallion he had bought at auction. It was a big horse and should be a good ride for a big man. As Colton swung himself up into the saddle, the horse danced a little to the side. *Not his usual rider.*

Colton rode him around the corral, keeping to an easy gait.

Ears back, the horse maneuvered close to the railing, scraping Colton's leg against the wood.

Colton yelled and pulled the reins to the left, forcing the horse's head in the other direction. But when Colt eased up on the reins, the horse tried to disgorge him again.

"That horse sure doesn't want a stranger on his back," Big Jim called.

Colt grinned. "Apparently not. It's going to take a while for Sam to get used to me."

Big Jim saddled his favorite horse and led him out of the stables. "Hold up, Colt. Do you want to go for a ride? We can go take a look at the cattle I have in quarantine."

"Sure, Dad." Colton maneuvered Sam out of the corral through the stables and joined Big Jim.

They headed to a pasture where the newest acquisitions were quarantined until the veterinarian could get by to take a look at them. Big Jim had to be sure they were healthy before he allowed them to mingle with the rest of his herd.

"So, what are your plans for the Dalton place?" Big Jim tried to keep his tone easy. He didn't want to get Colt's back up.

"I talked to the foreman. I think we're going to plant a crop of feed for the cattle. That's the first thing."

"There's time," Big Jim agreed. "You could put in some winter rye and let the herd graze on that."

Colton gave him a sideways glance and then nodded. "Good idea. I had thought a grain crop."

Big Jim shrugged. "You can do both. Harvest a grain crop and leave the rye for forage. That should get you through the winter just fine."

"Thanks, Dad. I really hadn't had a chance to think this through."

Big Jim was amazed that Colt admitted that to him. He bit his tongue to keep from roaring that he'd been a danged fool to make that kind of investment without thinking it through. He sucked in a deep breath, filled his lungs, and let it out slowly. He didn't want to have the kind of breach with Colt that he'd had with his middle son, Tyler.

It was a miracle that they had resolved their issues over Ty's music aspirations. It wouldn't have happened at all if Ty hadn't gotten involved with Leah and her daughter. *Yeah, better keep my opinions to myself.*

"Heck, Dad. The Dalton ranch is good land...and it's a decent-size spread. I thought that I'd made a pretty good deal just paying the loan up to date. Besides, Misty and her little brother haven't got the knowledge or ability to make a go of the place on their own." Colton turned to grin at him impudently. "I don't see how this can be a losing proposition."

"You could be right. At least I hope so."

Colt heaved a deep sigh. "And I suppose you know I couldn't stand by while Misty and Mark lost their home."

Another surprise. Big Jim congratulated himself on not going off on a rant. Maybe this slow and easy approach was paying off. "I know, Son. You've got a good heart. At least you made sure to get a legal agreement, all drawn up and signed. Good thinking."

Colton's expression grew grim. They rode along in silence for a moment. "The main reason I got Breck involved was because I was getting the runaround from Fred Hamilton at the bank. It was like he didn't want me to pay up the loan. He told me the ranch was already in foreclosure, but it wasn't. I told him I would be back in the afternoon to take care of the loan, but he skipped out on me. Next thing I know, I'm staring at him, speared through the gut in the Dalton hayloft."

Big Jim drew up on the reins, staring hard at his son. "So, you're telling me you might have been one of the last people to see Fred Hamilton alive?"

Colton reined in the big Appaloosa. "I guess so. I

hadn't thought about it that way. I thought he was just trying to dodge me." He frowned. "But, at the time, I did think he was acting strange...evasive...shifty. I thought he had some ulterior motive concerning the Dalton place, like maybe he wanted to snap it up for himself."

Big Jim swallowed hard. "Do you think his death has anything to do with the Daltons or their property?"

"I can't say, Dad. It was just a feeling. Like there was something going on beneath the surface... Hey!" Colton lurched to one side as his mount scraped him against a mesquite tree. The rough bark and thorns dug into his calf, tearing the dense fabric of his Wranglers. He let out a mild curse. "This damned horse hates me."

Big Jim chuckled. "Looks like it. Maybe you ought to pay a little attention to where you're going. You're the rider. He's the horse. You're supposed to be giving him directions. Remember?"

Colton glanced at the torn denim and blood oozing out of his wound. "Yeah, thanks, Dad. I didn't think of that."

Big Jim huffed out a breath. "Was that sarcasm I just heard?"

Colton grinned. "You have the hearing of a bat, Dad."

The return ride to the Garrett ranch house was silent for the most part. It seemed each man had a lot to consider.

Big Jim was thinking about Fred Hamilton, wondering if his death was tied to the Daltons. It seemed unlikely that their barn had been a random choice for a murder scene, but what was the connection?

He reminded himself that Misty's brother had been murdered. *Shot in the head.* Was Joe's death in any way tied to that of Fred Hamilton?

When they rode up to the stables, young Mark was

there. He greeted them with a wave of his hand and a grin. *A really good kid*.

Big Jim watched Colton interact with the boy. Both men dismounted and handed the reins over to Mark, who promised to give the horses a good rubdown.

"Did you know your horse hates me?" Colton asked. "He really hates me. He tried to kill me a few times."

Mark's face reflected concern. "Oh no. He must have been having a bad day. He's not like that. Sam is a good horse."

Colt broke out in a grin. "It's okay. He just has to get used to me. He doesn't want anyone on his back except you. It will take a little time." He ruffled Mark's hair and headed out of the stable.

Throwing an arm around Colton's neck, Big Jim trudged toward the house, his oldest son in tow.

Big Jim didn't want to mention it, but he thought his son would make a great father someday. He just wanted Colt to wait for the right girl.

"It's really beautiful here." Misty stretched out her arms and turned around.

Leah had invited Misty to join her to inspect the home being constructed for her family. The site was beautiful, a modest rise overlooking a lush valley.

"You are so lucky." Misty gulped in deep breaths and blew them out through her pursed lips.

Leah chortled. "You bet I am. My Tyler is the best man on the planet."

Gracie ran to Misty and grabbed her hand. "C'mon with me, Misty. I want to show you my room."

Leah and her grandmother followed into the shell of a house. The roof was covered with yellow Tyvek in preparation to have an outer layer applied. There was no electricity, but the windowpanes were in place, allowing sunshine to brighten the interior.

"Oh, this is quite spacious." Misty stopped to look around the front room.

"The kitchen and den are back there, and the bedrooms are off to this side." Leah gestured to a doorway opening off to the left.

"Except for my room," Gran said. "They gave me a nice-sized room and my own special bathroom on the other side of the house."

Leah laughed. "We thought you might like some privacy."

Gran's expression was amused. "I think that you might like some privacy too."

Leah sucked in a deep breath and released it with a grin. "Yeah, that too."

Gracie pulled Misty down the hallway to show her a room she was claiming as her own. "Mommy said I could pick whatever color I want. I want purple."

Misty visualized a gloomy purple shrouding the space. "That sounds—nice. Very nice."

"This is the color we're going for," Leah supplied, pointing to a paint swatch taped to the wall. It was a pale lilac. *Much better*.

"Even nicer," she said. "How many bedrooms do you have here?"

"Um, we have one master suite, Gracie's room, Gran's room, and two more guest rooms."

Misty grinned. "Planning on having a few guests?"

"Maybe." Leah glanced at Gracie, who was dancing around her future room. "We hope to make some more little Garretts some day."

"That's a good plan. I wish you the very best." Misty was happy for Leah and her family, but she felt a twinge of envy. She hoped that, someday, she might have a plan for the future that included Colton as well as Mark.

Just to be able to live every day with the people she loved and not be afraid of what the next day would bring was her idea of heaven on earth.

Chapter 13

COLTON SNAGGED A COUPLE OF APPLES OUT OF A bowl on the kitchen table. He had a sneaking suspicion his talented sister-in-law had polished them to a high gleam and arranged them in this pyramid of perfection. They looked ripe and delicious, but he had another purpose for them...seduction was on his mind.

He headed for the stables where Sam, the big Appaloosa, was king. Mark was still at school, so Colt thought he would take another solo run at breaking down the stallion's prejudice against him. At best, he hoped to be able to win the horse's acceptance and trust. At worst, it would be an opening overture in a courtship of man and horse.

Colt tromped out the door, intent upon his path to the outbuildings. He knew Sam was important to Mark and Mark was important to Misty...so it made sense for him to try to bond with the horse they had in common.

Entering the stables, he heard the sound of horses' hooves moving around in their stalls. They must know that he intended to confront Sam. The Appaloosa must be antsy, dancing in anticipation of the next time he got to put Colton, his foe, in his place.

Colton turned the corner, gazing down the line of stalls. Two of the horses were peering at him, leaning as far as they could out of their stalls. But not Sam. He was playing hard to get.

"Hey, big fellow." Colt approached him slowly, speaking in a low voice. "You're such a big, strong fellow."

The horse's ears went back, and he moved to the far side of the stall. His hooves moved rhythmically on the floor, tromping the hay underneath.

"That's okay, Sam. You can stay over there. I'm just going to hang out here and eat this apple." He displayed one of the apples and took a big bite out of it. He made a show of crunching it open-mouthed. He leaned against the door to the stall, holding the apple in one hand.

The horse nickered, his ears flicking from front to back. He stared at the apple in Colton's hand.

Horses have a keen sense of smell, and Colton counted on the fact that the tantalizing aroma of fresh apple would entice his prey. "C'mon over here, Sam. I'll share with you." He waggled the apple enticingly.

Sam snorted and took a couple of steps closer.

"That's a good boy. Come on over." He extended the apple to the horse.

Two more steps and Sam stretched his neck out to accept the treat. His big horse teeth crunched the fruit, much as Colton had.

"Pretty good, huh?"

Sam shook his head, sending his mane flying in all directions, and took a couple of steps to the back of the stall.

"I see. You just want me for my apple…well, I have another one." He displayed the second apple and waggled it for Sam to notice.

Sam tossed his head and neighed, then closed the distance between them. He reached for the apple, but Colton drew it out of reach.

"Be patient, big boy. There is a price to pay."

Sam stared at him, intelligent horse eyes regarding him.

Colton stretched out his other hand and stroked it over Sam's neck. "That's a good boy. Yes, good boy." He continued to stroke the horse's neck with one hand and offered the apple with the other. "There we go. See, we can be friends. I'm not Mark, but I am the guy who paid top dollar to give you a home where you can be with Mark every day."

Sam gobbled the apple but didn't move away.

Colton stayed in the stable a while, just rubbing the horse's neck and talking softly to him.

Small victories.

—◦◦◦—

When Misty got to the Garrett ranch that evening, she wasn't sure what to do about the photos Joe had hidden away. She was certain they were something her big brother hadn't wanted her or anyone else to find, but for the life of her, she couldn't figure out why. They were just snapshots of Joe and his four best friends from high school. They had remained friends up until Joe's death…at least the four of them had. Not Nate Blair, since he had gone missing all those years ago.

She frowned. *Two gone out of five.* Those weren't very good odds. But maybe the Blair boy was alive and well somewhere else. He could easily be living a normal life in an alternate universe…one that didn't include crops and cattle and small-town life. One that didn't include his father, Levi Blair, the man who had directed that his will be revised to name his nephew, Eddie Simmons, as his sole heir.

Did that mean Levi Blair had given up on his son, Nate? Did he know for certain that Nate wasn't going to return to Langston, or worse yet, that Nate was dead?

An involuntary shiver spiraled down her spine. Misty stared at the packet of pictures she'd found. She opened a drawer in the guestroom bureau and stuffed in both the packet of photos and the gun wrapped in the old T-shirt.

Misty heaved a sigh. Just getting those two items out of sight made her feel better. A lot better.

She headed for the kitchen to see what she could do to help Leah with dinner. She found Gracie at the table, diligently doing her homework, and Leah chopping vegetables.

"What can I do to help?" she asked.

Leah greeted her with a grin. "Not a thing. Sit down and have a glass of iced tea. You're the one who has been working all day." She nudged a pitcher of tea toward her.

Misty claimed a stool on the opposite side of the granite counter. "That sounds great." She reached for a tall glass and filled it with the cold liquid. She glanced at the little girl at the table, her head bent over her textbook and tablet. "Gracie sure is hard at work."

Leah heaved a sigh. "Intro to some kind of new math. It's nothing like the math when I was in school. Not a fun place to be."

"That's okay, Mommy," Gracie called out. "Mark said he would help me when he gets done with his chores."

Leah rolled her eyes. "I'm so very thankful for your little brother."

Misty grinned. "Yeah, me too. He comes in handy sometimes." She leaned forward on her elbows. "Listen, Leah, I want to thank you for helping me clean out my dad's room and Joe's. It would have been so much harder for me to face the work alone."

Leah flapped her hand. "Think nothing of it. I dropped the boxes off at the church today, and the secretary said to thank you for your donation. The ladies auxiliary will see that the clothing and other items are distributed to needy people in the area."

Misty felt a pricking sensation behind her eyes and blinked rapidly to keep from tearing up. "I'm just glad someone could use them."

Leah leaned across to squeeze her hand and then went back to chopping vegetables for a salad.

Colton and Big Jim came into the house together. She heard their voices first, and they sounded like they were in a good mood. When they entered the kitchen, Colton came right to where she was sitting and planted a kiss on her lips. Suddenly, all her earlier worries melted away. It seemed that everything got better by the mere fact of Colton's presence.

He stood beside her, his arm around her shoulder. "How did it go at work?"

"Great," she said.

He cocked an eyebrow. "Great?"

She shrugged. "Well, not great, exactly. It was boring, but I can handle it. Just a stack of paperwork Breck left for me."

Colton frowned. "So you're alone all day?"

"Usually. Breck is off doing other things. He leaves me notes of things to do and calls in occasionally."

"I hope you're safe there. Anyone could just walk right in."

She gave him a smile. "Well, that's what they're

supposed to do. Walk right in. It's a law office, not a bank vault. People can walk in when they need to see Breck...and then I tell them he's not in and make an appointment for them." She shrugged. "Not that it happens very often. Mostly, people call ahead when they want to make an appointment."

Colton nodded, but he looked worried.

Misty felt a chill of apprehension as she wondered if his concerns were well-founded.

⌁⌁⌁

It was at dinner that Misty announced her intentions of moving back to the Dalton ranch.

Colton could not have been more surprised if she had smacked him in the face.

Gracie and Mark were sitting at the breakfast bar for their meal, having finished their respective homework, and were too far from the table to overhear.

There was a chorus of disappointment, but Misty seemed to have made up her mind.

Colton was angry. He tried not to show it, but he speared his food and shoveled it into his mouth in silence.

"Do you think it's safe?" Leah asked, giving voice to his concerns.

Misty shrugged. "I don't know why it wouldn't be. Mark and I don't know anything about the banker's death or why he wound up there."

Leah's brow puckered in a frown. "But what about Joe? The killer is still out there. As I understand it, the sheriff doesn't have a lead on the person who shot him."

"Trust me, Joe's death is on my mind all the time." Misty's lips trembled before she pressed them together in a firm line. "I—I don't know anything about that either. I mean…" Her voice dropped to a lower register. "Mark and I weren't in the loop. Joe didn't share his thoughts or his activities with us."

Colton swallowed hard, his food going down like a load of concrete. "Yes, but whoever shot him might not know that. I don't think you'll be safe there."

Her large, dark eyes appraised him, as though wondering at his motives, causing him to wonder what his own motives were. "Well, we can't keep imposing on Garrett family hospitality forever. We need to get back home and try to pick up the pieces."

Colton stabbed a piece of meat and poked it into his mouth, thus ending his commentary.

Later, he asked Misty to take a walk with him.

She hesitated but took the hand he offered.

It wasn't fully dark outside, but the sky was streaked with purple and crimson from the setting sun. Crickets chirped, and the smell of damp earth and grass wafted on the light breeze.

Colton tucked her hand in the crook of his arm and laid his hand on top of hers. It always felt so small and soft when compared to his.

"What did you want to talk about?" she asked.

He sucked in a breath and blew it out in a huff. "I'm concerned about you and Mark moving back to your home so soon after all the violence. I wish you would give the sheriff a chance to find out who's behind the murders of your brother and Mr. Hamilton."

Misty hung her head but stayed in step with him as they made a wide circle of the house and outbuildings. "I feel like such a moocher staying here. I appreciate you for taking us in when we were about to be thrown out. I appreciate you even more for all the sweet things you do without even thinking about it."

He stopped, turning to face her, and lifted her chin. "Misty, honey—you've got to know how I feel about you."

She gazed up at him solemnly. "No, I can honestly say I don't have a clue. I think you like me, but maybe you need to spell your feelings out for me." The silence that followed was like a black vortex sucking him inside.

Colton's chest tightened as though a steel band was constricting his lungs. He swallowed hard. "Well, I guess you could say I love you."

She raised her brows, "Guess you could say? What the hell does that mean?"

He grinned. "Damn, you're a tough woman. I love you. There! Are you satisfied?"

"Well, I don't know. Why was that so hard to say?"

"Because I've never said those words to any other woman before. It's you. You're the one I love." He stroked her cheek with the back of his fingers.

She broke into a wide grin of her own. "Now I'm satisfied." She slipped both arms around his waist and delivered a fierce hug.

Colt wrapped his arms around her, holding her tight against him. *Now she knows*. He pressed a kiss against the top of her head, rocking her slightly.

"Oh, Colt. I've been hoping you felt that way about me."

He snorted indelicately. "Well, if you didn't know, you were the only one. I've been taking heat from Beau and Leah…and my dad."

She gasped, raising her head. "Your dad?"

"Yeah, everyone knew but you."

She ducked her head again, but she was grinning. He thought she was blushing, but the diminishing light hid her embarrassment. "So, now what?"

"So now I ask you again, as the man who loves you, please don't move back to your house until the sheriff has caught whoever murdered your brother and Fred Hamilton."

"Well, since you're the man who loves me, I'll take your concerns very seriously." She blew out a breath. "Do you suppose we could go talk to the sheriff tomorrow and see if he has anything new to tell us?"

He kissed her forehead and then her nose. "Sure thing. As long as you promise to give him a little time to solve the murders."

She broke loose with an impudent smile. "Why, Colton Garrett, I do believe you like having me around."

"More than you know." He gave her a little squeeze. "Now promise to let the sheriff get to the bottom of the violence before you go moving back to your ranch."

"It depends on what he has to say."

The next morning, Misty was pretty sure she could fly. At least that's what it felt like. The floaty feeling in her gut kept her off balance. She kept breaking out in a grin for no good reason other than the fact that Colton Garrett had finally declared his love.

It was a good thing she was alone in the law office. Otherwise, Breck would be thinking he'd hired a crazy woman.

She attempted to clear her head and focus on the

filing she had to do. No sense stuffing the papers in the wrong place just because she was distracted.

Colton's handsome face remained seared into her brain. She replayed his deep, resonant voice telling her he loved her over and over again in her mind. That seemed like a miracle in itself.

It seemed remarkable that Colton Garrett had not been snagged by some lucky woman before now. Someone with far more to offer than herself.

There were tons of photos of him in almost every room in the Garrett house. Pictures of Colt receiving academic awards decorated the walls and tabletops, as did pictures of him participating in various athletic events. He looked awesome decked out in the team uniforms, but not as good as he looked every day in the Western shirts that accented his broad shoulders and the Wranglers that emphasized his muscular thighs and backside.

Heaving a happy sigh, she reflected on their conversation the night before. He'd confessed she was the only woman to whom he had ever uttered the words "I love you." That in itself seemed remarkable. And she had no idea why he had found her worthy of his love. To her way of thinking, she was a completely ordinary woman. No particular talents. Not especially attractive. Certainly no possessions to give her added value.

"Hello, Misty!" Breck opened the door, clanking the bell against the glass. "Anything happening?"

Misty turned, still grinning like an idiot and blushed as though he had caught her in a misdeed. "Not that I'm aware of."

"I've been busy with the ranch," he said as he crossed the width of the room to approach his office.

"I've almost reached the bottom of the stack of things you left for me."

Breck cast a sideways glance at her, grinning. "Good. I'll have to come up with some more tasks for you. I don't want you to get bored." He entered his private office but left the door open, which was a little more companionable than he usually was.

"Is there anything in particular you would like me to do right now?" she asked.

"Just keep an eye out for Levi Blair. He's coming in to sign the new will you typed up." Breck made a disgusted noise in the back of his throat. "He's given up on his son ever returning to Langston. Boy disappeared when he was just a teen. Young Nate." Breck shook his head. "Ran around with a bunch of other wild boys, your brother Joe included."

"So you're saying Joe was one of the wild ones?" Misty stood in the doorway to Breck's office and braced herself against the woodwork.

"Come sit down." He gestured toward a chair in front of his desk. "I think all those particular boys have been in trouble at one time or another." Breck narrowed his gaze. "Except for Nate and your brother. I never got called to get either one out of jail."

Misty sighed and sat down. "You can blame that on my mama's constant prayers and my strict papa."

"Not a bad combination at all."

"I don't really remember much about Nate," Misty said. "But I recall Joe mentioning him…and then I heard about the disappearance."

Breck raised an eyebrow and shook his head. "Bad business. I'm pretty sure the boy met with foul play, but old Levi has kept his hopes up all these years. I think now that he's decided to name his good-for-nothing nephew as his sole heir, it's a pretty sure sign he's given up. If Nate were out there, with everyone on the internet, some sign of him would have turned up by now."

Misty bit her lip. "Breck, I found some pictures among Joe's things. I'd like to keep them, of course. But I think Nate Blair is in some of the photos."

"Really?" Breck was suddenly interested. "Digital images?"

Misty shook her head. "No, this was from Joe's old camera. The kind you loaded film in, so they had to be developed in a photo lab. They have a date stamp on them." She shrugged. "Maybe Mr. Blair would like to have a set."

"I'm sure he would. Why don't you bring them in, and we can scan them. That way you can keep the originals and Levi can have them printed, if he's of a mind."

Misty nodded. "I'll bring them tomorrow."

She went back to her desk and started on the next task in the pile.

About an hour later, Levi Blair entered the building. He appeared to have aged since the time Misty had first seen him. Indeed, his craggy face seemed to be even more morose than before.

"Hello, Mr. Blair. Mr. Ryan is expecting you." Misty stood and started to go to Breck's door to announce his client when Levi Blair raised his hand.

His eyes narrowed. "You the Dalton girl, ain't ya?"

Misty swallowed hard. "Yes, Mr. Blair."

He rocked back on his heels, surveying her. "Too bad about your dad. I don't suppose you're interested in selling off your property, are you? I could take it over and give you a little more than what you owe on it."

She struggled to draw a breath. "I—I have a partner in the ranch now, Mr. Blair."

A muscle twitched in Levi's cheek. "You do? Well, ain't that nice." He drew out the word "nice," ending it in a hiss.

Misty cleared her throat. "I'll just tell Mr. Ryan that you're here." She went to tap on Breck's door. "Mr. Blair has arrived."

Breck looked up. "Thank you, Misty. Please show him in."

Levi Blair gave her a nod of acknowledgment and swept his hat off as he stepped into Breck's private office, and closed the door.

After about ten minutes, Breck called Misty in to witness Levi's will.

"Misty found some photos that might include your son Nate," Breck said.

Levi looked up, his eyes darting from Breck to Misty and back. "Photos of my boy?"

"Yes, sir," Misty said. "They were taken a long time ago. My brother Joe died recently, and I was cleaning out his room."

Levi's face clouded even more. His fierce brows knit together. "Yes, I did hear something about that. Sorry for your loss, young lady."

Misty released a pent-up breath. "Thank you, Mr. Blair. I found some photos of Joe and his friends. There were a couple with your son, Nate. I thought you might like to have a set. Mr. Ryan said he would scan them for me."

Levi's expression softened. "That's mighty kind of

you. I think it's worse not knowing what happened to my son than if I had some idea of where he might be or if he's even alive." His eyes teared up, and he stood abruptly. "I'll stop by tomorrow afternoon to get those photos."

"You don't need to make a special trip," Breck said. "I'll scan them and send them to your email account. That way you can just download them directly without any delay."

Levi cocked an eyebrow at Breck. "That so?"

Breck nodded. "If you want to have them printed, you can forward them to the drugstore. They'll print a set right up for you."

He offered his hand to Breck and then turned to Misty. "Thank you for your kindness."

When Levi left, both Misty and Breck heaved a huge sigh of relief.

"It feels like he sucked all the air out of the room when he left." Breck straightened the papers on his desk. "Well, I'm outta here. I'll be in the office tomorrow afternoon to scan those pictures for you and send them to Levi's email." He left the office. Immediately after Breck departed, the phone rang.

It was Sara Beth. "Are you free for lunch?"

Misty giggled. "Free as a bird and twice as flighty."

"Well, come on down, girl," Sara Beth said.

Misty pushed her chair up close to the desk and turned off her desk light. She grabbed her purse and placed the CLOSED sign so that it showed in the beveled glass door insert. She made it to Sara Beth's store in record time and pushed open the door. The cowbell clanked against the glass to announce her arrival. "Hello?" she called out, not seeing Sara Beth immediately.

"Get in here, Misty. I have something to show you." Sara Beth popped up from behind the counter and ran to wrap both arms around her.

Misty returned the embrace. "What's up? You look like you're bursting with excitement."

"That I am." She extended her left hand, showing off a sparkling diamond engagement ring. "Frank officially proposed, down on one knee and everything. I about died."

Misty stared at the ring, thrilled for her friend. "That's so beautiful."

Sara Beth gazed rapturously at her extended fingers. "I told Frank I didn't need an engagement ring. I would be happy with just a plain gold band, but he surprised me."

"When is the wedding?"

Sara Beth grabbed her by the shoulders. "Two months, and I want you to be my maid of honor."

Misty felt a flush of pride. She had never had a friend this close. "Me? That's awesome. I'm so honored."

"I'm going to ask Leah to be my matron of honor, so I'll have my two best friends in the whole wide world to walk down the aisle with me."

The two women hugged again. "Thanks so much for thinking of me."

"Thanks for standing up with me." Sara Beth made a "follow me" gesture and led the way back to the counter at the rear of the store. She had containers of food spread out on top of the scarred glass case. "I made fried chicken last night and brought some cold for us to gnaw on. There's potato salad too."

"Oh, what a treat. Thanks for inviting me." Misty

seated herself and watched as Sara Beth arranged two portions on paper plates. "What about your father? Is he coming to give you away?"

Sara Beth's shoulders sagged. "My dad hasn't spoken to me since I married Nick Jessup and moved to Texas. He blames me for breaking my mother's heart."

Misty frowned. "Well, he needs to get over that. He has a beautiful and sweet daughter and an adorable granddaughter. Your dad is missing out on all the good things happening in both of your lives."

Sara Beth blinked and looked down. "I wish he would realize that, but I'm tired of being stonewalled." She met Misty's gaze. "If he doesn't want to love us, it's his loss. I've had my share of rejection."

A wave of remorse swept through Misty's gut. "I'm sorry. I didn't mean to open up old wounds." She reached out to give Sara Beth's hand a pat. "I'm truly sorry."

Sara Beth sucked in a breath. "It's okay. You expected my father to be a normal dad with normal feelings, but he's not. He cut me off entirely." She shrugged and pasted on a smile. "It's really okay. I found my own family right here in Langston. It's my baby girl and Frank." Her smile became more genuine. "And Leah...and you."

Misty squeezed Sara Beth's hand. "I'm honored."

When Misty returned to the law office, she found Colton waiting for her in his truck. Grinning, he swung out of the cab of his pickup and stepped up onto the sidewalk.

"I hope you haven't been waiting long," she said.

"Not long." His voice was deep and rich in timbre, sending a tremor of excitement along her flesh.

"I—I had lunch with Sara Beth. She invited me."

"Nice," he said encouragingly.

"She's getting married." Misty felt her cheeks flushing. "She asked me to be her maid of honor." She knew she was babbling, but she couldn't seem to stop. "Sara Beth is really excited. I met her fiancé, Frank, the other day, and he is so nice."

Colton grinned even wider. "Getting married, huh? That sounds like a good thing."

A thrill surged through her stomach. "She's very happy." She pulled the office keys out of her purse and immediately busied herself with opening the lock. Anything so she didn't have to bear the brunt of those all-too-knowing blue eyes. Her hands were shaking, and she couldn't seem to get the key to fit.

"Let me help you." Colton took the keys from her fingers, inserted the right one in the lock, and gave it a twist. The lock opened with a click, and he pushed the door open for her to enter.

She felt a rush of color flood her cheeks. *What an idiot.* Just mentioning Sara Beth's upcoming wedding in front of Colton gave her the jitters.

"I asked the sheriff to meet us here," Colton said. "I thought it would be easier for you."

"Thanks," she squeaked out, her voice barely above a whisper. She had intended to take a seat behind her desk but found herself folded in Colton's embrace.

He lifted her chin and gazed into her eyes. "Is there something wrong? Something I should know about?"

Misty made a negative grunt and shook her head. "I guess I was just thinking about Sara Beth's wedding and forgot about all my own problems."

Colton grazed a kiss against her lips and gave her a squeeze. "Every problem has a solution."

"I know, you're right. I was just feeling a little down." She tried on a smile that felt fake even from her standpoint. "That's why I want to move back to our own place and try to sort things out. There's so much I don't know."

Colton's brows knit together. "That's what scares me."

They both sprang apart when the sheriff barged in, clanking the bell against the glass. "Hello, you two."

"Sheriff." Colton extended his hand, and the two men exchanged a hearty handshake.

The sheriff glanced at Breck's darkened office. "Mr. Ryan is out?"

Misty nodded. "He's gone for the day."

"We can sit down here in the back." Colton gestured to the long table Misty used for sorting files and collating papers.

They all trooped to the rear of the office and took a seat.

Misty gripped her hands together in her lap, hoping her anxiety didn't show.

Colton glanced at her and then cleared his throat. "We wanted an update, Sheriff. Have you made any progress in Joe Dalton's murder investigation?"

"I wish I could tell you more." The sheriff huffed out a deep breath. "The medical examiner recovered the bullet that took Joe's life. It hasn't been matched to any other cases, but at least we have the information on file. The ME also made a determination, from the angle of entry, that the shot was fired from the passenger window of another pickup or SUV of approximately the same height that must have pulled up alongside Joe's truck. That means someone else may have been driving, so we're possibly looking for two individuals."

Misty pressed her lips together to keep them from

trembling. She felt the sting of tears and bit the inside of her lip to keep them from pouring out. She couldn't bring herself to meet Colt's eyes, but she felt the weight of his gaze upon her.

"And that's all you have?" Colton's arm came to rest on the back of her chair, but he turned to gaze at the sheriff, his brows drawn together in a frown.

"The murder of Joseph Dalton remains an open case. We're still investigating." The sheriff blinked and glanced at Misty and then back at Colton. "We're looking into Joe's activities the days prior to his death."

Misty felt a choking sensation clog her throat. Sucking in air, she gasped.

Colton's hand clasped hers under the table. "What have you found?"

The sheriff shook his head. "Nothing out of the ordinary. He was in the company of his usual local friends the three days preceding his death. He attended the stock auction at the show barns, and afterward he met three of his friends at a bar for some drinks and then went to the Eagles Hall. The next night he met the same friends at the roadhouse a few miles west of town." The sheriff glanced at Misty before going on. "It's a biker bar called Wally's. The bartender remembers Joe being there. He left about midnight and appeared to be on his way home when he was apparently overtaken by the perpetrator or perpetrators and killed."

A tremor shook Misty's body, chilling her to the core. Involuntarily, she wrapped both arms around herself, but Colton's arm quickly encircled her shoulders.

"His friends," Colton said. "Are you talking about Stan Lynch, Ron Diaz, and Eddie Simmons?"

The sheriff nodded. "His usual companions."

Colt blew out a breath. "And you questioned them?"

The sheriff looked a bit peeved. "Of course. All three said they stayed at the roadhouse long after Joe left."

"What about Fred Hamilton? We found his body skewered in the loft of the Dalton barn. What can you tell us about his death?" Colton's strong fingers stroked Misty's shoulder rhythmically.

The sheriff cleared his throat. "According to the crime scene technicians, Mr. Hamilton was not killed in the Dalton barn. His body was transported there and arranged with the pitchfork stabbed through his entrails, but he had been dead for some hours before this happened."

"How do they know he was killed elsewhere?" Colton asked.

A muscle in the sheriff's cheek twitched. "I'm not into all that techie mumbo jumbo, but it all boiled down to the fact that there was no fresh blood at the scene. The secondary wound from the pitchfork didn't yield a blood spill. It was all for show, so we figured it had been staged to scare or intimidate someone... Got any ideas about that?" He glanced from one to the other.

A tremor shook Misty's entire body. "But why?" she cried out. "Why would someone do that?"

"That hasn't been determined as of yet, but maybe someone was sending a message." The sheriff leaned forward, resting his forearms against the table. "Miss Dalton, what kind of dealings did you have with Mr. Hamilton?"

Misty blinked rapidly before heaving a sigh. "I really didn't have any dealings with him personally. My father obtained a loan against the ranch after my mother died. Then when his health failed, my daddy couldn't make the ranch profitable, so we were in the process of losing the property." She shot a glance at Colton, finding courage in the kindness reflected in his eyes. "Colton met with Mr. Hamilton and paid the past due payments and late fees."

The sheriff glanced from one to the other.

Misty felt Colton's grip tighten, and her blush reflex kicked in.

The sheriff's expression changed from confusion to knowing.

"Mr. Garrett is our partner in the ranch. My brother Mark and I. We signed the papers."

Colton continued stroking her shoulder, as though he had no problem letting the sheriff know he had feelings for her.

Misty sucked in a deep breath and laced her fingers with Colton's. *Might as well step up and admit my feelings too.*

Colton looked grim but pressed a kiss against her temple. "Actually, I met with Mr. Hamilton at the bank and was supposed to meet with him again that same afternoon, but when I returned, I was told he had gone for the day." A muscle twitched in his jaw. "I was pissed off. I came to see Breckenridge Ryan the next day, and Mr. Ryan accompanied me to the bank, where the loan was secured from the vice president. I never saw Hamilton after that."

The sheriff looked grim. "Neither did anyone else. Apparently, after your visit, his employees report that he appeared to be agitated. When he left, he claimed he wasn't feeling well, so when he didn't show up the next day, they thought he was still sick. Nobody checked on him until a few days had passed."

Colton shrugged. "He was, after all, the president of the bank. They were probably a little afraid of him."

The sheriff nodded. "I suppose you're right, but he didn't go to his house after you left the bank. Wherever he went, that was when he was killed. Whoever he met with shot him and then staged the scene in Miss Dalton's barn."

Misty sat up straight. "Shot him?"

"Yes, the ME recovered a single bullet in his chest. Not a match to any crimes on record at this point." The sheriff pushed his chair back. "If you good folks have anything to add, let me know."

Misty felt her lips tremble. She started to tell the sheriff about finding the photos and the gun among her brother's personal things but somehow couldn't bear to bring any possible shame on him. Breck had said Joe was the only one of the surviving friends from his school days who hadn't run into trouble with the law, and she hoped to keep it that way. It was bad enough everyone in the area knew about her father's drinking after her mother's death and the subsequent financial mess. No reason to smear more mud on the Dalton name. After all, she and Mark would have to live it all down.

Colton stood and leaned across the table to shake the sheriff's hand. "I just have one more question, sir."

"Shoot," the sheriff said, pumping Colton's hand.

"Misty and her younger brother have been staying at the Garrett ranch, but she wants to return to her home. I'm dead set against it." He swept her with his fierce gaze. "I think it's too dangerous. She's welcome to stay with us for as long as she needs."

The sheriff fixed her with a stern glare. "You might want to listen to Colton, young lady. The Garretts are good people. There's a murderer on the loose. At least one killer plus an accomplice in the case of your brother. We don't have any good leads on the murder of Fred Hamilton, nor do we have any clue as to why his body was staged to be discovered in your barn."

"Do you think the two deaths could be related?" Colton asked.

The sheriff ran his hand over his thinning hair before carefully replacing his hat. "Could be. The weapons are different and the methodology is different." He shifted his gaze to Misty. "The Daltons are the only common denominator."

Chapter 14

AFTER THE SHERIFF HAD DEPARTED, MISTY FELL silent. She seemed to have withdrawn into herself.

"Are you okay?" Colton asked, certain the sheriff's revelations had upset her and not wanting to cause her more distress.

She pressed her lips together and nodded. "I'm fine."

"You don't look fine."

A hint of a smile graced her face. "Thanks."

"No, I mean—"

"It's all right. I'm just feeling sad is all." She took a few paces across the room before turning back to face him. "I wanted so badly to be able to get on with my life. To help Mark get past Joe's and Daddy's deaths. We both need this to be over and done with."

"I understand. But you can't rush these things. You heard what the sheriff had to say. Just try to be patient."

She shook her head. "Sorry. Patience is not one of my virtues."

"Apparently not." He grinned and tickled her cheek, eliciting a giggle in return. "I need to get back to the ranch. Have I convinced you not to move back to your home just yet?"

Misty heaved a sigh and lifted her shoulders in a shrug. "I guess, but I'm going to go by and check on Rosa and Paco after I get off work. I'll just stop by to see if they need anything."

Colton tried to quell the anxiety gathering in his chest.

He had no right to tell her what to do, but he felt greatly concerned about her hanging around a place where so much tragedy had occurred. "Can't you just call them?"

She raised an eyebrow. "No. Rosa doesn't want to impose, and she won't tell me when they run low on food or basic supplies. I'll have to check for myself."

"Just promise me you'll be careful. Come home quickly."

Misty made an exasperated noise in the back of her throat. "That ranch is my home, Colton. I was born and raised there."

He huffed out a deep sigh. "I know. I want you to come to my home. I want you tucked up safe with me."

"Sounds like you care." She gazed up at him, her eyes shining.

"You know I do. I love you, remember?"

"I remember, and I love you too."

He planted a kiss on her lips that quickly deepened as her arms circled his neck. There it was. She admitted she loved him too. Now what? Did that give him the right to forbid her to go to her ranch? He thought not.

Colton kissed her on the nose. "Well, I'll be at home… my home…when you get there. Hurry up and come to dinner. We can go for a moonlight drive after we eat."

She flashed him a grin. "That sounds very romantic, Colt. I'll see you later." She gave him another kiss, and he left the law office, climbed in his truck, and headed back to the Garrett ranch. Now, if he could just stop worrying until she joined him there.

~~~

Misty stopped at the Food Mart to pick up a few fresh things. Milk, bread, and orange juice plus some fruit and vegetables. She figured Rosa and Paco would be running low on these supplies. The freezer was well stocked with meat.

When she pulled up close to the front door of the Dalton ranch house, the door flew open, and Rosa clasped her hands together. "Oh, Miss Misty. I'm so glad to see you. Paco hasn't come home yet, and I'm very worried." She cast a glance in the direction of the road, and her lips tightened. "He always come home before this time."

Misty noticed the battered old truck was missing. "When did he leave?" She climbed out of Leah's car and removed the bags of groceries from the back seat.

Rosa reached for some of the bags and led the way inside. "He come home for lunch and then go back out. He say Mr. Colton talk to him about planting a crop before winter sets in. He drive off toward the east field about one o'clock."

It was just after six, and Misty felt a twisting in her gut. If something had happened to Paco, she didn't think she could stand it. "Put the cold things away, and we'll go look for him. Maybe the truck broke down."

Rosa's brow cleared. "Ah, yes. The truck." She put the milk and other cold things into the refrigerator and slipped on a cardigan sweater.

"I'll meet you in the car." Misty went back outside and climbed behind the steering wheel, with Rosa following. When they were both settled, Misty started the car and pulled out onto the road. "He drove this way?"

"*Sí*. He go to see where best place to plant crops for feed the cattle." She flashed a smile. "Paco very happy that Mr. Colton would buy seed."

Misty gnawed her lower lip, staring out the windshield. She didn't see the old truck or any other vehicles on the road. The sun was getting low in the sky. She hoped they could find Paco soon and that he was safe.

They reached the property line, and she turned east onto a smaller farm-to-market road.

Rosa's lips were moving silently, and Misty realized she was praying.

"There!" Misty pointed up ahead to where the truck was partially hidden behind the old abandoned farmhouse on the property her father had acquired when she was just a child. The outbuildings looked as though they were about to fall down.

She pulled in and turned on the headlights.

Paco was not in the truck, but the driver's-side door was open.

Misty barely had time to bring the car to a full stop when Rosa was out the door. "Paco," she called.

Misty grabbed the flashlight she had seen in the glove compartment and followed. She washed the inside of the truck with the beam, her stomach catching when she saw blood on the seat and doorframe. "Oh no!"

"*Dios mío!*" Rosa covered her mouth with both hands. Tears sprang to her eyes, and she began shaking all over.

Misty put an arm around her, not sure what to say to comfort Rosa when she was so terribly frightened herself. She swallowed hard, wishing Colton was with her. "Let's look around. He has to be nearby." She hoped this was true. It appeared Paco had been in an accident or injured himself in some way.

She shone the flashlight around, playing the beam over the ramshackle sheds and falling-down barn. There was no movement, and she heard nothing. Turning toward the house, she rounded the truck with Rosa still encircled in her arm.

A slight movement caused her to start. Something on the passenger side of the truck made a noise. She picked out a form slumped against the rear wheel well. It was Paco.

Rosa rushed toward him, her arms outstretched. "*Papa!*" she moaned.

Misty went to kneel on the other side. Paco's head was bloodied, and he appeared to be covered with dirt and dried blood. "Let's get him in the car." She helped him to his feet, and the two women half carried him to lie down in the back seat. Rosa climbed in beside him, cradling his head in her lap.

Misty drove away quickly, calling Colton on her cell phone.

"Where are you?" he asked. "Everyone is waiting dinner on you." He sounded a little irritated.

"Colton, Paco has been injured. He and Rosa are with me in Leah's car. I don't know what happened to him, but he needs a doctor right away."

"Can you come straight here? I'll call the doctor to meet you here."

"Yes, we're headed there now." She disconnected and drove as fast as she could to the Garrett ranch. When she arrived, Colton, his father, and his brother Beau were waiting outside.

The three men rushed to open the door and carefully lifted Paco from the vehicle. They bore him gently into the house, with a weeping Rosa following close behind.

Misty turned to see Breckenridge T. Ryan's truck veer into the drive and make a hard stop. Breck jumped out on one side, and his wife, the local doctor, leapt from the passenger side carrying a leather bag.

"Where's my patient?" she demanded.

Misty pointed to the house, and the woman shot through the open door.

"Misty, that is my wife, Cameron, better known as Cami. What happened?"

"I went to my ranch after work to take some supplies, and Rosa said Paco hadn't returned. We went to look for him and found him all bloody. I don't know what happened to him."

Breck gestured toward the house, and they entered together.

Mark met her in the front room, his eyes wide. "What happened to Paco? He looks awful."

Misty embraced him, glad to hold onto her young brother. "I don't know. We found him like that."

"They took him to one of the guest rooms. The doctor is checking him over now, but they told me to step out." Mark's brows drew together. "I hope he's going to be okay."

She kissed his cheek. "Me too, honey. Me too."

Colton came down the hall toward them, his face grim. "I'm going to call the sheriff. It looks like someone attacked this man."

"Oh no!" Misty fought against the constriction in her chest. "Who would do such a thing?"

"Who indeed?" Breck asked.

———

Colton made the call to the sheriff's office and waited for him to arrive. He was gripped by a combination of fear, anger, and relief.

His fear was for Misty, who seemed oblivious to the fact that some person or persons were focused on eliminating everyone associated with the Dalton ranch.

He was angry that someone had brutalized an elderly man, but he was relieved that Misty hadn't been the victim of the attack.

Maybe she would listen to him now and stop thinking about returning to her place until the criminals had been brought to justice. *Maybe.*

Breck Ryan paced around the front room, glancing outside every few minutes, as if that might hurry the sheriff's vehicle.

Misty looked as though she might fall down in a heap, but Colt stood with his arms around her. She felt small and fragile in his embrace.

Big Jim and Beau joined them, each with his own grim expression.

"I just don't know what this world is coming to." Big Jim raked his fingers through his thick silver hair. "What kind of person would attack an old man? Just makes me sick."

"Where did you find Paco?" Colton asked Misty.

She pulled herself out of his arms, turning to face him. "Rosa was worried because he hadn't returned, so we went looking for him. The truck was at the old abandoned house on the east half of our property. When we drove up, we could see the driver's-side door was open and there was blood on the seat. We found him on the ground all bloody, and he couldn't speak." A single tear rolled down her cheek, and Colt reached to wipe it away. Misty leaned against him, burying her face against his chest.

"It's a good thing you went looking for him," Big Jim said. "Poor old fellow probably wouldn't have made it through the night."

Colton felt a shiver wash through Misty's small frame. Her dark eyes contrasted sharply with the paleness of her skin.

Leah poked her head in. "I know you may not feel like eating, but I made some fresh coffee."

One by one, the others made their way into the kitchen. The sound of muted conversation filtered out to the front room.

Only Breck Ryan waited with Misty and Colton.

Colton's attention was caught by the sound of vehicles approaching the ranch house. Two sheriff's department cruisers arrived, lights flashing but no sirens. The red and blue lights swirled through the windows, washing the walls with color as car doors opened and slammed. The sound of booted feet stomping up the walk caused Breck to move to the entrance. He opened the front door to admit the sheriff and three of his deputies.

The sheriff shook hands with Breck and looked around, taking in the sight of Misty in Colton's arms. "Where's the victim?"

"Sheriff." Colton tightened his grip on her. "The doctor is with him now."

"Who found the victim?"

Misty raised her hand, like a schoolgirl. "I did. Rosa, his wife, said he hadn't come home, so we went to look for him. We thought perhaps his old truck had broken down." She recounted how and where they had found the injured man.

The sheriff dispatched two of his men in the second

patrol car to check out the crime scene and keep it secure. "I need to see the victim," he said.

Colton released Misty and gestured to the sheriff. "Come with me."

Misty looked as though she wanted to follow, but he stopped her. "I'll send Rosa to you. The two of you need to get some supper. Try to make sure she eats."

Misty nodded and stepped back.

Colton led the way down the corridor to the bedroom wing. He rapped lightly at the door and twisted the knob.

Dr. Cami and Rosa looked up when Colt entered with the sheriff.

"The sheriff is here to see how Paco is doing."

Cami nodded, her mouth set in a firm line. "Come in, Sheriff. I called for a medical transport helicopter to pick up Mr. Hernandez. I've cleaned him and patched him as well as I can here, but I suspect there's internal damage, so I want to fly him to the hospital in Amarillo for further tests and treatment."

Tears streamed silently down Rosa's cheeks. She rocked a bit in her chair, clasping Paco's hand in hers.

"He hasn't regained consciousness?" the sheriff asked.

Dr. Cami shook her head. "No, but he sustained a vicious beating. More than likely, it took two or more persons to do this to him."

The sound of a rotor beating the air grew louder.

"That's our ride." Dr. Cami lifted her head and pushed to a standing position. "Sorry about the bedspread." She directed her gaze to Colton. "A little hydrogen peroxide should take the blood out."

"Not a problem," Colton replied. "Mrs. Hernandez,

Misty is waiting to get you a bite to eat. It's been a long night."

Rosa shook her head. "I want to go with my husband."

Dr. Cami put her hand on Rosa's arm. "You need to eat. Breck will drive you to the hospital. He'll be following the helicopter right away."

Rosa nodded and allowed Colton to show her the way to the kitchen. As they made their way down the hallway, the EMTs assigned to the helicopter passed by them, led by young Mark.

Colton was glad everyone was working together to help the Hernandez couple. He hoped the man survived. An angry fist gripped his stomach when he thought about someone injuring an elderly person.

When he reached the kitchen with Rosa, Misty opened her arms and took charge of getting the woman something to eat. Leah and Misty surrounded her, speaking to her in soothing voices.

Colton caught Breck's eye. "Cami said you would be driving to Amarillo."

Breck nodded. "When my wife takes to the skies with a patient, I'm the ground crew."

"Good partnership," Colton said. "She asked that you transport Mrs. Hernandez so she could be with her husband."

Breck chortled. "No, I'm pretty sure she ordered that I do it."

Colton thought about it for a second. "Well…"

"That's okay, son. I know when to lead, and I know when to follow." Breck nodded to where Rosa was being tended by the two women. "As soon as she has a chance to eat something, we'll take off."

Colton turned as the sheriff and his deputy entered the kitchen. "We got some images of the wounds, and now we're going to the scene of the attack. The other deputies are there now and have secured the scene." He shrugged. "It's going to be a long night."

"Take care, Sheriff, and find the sons of bitches who did this." Breck clapped the man on the shoulder. "I'll check in with you when I get back from Amarillo."

"I'm sending my deputy to collect the victim's clothing. If the hospital staff will bag them, I'll get them to the crime lab to see if there's any evidence to be recovered."

Breck nodded. "Anything I can do to help. You've got my cell."

There was a moment when the group drew a collective breath. The EMTs strode down the hall with Paco strapped to a stretcher and Dr. Cami bringing up the rear. She sought out Breck, gave him a curt nod, and then left. In a matter of minutes, they heard the helicopter lift off.

Rosa's face looked strained, and Misty patted her on the shoulder.

"Whenever you're ready," Breck said to Rosa.

"Wait," Leah called. "I packed you some extra food. The hospital may not be serving when you're ready to eat."

Rosa fell into Leah's arms, her shoulders shaking. She thanked everyone for their kindness, and Breck escorted her to his truck for the drive to Amarillo.

When Colton turned, he saw that Mark and Misty were clinging to each other, Mark's face ravaged by tears.

Too much had happened in this young man's life in such a short period of time. And in Misty's.

Colton was determined to stop them both from

returning to the Dalton ranch until whoever was behind
the violence had been arrested.

He met her gaze, and she nodded silently. He figured
she was reading his mind.

Big Jim crossed the room to lay his hand on Colton's
shoulder. He drew him into the front room. "Things
just keep getting crazier and crazier. I think you better
keep an eye on your little girlfriend. I don't know who's
got it in for the Daltons, but whoever it is needs to be
stopped."

"I agree, Dad, but the sheriff doesn't have any idea."

Big Jim shook his head. "Whoever it is, the sumbitch
is meaner than a snake. Why beat up an old man?"

Colton had to agree. "The sheriff said there had to be at
least two perpetrators involved. Maybe more. He couldn't
even say if the murder of Joe Dalton was tied to the murder
of Fred Hamilton. Different weapons and methods."

"Damn!" A muscle in Big Jim's jaw twitched. "I
don't know which would be worse—to have two different killers running loose or to have one very bad pair
responsible for all of it."

Colton heaved a sigh. "I hope Paco regains consciousness and can tell the sheriff who attacked him."

Big Jim's hands were drawn into fists. "I'd just like
to get my hands on those sumbitches first."

———

Misty busied herself around the kitchen. She needed to
stay occupied. She needed to focus on the little tasks so her
brain wouldn't explode with all the pain she had witnessed
lately. The image of Rosa's tear-ravaged face sprang to
mind, and she almost dropped the glass she was drying.

"Don't worry about the dishes," Leah said. "I can put them away."

"I—I need to do this."

Leah gave her shoulders a squeeze. "I understand." She turned to leave. "I'm going to help Gracie get ready for bed. She's hanging out with Gran, who is keeping her entertained. This has been a scary evening for her too. I know she's going to want me to be with her while she's going to sleep."

Misty nodded. "That's sweet. You're so lucky."

"I have been lately," Leah agreed. "But six months ago, I was the original bad-luck kid. It seemed as though everything I touched turned to crap."

Misty turned to face her, surprised to hear this admission. "What happened? Everything seems to be going well for you now."

Leah flashed a grin. "My whole life changed. I met Tyler Garrett and found out what love is really about."

Misty felt a twinge of envy. She wondered if she could possibly have a life filled with love and stability.

Leah gave her a brief hug. "Things will work out. You'll see." With that, she turned and left the room.

Misty finished putting away the dishes and wiped down the countertops. When she turned around, she found Colton slouched against the doorframe, watching her.

"Oh, you startled me." She sucked in a deep breath and let it out.

"I didn't mean to." He pushed away from the door and came toward her. The expression on his face sent a current of heat swirling through her lower regions.

"I know this has been a tough evening for you." He lifted her chin and placed a soft kiss on her lips.

She nodded. "You can say that again. Why can't the bad things just stop happening?"

"Because there are some very bad people out there, and we don't know why they're targeting anyone associated with the Dalton ranch, but I want you to stay safe."

Misty swallowed hard. "Me too. It's just Mark and me now. We're the only ones left."

Colt wrapped his arms around her and pulled her close. "And me. I'm with you. Don't forget that, ever."

"I know, and I love you," she whispered.

"I love you more." He kissed her again, this time wrapping his arms around her and holding her close. "Please don't take any chances. No more trips to the ranch. Promise me."

Her lips trembled, but she nodded. "I promise."

The next morning Misty drove off to the law office of Breckenridge T. Ryan, Esquire, while Colton drove in the other direction to the Dalton ranch. He wanted to see for himself what was going on. He was a partner, after all. He made a growling noise in the back of his throat. It wasn't about the ranch. It was about Misty. He wanted her safe. He wanted all threats against the Daltons to be stopped, contained, or neutralized.

He cruised by the Dalton home, but it was locked up and silent. Following along on the road, he came to a dead end and turned toward the old abandoned house on the property. It would probably be best to try to demolish it and the outbuildings. Maybe something could be reclaimed, but the current derelict condition was nothing but a liability.

He saw two sheriff's department vehicles pulled into the open area between the old house and the outbuildings, along with the rusty truck Paco had been driving.

Colton parked his own truck a good distance away from the crime scene and walked toward the deputies.

He knew one of them and raised a hand in greeting. "Hey, Jason. Have you been here all night?"

"'Fraid so. We've secured the crime scene, which seems to be this old truck." He jerked his head toward the faded vehicle.

"Good job," Colton said with a grin.

"Hey, I'm on overtime. My next paycheck will make my wife happy, anyway."

Colton jammed his thumbs in the pockets of his Wranglers. "So, what's going on?"

"Why do you care?" Jason raised a brow and gave him a questioning look.

"I care." Colton shrugged. "I'm going with Misty Dalton. She and her little brother are staying with us."

Jason straightened. "Oh, I didn't know you and Misty were together. I haven't seen you two around town."

Colton blew out a deep breath. "It's been tough, what with her brother getting killed and her father dying. Not a good time."

"Oh, yeah. I knew Mr. Dalton was sick, but Joe…I didn't see that coming." Jason leaned against his patrol car. "How old is Misty, anyway?"

Colton grinned. "Just turned twenty-two."

"You dog." Jason grinned too. "She's barely ripe."

Colton leaned against the passenger-door panel. "She's perfect."

"Serious?"

"I am. Not pushing her. She and her younger brother have been through a lot." Colton turned to give Jason his full attention. "I'm hoping you guys can clear up the mystery of Joe's death and now find out who attacked their ranch hand. It was a pretty brutal beating. The doc took him to Amarillo last night."

"Sorry for the old guy."

Colton gestured to the truck. "So, did you crime-fighter types discover anything? Like who did it?"

Jason let out a guffaw. "Not us lowly deputies, but the crime scene techs drove in from Amarillo and took blood samples. They found several sets of boot prints too. Not much else they were willing to talk about."

The other deputy came over to join them and introduced himself. "Clyde Allen." He gestured around at the decrepit buildings. "What is this old place, anyway? Doesn't look like anyone's lived here for a long time."

"You're new to Langston," Jason said. "This place used to belong to the Simmons family, but they went belly up about ten, twelve years ago. Most of them moved away, except for Eddie. He's lived with his uncle, Levi Blair, since he was a teenager."

That registered with Colton, who recalled what Misty had told him. "And Eddie was one of Joe's running buddies, wasn't he?"

Jason nodded, his brow furrowing. "Yeah. Eddie's a complete asshole. Been in a little trouble, but nothing serious."

Colton gazed around. "In broad daylight, it doesn't look like this would be a place where an old farmhand would get beaten up. Wonder what went down."

Jason twitched his shoulders. "Something bad, for sure."

Chapter 15

MISTY ARRIVED AT THE OFFICE, AND ABOUT AN HOUR later, Breck walked in, looking tired. She jumped to her feet. "How is Paco? Did your wife say?"

Breck tossed his Stetson on the bentwood coatrack by the front door. "He's holding his own, but he hasn't regained consciousness." He huffed out a long sigh. "I brought her home late last night, but Cami drove back to Amarillo right after breakfast. She'll let me know how he is."

Misty felt the tightness in her chest ease a little. "I brought the pictures. The ones I found in Joe's room." She indicated the photos inside the envelope on her desk.

Breck picked them up and examined the envelope. It was slit at the top where Misty had opened it. He turned it upside down and let the images slip out onto her desktop. "These were taken a while back, weren't they?" He leafed through the photos and selected one, holding it aloft. "Young Nate Blair. Handsome young devil."

Misty gazed at the image. "I kind of remember him. He was always nice to me."

Breck shuffled through the photos. "Hmm... It looks like these two got into a scuffle." Breck's brow furrowed as he gazed at the picture of Nate and Eddie in a clinch. "Probably just boys being boys, but..."

Misty peeked over his shoulder. "Yeah...I wonder what was going on."

"Hey, what about this one? It's Eddie with a gun." He shook his head. "I guess if your brother was taking pictures, they must have been acting out something. Looks grim."

"Yeah, and Joe had them hidden. I have no idea why."

Breck gave her a sharp look. "Hidden? Where did you find these?"

"They were in that envelope and taped to the underside of his bottom dresser drawer. I would have missed them, but I couldn't get the drawer to open."

Breck looked concerned. "And judging from the ages of the boys, this was taken just before Nate disappeared. I wonder if there's some connection."

Misty shrugged. She wondered too but didn't venture a guess.

"It's thought that Nate ran away, but that begs the question as to why he would do so. Maybe some trouble with Levi. The old man was known to be pretty strict." Breck placed the photo in with the others and shuffled through, giving those on top a cursory glance.

Misty pressed her lips together. Her brief encounters with Levi Blair had not filled her with warm fuzzies. He could slice right through a person with a single glare. She heaved a sigh. "That would be enough to cause a boy to run away."

"I guess so," Breck said. "But since Levi recently cut him out of his will, it would be unfortunate if young Nate turned up after Levi kicks the bucket."

Misty stifled a shiver. Not a pleasant thought. She had experienced enough deaths lately to give her nightmares.

Breck carried the photos to the combination copier, scanner, and printer near his desk and fed them in. He sent them to Levi with a brief message. Turning to Misty, he gave her a nod. "I hope these photos bring Nate's old man some comfort."

—⁓—

Colton killed time with Jason and Clyde for a while, hoping to learn something about the attack on Paco Hernandez. Even more important, he hoped they might be able to tell him if there were any clues in the murder of Joe Dalton. He relied on his friendship with Jason and with the deputies' boredom to perhaps loosen their lips about the crimes related to the Dalton family. Good to be a member of the Good Ol' Boys Club.

He was determined that Misty would have closure and learn the true reason behind her brother's murder, and he wanted to be able to give her hope that the authorities were following up on substantive leads.

She had grudgingly agreed to remain at the Garrett ranch because he had convinced her she and Mark were in danger. The attack on Paco had driven his point home, but at what cost? He hoped the old man would recover without any permanent disability.

"I heard this ranch was circling the drain," Clyde said.

Colton lifted his head, giving Clyde a sharp glance. "Where did you hear that?"

"Oh, just around. It looks like really good land. Someone was saying this place was in foreclosure." He cocked his head to one side. "Do you suppose that's true?"

Colton scuffed the toe of his boot in the dirt. "Maybe it was true, but it's not anymore."

"What happened?" Jason asked.

"I paid off the past due part of the loan."

Both deputies exchanged a speculative glance and then turned their attention back to Colton.

"Because you're the boyfriend?" Jason asked, a wry grin on his face.

"Partly, and partly business. We have a legal agreement. I'm a partner in the Dalton ranch now. It's in my best interest to help them turn this place around."

"Sweet deal," Clyde said.

Jason just shook his head. "Sounds like this love thing is getting expensive."

"Maybe." Colton tried to keep his temper in check. "She's worth it." He took a few steps away from the deputies' vehicles. "Is it okay if I take a look around?"

Jason appeared to be sizing him up. "Technically, isn't this sort of your land?"

"Yeah, I guess you could say that."

"Well, you can look around. Just stay away from the truck. That is what the big city experts identified as the crime scene. Looks like the old guy was dragged out and beaten up pretty badly."

"I only wanted to check the outbuildings. I'm thinking they need to be torn down and hauled away."

"Be careful," Jason advised. "I do not want to have to answer for it when the whole place comes crashing down on your head."

"Gotcha." Colton headed for the largest structure, an old barn. The door was ajar since one of the hinges had broken loose, allowing some light to penetrate the dim interior. He stepped inside, inhaling the musty odor of dust, mold, and some kind of animal excrement. An old International Harvester tractor was quietly rusting in one corner along with a cultivator attachment beside it. Some of the tines had come loose and were lying in the dirt.

The scurry of tiny feet attested to the presence of rats or field mice. Rotted bales of hay were moldering against one wall.

Colton checked out everything before returning to the door. The wood in the structure of the barn could probably be reused, but he wasn't sure how to best make use of it. He was pretty sure Big Jim would have some ideas. *He always does*.

He checked out a smaller building. It was in better shape and had stalls inside. *Must have had horses here at one time*. He exited via the door at the rear of the stable and walked through a spiderweb. The crawling sensation had him tearing off his Stetson and flailing at his face to remove the last traces of web. He gave an involuntary shiver as he took a few paces away from the spider's domain. Slapping his hat against his thigh to knock off any vestiges of the web, he stepped backward and stumbled over a slightly raised pile of wood.

Falling backward, his weight crashed through the aged lumber and sent splintered boards falling beneath him. He scrambled off the pile on his hands and knees and heard the broken planks land far below. The sound of the wood splashing into water sent a chill skittering across his skin.

Colton's heart raced, thumping against his ribs like a drummer on speed. When he could draw a ragged breath, he crawled back to the edge of the gaping hole to see what he had almost fallen into.

Under the pile of lumber was a circle of stones set in concrete. The top part of the stones had crumbled, and only about a foot remained aboveground.

Colton leaned over the edge, peering down into the shadowy interior. The pit appeared to be bottomless. He thought it was an old well or cistern of some kind. The stench of brackish water reached his nostrils, causing him to draw back. *Ugh!* The disgusting odor cut his breath. *Phewww…smells like something fell in and died down there.*

He recoiled when he realized he could have met the same fate. This was a big liability. He would make sure to have it filled in. He wondered if Misty knew about the existence of the well. *Probably not.* But he would be sure to talk to her about it when she got home from work that evening.

When he climbed to his feet, he was still shaking. He sucked in a deep breath to steady himself and then stacked the longer boards back across the opening. It wasn't safe, but at least this might prevent someone else from falling in accidentally. If he hadn't been distracted by the spiderweb, he would have been more alert.

He brushed his palms against his Wranglers and then tried to beat the dirt off the denim when he saw what a mess they were. *Great! I look like I've been dragged through the dirt. It could have been worse.* He could have fallen into the abandoned well and never been heard from again. He imagined with the two deputies standing guard over the "crime scene" someone would have come looking for him eventually, but it would probably have been too late.

He needed to make sure this hazard was permanently sealed, and quickly.

Breck had left the office, telling Misty he was headed to his ranch to confer with his foreman, T-Bone, and that the local veterinarian was coming out to join them. It all went over Misty's head because she tried to ignore all things having to do with cattle.

An involuntary shudder racked her body. She could still see the sweet face of the calf she'd fallen in love with as a child...before she'd learned that the beef on their table had been born on their property.

Not ever going to get involved with a cow on a personal level again.

She tried to focus on the stack of clerical assignments piled on a corner of her desk. She turned the pile over so as to attack the task that had been there longest.

The door to the office opened with such force as to swing back and knock the bentwood coatrack to the floor with a loud clatter.

Startled, Misty jumped, half rising from her chair.

"Let me see 'em!" Levi Blair strode into the office without bothering with the felled coatrack. He stomped toward her and stopped right in front of her desk, taking a wide stance and fisting his hands at his waist.

"Sir?" She gazed up at him in confusion. "May I help you?"

"Yes, you certainly may, young lady. I want to see those pictures you sent me. The ones with my son in 'em."

She frowned. "Certainly. I've got them right here." Her hands fluttered around her desk, and then she clasped them together in dismay. "Oh no! They're still in Mr. Ryan's office. He scanned them and then emailed them to you." She gave him a nervous smile and shrugged. "I'm sorry, but he's gone for the day."

Levi raised one of his fearsome shaggy eyebrows, glancing from her to Breck's office door. "No problem." He grabbed the stapler off her desk and in three strides was in front of the pebbled-glass inset in Breck's door. He covered his eyes with one arm and smashed the glass. Shards flew everywhere. Levi reached inside to unlock the door and then stepped through, fragments of glass crunching underfoot.

"Tell Breck to have the door repaired and to bill me." He reached Breck's desk, his gaze fastened to the envelope with the photographs inside. "Is this all of 'em?"

Misty swallowed hard. "Y-yes, sir. They're all there."

He grabbed the packet and exited Breck's office, grinding more glass into the polished wood floors. As he passed Misty, he sent a chilling glance her way. "You seen 'em? You know what they mean?"

Misty felt a squeezing sensation in her chest. "I glanced at them. It's just a bunch of Joe's high school friends horsing around."

Levi's eyes narrowed. He let out a snort that sounded more like a bellow. "It's more than that. Come here." He strode to the long table at the back of the office.

Uncertainly, she followed him, wishing Breck hadn't left. Wishing Colton was there. Wishing she wasn't.

Methodically, Levi laid out the photographs. He moved them around, changing the sequence. "Y'see this?" He laid his large forefinger on one of the images. "That's the date your brother had these pictures developed at the drug store. They used to put a date on them, and this was just three days after Nate disappeared." He turned his fearsome gaze to Misty. "Do you know what this means?"

"No, sir." Her voice was barely audible, almost a whisper.

He slammed his hand on the table, causing her to jump. "These photos was taken the last day Nate was seen around here. And you know what else?" His dark eyes crackled with an inner fire.

Misty pressed her trembling lips together, not trusting herself to speak, but shook her head as a reply.

"It means every one of them damned boys lied to me. They all said they hadn't seen Nate that day or for a couple of days before. They was damned liars." And he slammed his palm down on the table again.

Misty jumped again in response, nodding her head nervously.

"And I'm a-gonna get to the bottom of it." He turned on her fiercely. "Did your brother tell you about the day Nate disappeared?"

"No, sir." Her heart pummeled her ribs without mercy.

"Now tell me the truth, girl. How did you come to get these pictures?" He shook his giant ham of a fist in her face.

She realized he could snap her neck with one hand. Her mouth felt dry, but she sucked in a breath, trying to gain control of her fear. "I was cleaning out Joe's room." She felt tears gather and blinked them away. "After he was m-murdered. I found the photos hidden and brought them to Mr. Ryan."

Levi's glare softened. He turned back to the photographs. "These boys was always hanging around Nate. Getting into trouble." He blew out a breath. "But I thought 'boys will be boys' and didn't put my foot down." He placed his finger on one of the faces in a group photo. "This here's the Lynch boy, and that'n is a Diaz." His brows drew together in a furious V. "And this'n is my nephew, Eddie. If anybody owes me the truth, it's him."

Misty nodded. As Levi advanced toward her, she backed away.

Instead of grabbing her with one of his big hands, as she had feared, he sidestepped her and headed for the front door. "You be careful, young lady. You may know more than you think you do."

He trudged straight to the door, still standing open, and walked through to the daylight, his silhouette dark in contrast to the brightness. The cowbell clanked against the glass as he slammed the door behind himself.

Misty slumped into one of the chairs at the long table. She was shaking all over. Her encounter with Levi Blair had left her weak and confused. What had happened to Nate Blair? What had Joe known about Nate's disappearance?

She gripped her shaking hands together to steady them and drew a deep breath.

Levi was gone, and he had left a path of destruction in his wake.

Misty debated what to do and decided she needed to call Breck about the encounter. He should know about Levi's actions. Especially since he needed to replace the glass in his office door.

She returned to her desk and punched in the number to Breck's cell. When he answered, she quickly recounted the events that had occurred since he'd departed his office.

"Broke the glass?"

She heard the vexation in Breck's voice and could imagine the angered expression on his face.

"You stay put. Don't touch a thing. I'll be right there." He huffed out an impatient breath. "Misty, honey... don't you worry. I won't allow that old bully to come back to the office, even if I have to send him packing as a client." He rang off.

Misty felt a little calmer after that. All she had to do was wait for Breck to arrive, and he would take over. Straightening her spine, she picked up the task from the pile she had been about to tackle when Levi had first hit the front door.

———

Colton poked around a bit more and then made his way back to where the two deputies stood guard. "Well, it's nice to see that my tax dollars are getting put to good use." He grinned as he said it, but Justin rolled his eyes.

"Yeah, somebody has to keep the crowds in check."

"Hey, we love to stand around in the sunshine, with not another vehicle in sight, guarding a crime scene." Clyde removed his hat and wiped his brow.

"Don't work too hard, fellas." Colt took a couple of steps toward his truck but stopped when Jason asked a question.

"Did you find anything interesting? Something worth saving this old place?"

Colton cocked his head to one side. "It's all about the land. This is valuable acreage for grazing and for producing crops."

"Yeah, I suppose so," Jason agreed. "And if you knock down all these decrepit buildings, you'll have a little more."

"I suppose," Colton said. "I just want to make sure it's

safe. I found an old well out back. If you two are poking around, don't fall in. It needs to be covered." Colt bade them goodbye and took off, thinking he hadn't learned anything new about the crimes involving the Daltons or their property, but he was glad he had a chance to tromp around the outbuildings. He hadn't looked at the little house, but maybe it could be renovated and Misty could use it as rental property. Maybe not. He needed to call someone to check out the well. Perhaps it could be restored to a useful source of clean drinking water.

He shook his head and pulled off the graded caliche road and onto the paved farm-to-market road. *Ridiculous. It would be better to clear that corner of the Dalton land and get it over with. Not everything can be saved.*

By the time Breck reached the law office, he was in full warpath mode, his temper raging just below the surface. "What the hell?" His eyes lit on the overturned coatrack just inside the front door.

Misty held up her hands. "You said not to touch anything, so I've been sitting right here, minding my own business and working on a statement for the billable hours to send to the Slaytons."

Breck's eyes narrowed, focusing on the broken glass strewn on both sides of his office door. "That bastard. This makes my blood boil."

"Mr. Blair was more than a little boiling when he came in here. It was the pictures you sent that set him off." She gave a shiver in remembrance. "He was just plain scary."

Breck pulled his cell out of his pocket, punched a number, and then began talking. "Sheriff, come over to my office. It's been vandalized." He spent his waiting time pacing around the front office.

In due time, the sheriff parked in front and strode through the door. "What's going on here?" he asked, gesturing to the fallen coatrack. He frowned, fisted his hands at his waist, and surveyed the broken glass. "What the hell happened?"

Breck stepped forward to shake the sheriff's hand. "Your friend and mine, Levi Blair, came in the office a short time ago, scared the devil out of poor Misty, and deliberately broke my private office door."

The sheriff eyed Misty uncertainly. "Are you all right, Miss Dalton? Were you injured?"

Misty swallowed. "Mr. Blair didn't hurt me. He just frightened me."

"Come on, Misty," Breck said, gesturing for her to join them. "Tell the sheriff exactly what happened. Don't leave anything out."

She pushed back from her desk and retold the story in detail. She answered questions when they stopped her but managed to get all the way through.

"So, Blair never touched you?" The sheriff gazed at her, one brow raised.

"No, sir. He grabbed my stapler to break the glass, and he got the packet of photos off Mr. Ryan's desk."

"And then he spread them out to look at them?" Breck pointed to the table in the back of the room.

She nodded. "He laid them out and then rearranged them. That's when he got real mad. He said the boys lied to him."

Breck led the way back to the table, and all three surveyed the photographs.

"And you say the date these pictures were printed was a couple of days after young Nate disappeared?"

"That's what Mr. Blair said." Misty felt a shiver spiral down her spine. "He was really upset. He said he was going to talk to his nephew, Eddie Simmons."

"And that's when he left." Breck gazed down at the photos. "There's a story here if we just knew how to read it."

All three stared down at the images. In the order Levi had placed them, it appeared the boys were just horsing around to start, but the blurred pictures of two boys fighting were followed by the image of Eddie, his shirt smeared with something dark, maybe mud. He was holding a gun.

Misty covered her mouth with both hands. "Oh, I wonder if that's the gun I found in Joe's room?"

Breck and the sheriff both turned to stare at her.

"A gun, you say?" Breck asked.

"What kind?" the sheriff asked.

Misty shrugged. "I don't know. A handgun of some kind. It's all wrapped up, so I didn't disturb it."

"Where is that gun now, young lady?" the sheriff's voice boomed.

"Um—I took it to the Garrett ranch with me after I cleaned out Joe's room. I-I thought it was Joe's." She glanced from one man to the other. "He had taken such care to hide it. I didn't want to leave it behind."

"You did the right thing, Misty. It should be safe at the Garrett place," Breck said. "If you like, I could follow you and take charge of it until the sheriff determines if it's the same weapon as in the photograph."

Misty gazed down at the image of Eddie Simmons

holding the handgun aloft. His expression was difficult to read. She thought he might have been frightened...or angry. *Maybe both*. Heaving a deep sigh, she nodded. "Yes, that would be good. I thank you for taking it off my hands."

"We can leave right away," Breck said. "I won't short your pay."

"I think I'm headed out to Levi Blair's ranch," the sheriff said. "I want to talk to Levi, and I want to talk to his nephew, Eddie. Someone is going to tell me what's going on."

Chapter 16

COLTON WAS SURPRISED TO SEE MISTY PARK THE OLD car close to the Garrett ranch house very shortly after he had arrived home. He gazed out the window, and even at a distance, he could see she was upset. Her brows were drawn together, and her lips formed a tight line. She marched purposefully toward the front door, her back straight, her shoulders rigid.

Colton threw the door open, wondering why she had left work so early. Had she been fired? Surely Breck wouldn't do that without sufficient reason. "Hey, Misty. What's wrong?" He held out his arms, and she melted into them.

He glanced up in time to see Breck Ryan's big diesel club cab truck pull up behind Leah's old heap. "What's going on?" he whispered, burying his lips in her hair.

"Oh, Colt." Her voice came out small and edged with fear. "I've had just the most awful day."

Breck climbed out of his truck and strode toward the open front door of the Garrett house. His gaze flicked over Misty and Colton.

Misty drew away, running her fingers through her hair. "I'll be right back."

Colton gazed at her departing form, wondering where she was going and what was going on. "Come on in, Breck."

"Misty found something in her brother's things."

Breck answered Colt's unasked question. "I don't know if it has a bearing on anything that's happened recently, but I told the sheriff I would take charge of it."

Misty returned quickly holding something in a plastic bag. She extended it to Breck, who accepted it, his expression grim.

"Looks like an old .45-caliber revolver. It's wrapped up pretty good here." He gave Misty a stern look. "I think Joe was trying to preserve some kind of evidence, but we don't know what."

Misty heaved a shuddering sigh. "I'm just glad to be rid of it."

Colton couldn't imagine why Misty hadn't told him about finding the gun.

Breck held the weapon suspended in the bag, squinting at it with a raised brow. "I'll turn it over to the sheriff. He can have it checked against any recovered ammunition found at crime scenes...or recovered from the victims. Looks like this one still has some bullets in it."

Misty nodded, rubbing her hands over her arms.

When Breck departed, Colton scowled down at her. "Why didn't you tell me about the gun? We're not supposed to be keeping secrets from each other."

"Oh, I'm sorry," she burst out. "It's just that so much has been happening all at once. First the gun and photos turned up when I went through Joe's things, and then someone attacked Paco, and today Levi Blair came into the office and scared me to death."

"What?" Colt drew her close, a sense of rage gathering in his chest. "What did that old bastard do to you?"

She heaved out a sigh. "Nothing, really. He just came storming into the office wanting to see the pictures I found in Joe's room. Breck emailed them to Mr. Blair because there were some photos of his son, Nate."

"The boy who went missing?"

"Yes. Breck thought Mr. Blair would like to have them, but those photos were exactly what set him off. Something about the date. And he said Joe and the other boys lied to him about not seeing Nate the last day he was around."

"And this scared you?"

Her face crumpled, and she nodded wordlessly. She sniffled and then blurted out, "I told him the photographs were locked inside Breck's office, and Mr. Blair broke the glass in the office door."

Colton tried to grasp what she was saying, but tears rolled down her cheeks, and her words became garbled. "You said he was yelling at you? Why the hell would that old goat yell at you? You had nothing to do with Nate's disappearance. You were just a child then."

Eyes squeezed shut, she shook her head. "He wanted to know if Joe told me anything. He seems to think the boys who ran around together know what happened to his son, Nate. He said he was going to question Eddie. That's when he stormed out."

Colton drew in a breath and blew it out. "Good. They can keep it in their family, but stay away from mine."

Misty jerked her tear-stained face up to stare at Colton. "But I'm not your family."

A scoffing sound emerged from his throat. "Of course you're my family, Misty. You're the woman I love. The one I'm going to marry."

She appeared to be frozen in place and then blinked. "Was that a proposal?"

"Yeah. Not very romantic, but I'm asking you to marry me…as soon as possible."

A little smile flickered around her lips. "With all my troubles, you still want to marry me?"

"I do." He gazed at her intently. "What is your answer?"

"I will marry you." A wide grin spread across her face as she looped her arms around his neck.

"Wahoo!" Colt shouted. He lifted her off her feet and swung her around.

"What's going on?" Leah hurried into the room, wiping her hands on a dish towel.

"What's all the ruckus?" Big Jim demanded, close on her heels.

When Colt set Misty on her feet, he turned to see his entire family and Mark crowded in the doorway of the front room. They were looking at him quizzically.

"Misty agreed to marry me," Colt announced. He saw a dark expression cross his father's face, but in a flash, Mark sprinted across the room to throw his arms around Colt's middle.

"That is so great," Mark said.

"Yes, it is," Leah added, moving closer. She embraced Misty. "I'm so happy for both of you."

Beau heaved a sigh before stepping forward to extend his hand. "Congratulations, Bubba. You said you were going to marry her, and now it's official."

"Thanks." Colt shook his hand.

All eyes turned to Big Jim, who stood back with his arms crossed over his chest, leaning against the doorframe. "I don't know what all the rush is about. In my day, a courtship lasted a little longer." He pushed away from the door and extended his hand to his oldest son. "But I just want whatever's best for you both. Congratulations, Colt." He turned to Misty and opened his arms. "And welcome to the family, Misty."

She hesitated a second but stepped into Big Jim's embrace. "Thank you." Her voice sounded small.

Colton locked his gaze with Big Jim's over Misty's head. He could tell this wasn't the outcome his father had wanted, but at least he was willing to accept Colton's decision. Misty would become a Garrett. That was all that mattered.

"Well, we have a lot to celebrate," Leah said. "Gracie and Mark brought home their excellent report cards, and I baked a chocolate cake to celebrate their hard work. Now we have two reasons to party." She gestured toward the kitchen, and everyone moved in that direction, with Colton and Misty bringing up the rear.

He drew her close and kissed her forehead. "Are you okay?"

"Remarkably, yes. My horrible day just got a lot better." She gazed up at him, her face aglow.

"I'm here to make sure your entire life gets a lot better."

She let out a little sigh. "So, we're engaged to be married?"

Colt felt buoyant. "That's exactly what we are. Now we need a ring."

Misty's eyes lit up. "A ring? I get you and jewelry too? Oh, that would be lovely."

"We'll go to Amarillo and get you the prettiest ring in the city."

She giggled. "And I'll have to show it off to anyone who will take a look, even if it turns my finger green."

Colt let out a less-than-polite snort. "I guarantee you

your finger will not turn green." He led her toward the kitchen, where Leah was ladling up bowls of chili.

"I let the kids pick the meal," Leah said. "So, it's chili with hot dogs and chocolate cake."

"Good choice," Big Jim said. "And how about those report cards? All A's and B's."

"There's hope for the next generation." Beau gave Mark's hair a ruffle.

Mark responded with a grin.

Misty reached for the report card. "Awesome as always." She looped an arm around Mark's neck and leaned her head against his. "I'm so proud of you, Mark."

"Look at mine," Gracie said. "I got a B in math." She waved the report card in front of Misty's face.

Misty gazed at the card. "That's fabulous."

Gracie laced her fingers together and twirled back and forth. "Mark helped me with the problems I didn't understand."

"I'm proud of both of you." Misty hooked her other arm around Gracie.

Colton thought about his future with Misty. He thought she would make a great mother someday. She had been taking care of her entire family for so long. But first, she deserved to be a bride. To be a loved and cherished wife. That was the first goal he set for himself. And to keep her safe.

—⁓—

Big Jim walked out onto the enclosed patio to the rear of the house. He turned back to the kitchen, watching his family talking and laughing. He swallowed hard and looked away, taking great gulps of the cool night air.

Damnation! Now Colton's going to marry that girl. I should have put my foot down. I should have…

He heard the sliding-glass door open and close behind him. He huffed out a breath, wondering who was coming to lecture him.

"You did a great job of covering, Big Jim." It was Leah.

He shrugged. "I don't know what you're talking about."

"Hah!"

"Okay, so I know what you're saying." He shoved his hands deep in the pockets of his Wranglers.

"Well, what's the big deal, anyway?" Leah came to stand beside him, gazing up at the same countless stars overhead. "Surely you want Colt to get married and have a family of his own."

He glanced down at her upturned face. "Of course I do. I just wanted him to find someone…different."

"Honestly! What do you have against Misty? She's a lovely person." Leah grabbed his shirtsleeve. "She's sweet and smart…and most of all, she loves Colton with all her heart."

Big Jim made a grumbling noise deep in his chest. "You could have fooled me. I thought she was just looking for a savior. A man with enough money to bail her out."

"Ouch!" Leah stepped back, removing her hand as though she'd been scalded. "Makes me wonder what you thought of me when I first landed here in Langston. I sure didn't have a penny to my name, and yet one of the Garrett boys fell into my gold-digging trap."

Big Jim cringed at her scolding tone. "You know I welcomed you with open arms."

"I thought you did, but my story was even more

desperate than Misty's. I wasn't only broke. I brought big trouble with me."

Big Jim acknowledged that, indeed, Leah had brought a boatload of trouble. What was the difference? Why did he feel so closed-up toward Misty? He blew out a breath. "It's because she's a Dalton."

Leah turned on him, her hands fisted on her hips. "So what? Her last name is going to change very soon, if Colt has anything to say about it."

"I know." He scuffed the toe of his boot against the ceramic tiles. "I just realized what my problem is." He heaved another huge sigh. "Arnold Dalton and I lost our wives about the same time. I spent my time trying to focus on the boys and making sure they had something to call their own. I wanted to give them a leg up in life."

"And you've done a fine job," Misty said. "Tyler is a wonderful man. Best husband a woman could ask for." She gave him a dimpled smile. "Colt and Beau didn't turn out too bad either."

"Arnold Dalton turned to alcohol. He climbed into the bottle and ignored his kids. He let them grow up on their own with absolutely zero guidance from their father. He pissed away his children's inheritance. His son Joe was a wild one without a father there to guide him. Dalton let his entire family down."

Leah narrowed her eyes. "You're comparing yourself to Misty's dad? People express their grief in different ways. Maybe he wasn't as strong as you, but you can't let her father's weakness turn you against Misty. She's a wonderful person. She held that family together the past few years. You should admire her for her strong spirit."

"Are you done with your lecture?"

"Yes, I am. But you mark my words, Big Jim Garrett. If you don't climb down off your high horse, you're going to alienate both your future daughter-in-law and your oldest son. I'm pretty sure you want to be there for your grandchildren, so you better suck it up." With that she turned and stormed into the house.

Big Jim felt as though he'd been dealt a physical blow. Leah, his beautiful, sweet, and kindhearted daughter-in-law, had just given him a verbal smack upside his thick skull.

He considered her words. Surely Colton, his firstborn, wouldn't turn against him. The Garrets were solid. Big Jim had spent his entire adult life ensuring his family would stick together. And yet…

⁓

The next day, Misty drove into Langston and parked next to Breck's diesel truck, surprised that he was in the office so early. She entered the law office, the cowbell clanking against the glass.

She saw that the bentwood coatrack had been righted and the shattered glass swept up. A large metal wastebasket stood next to Breck's office door with a broom and dustpan nearby.

Breck was in his office with the door open. He looked up when she peeked around the corner. "Come in. Come in. The sheriff is on his way into town."

"I would have swept up this mess," she said.

"I was a bachelor way too long not to be able to wield a broom. And with my wife serving the entire county's medical needs, I can sure pitch in." He gestured to a chair opposite his desk.

Misty sat down, still clutching her purse.

"Cami said to tell you that Paco is improving. He sustained internal injuries, but he seems to be growing stronger. He was placed in a medically induced coma to keep him from thrashing around and opening his sutures."

Misty received the news with mixed emotions. Glad Paco was getting better. Sorry he was going through so much in the meantime. "What do you have for me to do today?"

"Just relax. The sheriff should be here shortly, and we can give him the handgun. Then it will be his responsibility."

She nodded anxiously, the reality of the situation falling like a wet blanket on her good mood.

The cowbell tinkled again, and Breck cocked his head to one side. "We're in here, Sheriff."

The sound of boots clomping across the hardwood floor was prefaced by a knock on the open door frame and Levi Blair was standing in the doorway.

Misty felt as though an icy hand suddenly squeezed her chest.

Levi was grinning affably. He swept off his hat and entered the room, extending his hand toward Breck. "I come to apologize for my behavior yesterday. I got a mite out of hand when I saw them photos."

Breck stood, a frown etched on his features. "Levi, what were you thinking? You scared the daylights out of this young lady."

Levi stood with his hand extended in the air and a frown on his face. He dropped his hand. "I was out of my mind when I saw the photos of Nate and those young jackasses playing around." He turned to Misty and extended his hand to her instead. "I didn't mean to scare you none, young lady. Please forgive an old man."

Reluctantly, she offered her hand, which was immediately enveloped in his large and work-callused grip. A deep sadness in Levi's eyes seemed to reach all the way to her soul.

He returned his attention to Breck. "I made arrangements at the hardware store for your glass to be replaced, Breck. I hope you can forgive me."

Breck blew out a deep sigh. "Well, of course I can forgive you, Levi. Just don't let anything like this happen again. You have to think before you act."

"I know, you're right." Levi shrugged, his big shoulders lifting and falling with the effort. "I'm plumb ashamed of myself. But if you'd ever lost your son, you would understand."

"Mr. Blair?" Misty spoke up. "When you talked to Eddie, was he able to shed some light on what happened to your son?"

Levi's gaze narrowed. "Funniest thing about that. It seems my nephew and his running buddies can't be located. Nobody seems to know where they are." He sighed again. "Probably a good thing. Give me a little time to cool down."

The cowbell clanked again, and the sheriff strode into Breck's office. His brows drew together when he saw Levi. "Levi, you aren't causing any more trouble, are you?" He glanced from Levi to Breck and back again.

"Not today," Levi said. "I come to make amends. I was a crazy man yesterday. I'm havin' the glass repaired too."

The sheriff's stern gaze returned to Breck. "Is this all right with you, or do you want to press charges?"

Breck glanced at Misty. "I guess there was no real harm done. Just stay out of my office unless you see my truck outside. I don't want you scaring Miss Dalton again under any circumstances."

Levi nodded. "Agreed. Again, I apologize to you and to Miss Dalton."

Misty felt a little better but thought she should get back to her desk. She started to rise, but Breck stayed her with a hand gesture.

"Sheriff, this is the weapon you came for." He indicated the gun in the T-shirt on his desk.

The sheriff stepped forward. "Hmm…a Colt .45. It looks like an old one."

Levi pointed at the weapon. "It can't be…but it looks just like the one my daddy used to own. He left it to my older brother, Jed."

"Really?" The sheriff glanced at him.

All three men bent over the gun. The sheriff picked up Breck's polished-brass letter opener and gently pried the cloth away. The fabric was an old, faded T-shirt, and it was covered with rust, but the gun didn't appear to have rust on it. The sheriff gingerly lifted the shirt, holding it between thumb and forefinger.

"Damnation! That there is my daddy's gun," Levi said. "See, right there. Those are his initials carved on the handle. V. E. B., Victor Elijah Blair." His fierce brows drew together, and his eyes locked with Breck's. "Where did you get this? It belongs in my family." He reached toward it, but the sheriff stopped him.

"Right now, it's going to be checked for fingerprints and other evidence. If it belongs to you, it will be returned to you."

Misty was glad no one mentioned that it had been found among her brother's things. She didn't want to be the object of Levi Blair's scrutiny again. But she needn't have worried. Levi's attention was fixed elsewhere.

"Where are them photos you have of the boys?" he demanded.

Breck fisted his hands at his waist. "They're right where you left them on the table in back. Why?"

Levi didn't answer but instead strode out of the office, his boots clomping to the table along the back wall. He returned immediately, clutching two of the photographs. "Y'see right here. This'n with Eddie holdin' that there gun. He must have taken it from his father."

Misty stared in horror, realizing the weapon appeared to be the same.

"And this here photo of Nate and Eddie wrestlin'…" Levi placed the second image atop the other. "Y'see? That's the shirt Eddie was wearin' in this here photo. It's the same."

All eyes fastened on the shirt in the photograph. The screen-printed image on the front was an old concert icon from a country singer's tour.

The sheriff carefully raised the T-shirt, still in his hand. He lifted it by the shoulders, holding it up for all to see.

It dawned on Misty that the rusty-looking stain on the shirt was probably blood. Her stomach did a tumble and roll, and she pressed her lips together to keep from crying out.

"What's going on here, Sheriff?" Levi demanded. "That's my nephew's shirt, and this is my daddy's gun. Just tell me what happened."

The sheriff cleared his throat. "Wish I could, Levi." He released a huff of air. "I think I need to be talking to your nephew Eddie and the other two boys he runs with."

A muscle spasm twitched Levi's jaw. "Not if I find them first."

"Now, Levi," Breck began, "don't do anything foolish. You need to let the sheriff do his job. Don't go taking the law into your own hands."

Levi tore his gaze away from the bloodstained T-shirt. His eyes reflected all the pain tormenting his soul. "Me?" His voice was smooth as syrup. "I wouldn't think of it." He nodded to Misty and stormed out of the office. Moments later they heard the cowbell clank against the glass in the front door.

"There's going to be trouble," Breck said.

———

Colton sat astride his favorite horse. Ostensibly, he and Beau were riding out with Big Jim to check on the cattle. In reality, nowadays they mostly did this in one of their trucks or in the Jeep 4x4 kept for going overland. Today's ride was all about the Garrett men being together. When all three boys were younger, Big Jim had led this ritual, performing it at least weekly if the weather was good. When the weather was bad, the boys had been bundled up and rode in the cab of the truck. The goal was always the same: "Check on the stock."

Big Jim rode just a bit ahead. He always liked to be in the lead, and his sons catered to his wishes.

Colton thought this ride was all about the available Garrett men spending time together. After his announcement last night, he sensed his father needed time to be able to accept Colt's engagement to Misty.

He was halfway expecting to receive a verbal beat-down from Big Jim, but Beau's presence reassured him that it wasn't in the cards. If his dad had something to say to him, he would have done so privately.

No, this was all about Big Jim spending time with his sons and, in some way, atoning for his negative attitude.

"So, have you and Misty set a date?" Big Jim's tone was easy, but Colt suspected he was holding his breath.

"Not yet, Dad." Colton chuckled. "I just ambushed the poor girl with my proposal last night. I'm going to take her into Amarillo to choose a ring on Saturday. She can be engaged for a little while."

A look of relief crossed Big Jim's face.

"Dad...I'm going to marry her."

Big Jim sighed. "I know. I'm just glad it doesn't have to be one of those hurry-up things."

Colt drew up on his reins. "What? You thought I got Misty pregnant? Dad, I wouldn't be that irresponsible. First things first."

Big Jim drew up on his horse too and raised his brow. "Well, what am I supposed to think? You're in such a danged rush. Slow down. Take it easy."

Beau kept riding. He glanced back, shook his head, and kneed his horse to a faster gait.

"Dad, I'm happy. Doesn't that mean anything to you? I'm really happy."

Big Jim leaned over and placed his hand on top of Colt's. "Trust me, Son. That's all I care about. Is this the woman you want to spend the rest of your life with?"

Colton gazed into his father's eyes and gave himself a mental ten-count before trusting himself to speak. "Yes. I want to grow old with Misty Dalton by my side."

Big Jim heaved a sigh. "Then that's good enough for me. This is the last time I'll question your judgment. If you're that sure, then you have my blessing." He released Colt's hand and gave him a grin. "Now, let's catch up to that rascal brother of yours." He slapped his heels against his horse's flanks and took off, leaving Colt to stare after him.

Colton shook his head, let out a chuckle, and followed after his father.

Chapter 17

WHEN MISTY STEPPED OUTSIDE THE OFFICE, SHE WAS more than a little anxious. A feeling of dread had been building in her gut the entire afternoon. She had half expected Levi Blair to return, throw open the door, and lambaste her about the gun and T-shirt.

Misty tried to understand his point of view. Certainly, in his position she would have been insane with grief... Well, maybe he had the insane part down pat.

Her hands shook as she tried to separate the keys and force the right one into the lock. She felt exposed and vulnerable.

Glancing around, she didn't see anything out of the ordinary. A few vehicles cruised by on the street, and a few were parked, but the only car in front of the law office was the one belonging to Leah. She squared her shoulders and managed to get the key into the lock, twisting it to secure the office.

Expelling a huge sigh, she turned to the car, waving when she spotted Sara Beth closing up her shop. The baby was safeguarded in an all-purpose carrier and car seat. Sara Beth finished locking up her place of business and picked up the carrier, looping it over her arm. She gave a hearty wave to Misty and strode purposefully to the pickup truck where her fiancé, Frank, stood waiting by the passenger door.

Misty watched as Frank gave Sara Beth a kiss on the

cheek and took the carrier from her. He secured the baby
and then held out his hand to assist Sara Beth up into
the truck.

Misty smiled, glad her friend had someone nice in her
life and even more grateful that she had Colton Garrett in
hers. She climbed into the car and fastened her seat belt
before starting the motor. It was always a relief when
the old car roared to life. True, it was a little loud, and it
started with a rough idle, but soon enough it settled into
a lesser growl as she pulled away from the curb.

Heading for the highway, she felt the dread give way
to anticipation. Soon, she would be in the arms of her
own fiancé. She knew Colton would be waiting for her
to return to the ranch. Maybe they would talk about
the wedding. He had indicated he didn't want a long
engagement. But how long was that?

"Misty Garrett," she said aloud. "Misty Dalton
Garrett. Mrs. Colton Garrett." She realized she was grinning like an idiot. Just driving along, thinking about Colt
and grinning bigger than Dallas.

She wondered if they would get married in church, or
would they just go to the justice of the peace? No, she
felt certain the Garretts would expect a church wedding.

Sudden tears sprang to her eyes. Who would give her
away? *Oh, poor Daddy. He would have been so proud
to walk me down the aisle.*

She was lost in thought when she glimpsed another
vehicle in her rearview mirror, and it was coming up
fast. No matter. There weren't any other cars on this particular stretch of highway, so whoever it was would have
plenty of room to pass. Just to make sure, she pulled to
the right as much as possible so the driver could see she

was driving at the posted speed limit and he could go right around her if he felt the need for speed.

It was a pickup truck, and sure enough, the driver swerved as if to pass, but when he drew up alongside, he slowed down to match her speed.

When she looked, she recognized Eddie Simmons in his truck. He glared at her and then jerked the steering wheel to ram his truck into the side of her car.

Misty's steering wheel jerked violently, spinning out of control, sending the vehicle veering sharply off to the side. Like a slow-motion nightmare, the vehicle plowed through brush and weeds and into the ditch.

With a sickening lurch, the old car went airborne before sliding to a soft landing on the passenger side.

The impact wrenched Misty from one side to the other, as though the car had been picked up by a giant hand and violently shaken from side to side. Now, she was suspended by her seat belt, her hands gripping the wheel and her heart throbbing against her ribs like a captive trying to break free.

She released a ragged breath, watching as the dust floated forward, swirled, and settled. Her ears were still ringing from the crescendo of metal on metal.

A sound escaped her throat, something like a kitten's mew.

Oh no! She'd had a wreck in Leah's car. How would she ever be able to pay? Insurance? Was there insurance?

Her thoughts were jumbled, rushing one on top of the other to crowd her brain and muddle her judgment.

The sound of someone pounding on the side of the car caused her to focus.

"Get outta there!"

Slowly she turned her neck to stare at Eddie Simmons. He was standing on the driver's-side door panel of the overturned vehicle.

"Come on. Get out!" He grasped the door handle and wrenched it open.

She felt vaguely relieved. Here was someone to help her. *Eddie…Joe's friend.*

Misty was late getting home.

Colton had been pacing back and forth between the kitchen and the front room, where he would peer out the window to check if she was pulling into the drive.

"I swear, you're going to wear a hole in the carpet, Son." Big Jim eyed him in passing.

"I know," Colton said. "There's just so much going on. I hope she didn't decide to go over to her ranch for some reason. I should have insisted she come here straightaway."

There was a snort from Big Jim. "Son, they don't mind us. They're women."

Colton turned, frowning. "What?"

His father shook his head. "You really are worried, aren't you?"

"You're damned right!" Colt exploded. "With everything that's happened, I have every reason to be worried."

Big Jim held up his hands. "I didn't say otherwise. Just calm down."

Colton released a deep breath. "I don't think I can. She should be here by now."

"Did you try calling her?"

"Yes, but it just goes straight to message." Colt gritted his back teeth together. He was pretty sure she would answer the phone if she could. She wouldn't worry him needlessly.

"If you think it will help, we can drive back toward town and see if she's had car trouble. I know Leah's old clunker concerns you." Big Jim got to his feet and felt around in his pocket for his keys.

"Aw…you don't have to go, Dad. I can drive myself."

Big Jim fixed him with a cool gaze. "I'm not sure you're focused enough to be driving. You've got to have a clear head to get behind the wheel."

Colton returned the stare. "I'm fine. I'll just take a drive back toward town to make sure she's okay. I'm not distracted."

Big Jim's expression said all too clearly that he thought otherwise. "Call me if there's anything I can do."

Colton knew what a big concession this was coming from his father. "Thanks, Dad. I'm just going to see if I can backtrack a little. I'll probably meet up with her on the way."

"Hope so," Big Jim said tersely.

Colton lost no time in driving back to the highway. Once he was out of sight of the house, he tromped a little heavier on the gas pedal. Turning onto the highway, his anxiety grew with each mile. It was getting darker, and still no sign of Misty.

His throat closed in fear as, up ahead, he saw red and blue lights flashing. He eased his foot off the gas as he slowed his truck.

Two Texas Highway Patrol cars were pulled off the road, and an officer was waving him by with a flare. His gut clenched as he recognized Leah's car on its side in the ditch.

Throwing the truck into park, he killed the motor and jumped out. He ran across the highway, his heart beating a staccato rhythm. He recalled all too well the incident with Misty's brother, Joe.

"Get back in your vehicle, sir," the patrolman ordered. "There's nothing to see here."

"My—my fiancée was driving this car tonight."

The officer shone his flashlight in Colton's face. "There was no one in the car, sir."

Colton sensed there was something the officer wasn't saying. "Please tell me. There's been a lot of trouble lately. Her brother was murdered."

The officer's mouth tightened. "It appears someone ran this vehicle off the road." He turned the beam of the flashlight toward the car. "And there are boot prints where someone climbed on top of the vehicle. There is no blood, but considering the evidence, we're treating this as an abduction."

His words settled heavily on Colton, prickling the back of his neck like ice. *An abduction?*

He had no doubt that whoever was responsible was the same person or persons who murdered Joe and Fred Hamilton and gave Paco a beating. Now the murdering scumbag had his hands on Misty.

Colton felt totally impotent. He had no idea which way to turn. His mouth was dry, and when his cell rang, he fumbled to retrieve it from his shirt pocket. "Misty?"

"Sorry, Son," Big Jim said. "You didn't find her?"

"No," he croaked. "The car... Leah's car..." He swallowed hard. "Someone ran her off the road and then abducted her. The Highway Patrol is here."

Big Jim uttered a curse. "The sheriff called here at the house. He said he had picked up one of Eddie Simmons's running buddies and he's singing like a canary."

"Eddie Simmons?"

"The Diaz boy told the sheriff that Eddie shot Nate Blair some years ago and that Joe Dalton helped him dispose of the body."

Colton walked toward his truck and opened the door. He had no idea where he was going, but he couldn't stay there. Climbing inside, he slammed the door. "So Joe was in on it?"

"Not the murder, but he did take part in the cover-up. The Diaz boy said Joe and Eddie had a falling-out recently over money and that Eddie shot Joe. Diaz has been laying low because he didn't want to get involved any deeper than he already was."

"It was Eddie Simmons?" An image of the wiry, red-faced kid formed in Colton's mind. "He's the one who must have run Misty off the road. He's got her." It was all starting to come together, but Colton still couldn't see why Misty would be taken. Surely Eddie didn't think she knew anything about his actions. Why would he kidnap her? Why would he run her off the road? Was he trying to destroy all things Dalton?

"Are you there, Colt?" Big Jim's voice was etched with concern.

"Yeah, Dad. I think I should drive to the Dalton place just in case he took her there."

"I'll meet you there." Big Jim disconnected.

Colton reached to start the motor but was aware the Highway Patrolman had come to stand outside the truck. He lowered the window. "Yes, Officer?"

"Sir, I need your information and information on the person who was driving the car."

Annoyed, Colton handed over his license and rattled off Misty's information. "I really need to leave. I have an idea where he might have taken her."

"Who?" The officer passed Colton's license back through the lowered window.

"You need to connect with the Langston Sheriff's Department. Between the two of you, you will be able to see the whole picture." Colton threw the truck into reverse and did a U-turn that sent his tires squealing. He glanced in his side mirror to see if he was being pursued, but apparently the officer didn't think he was worth the chase.

As he headed for the Dalton place, he pressed harder on the gas pedal. He figured that his dad would beat him to Misty's ranch. He hoped Big Jim didn't encounter the murderer or murderers before he could get there.

"Please be all right," he whispered, envisioning Misty's face. "Please be all right."

Misty could barely breathe.

Eddie had her in his truck. The windows were open, and he was singing to the radio. His fingers were tangled in her hair, and he held her pressed down onto the worn and ragged seat beside him.

When he had jerked the car door open and dragged her out, she had been too stunned from the collision to be scared.

But that had quickly changed.

He'd thrust her into his vehicle and then torn away from the site of the crash.

"What did you do?" he kept screaming at her. "What did you do?"

When she had no answer, he seemed to go into some kind of trance, where he was smiling and singing.

With Eddie's fist twisted in her hair and forcing her face onto the truck seat, Misty couldn't see which direction he was going, but she felt the truck slow and heard the change of road surface from highway to graded caliche.

The shock of the initial impact had worn off, only to be replaced by sheer terror. A thousand questions raced through her mind, but she was too petrified to speak. She wasn't even certain she was capable of speech.

The truck sped on, over the rough road, to a destination where she was pretty certain she would be killed.

The smell of the filthy old seat filled her lungs and roiled her senses. Years of dust and sweat had soaked into the fabric, and now it worked her gag reflex.

Eddie turned and slowed, the tires crunching gravel, before he came to a stop. He dragged her out through the driver's-side door, leaving it open as his eyes narrowed.

She stumbled to her feet, glancing around as best she could, given his fist gripping her hair. She recognized the abandoned farm structures on her own land.

"Home sweet home," he growled.

In her jumbled mind, she recalled that this property had once been owned by Eddie's parents. He had grown up here.

"Now, for damage control. You're gonna tell me what you told my uncle and the sheriff."

"M-me? I don't know what you're talking about."

He thrust her forward, and she fell to her knees. "Don't lie to me. I know you gave them the gun and the pictures."

"Yes," she said. "Yes, I did. I found them among Joe's things after he—died."

"Joe!" he spat out. "I killed that lyin', cheatin' bastard, all right. He told me he would never give me back the gun, and he told me he had pictures of me killin' Nate." Eddie turned, stomping around in a circle, shaking his fists and cursing.

Misty trembled all over, the truth causing her flesh to prickle with fear. *He killed Joe. He murdered my brother.*

Eddie turned on her. Squatting down, he shook his fist in her face. "And then he tried to get more money from me. He said he had the evidence against me and would give it to the sheriff if I didn't pay his gambling debt. But I was tapped out, so I had to kill him, don't you see?"

Misty stared at him, wide-eyed with fear, her heart pulsing in her ears. It suddenly became clear. The reason Joe had been so desperate for money. But hearing Eddie admit to killing him hit her harder than the impact of the collision.

He stomped his foot, emitting a yowl of rage. "And then you go and give the damned pictures to my uncle Levi. Do you know how hard I worked to get on his good side? I tried to be like a son to the old bastard, and he was gonna give me all his property when he croaked…but you ruined that for me." He slapped her, open-handed, sending her flying backward into the dirt.

Her cheek stung from the blow. She scrambled sideways to avoid the next one. "Please, I don't know anything about what happened."

Eddie leaned forward, his hands on his thighs. "Well, you do now, don't you? You don't know it all, but you do know that I killed Nate and Joe." He made a sound in the back of his throat as though he was being strangled.

"And that asshole Hamilton. He promised my uncle Levi he could have first pick at buying your ranch. That way it would have come to me in the end. But no. He came straight to my uncle's place to let him know that Garrett's oldest son was prepared to grab it up by paying off the loan."

"You and your uncle killed Mr. Hamilton?"

Eddie emitted an enraged roar. "No, you stupid bitch. My uncle wasn't home. I shot Hamilton and got my friends to help me hide the body in your hayloft. With old man Dalton circling the drain and Joe dead, I didn't figure anyone would find him up there right away. I was so angry at Hamilton, I used your pitchfork to skewer him to the wall. Hah!" His teeth were bared in a frightening leer. "Nobody's gonna cheat me out of getting what I want. I've worked for this land for years, kissin' up to that old man."

"But your uncle has a lot of land already. Thousands of acres... Isn't that enough?" She glanced around, seeking any kind of weapon she could use to defend herself. "I mean, how much land can one man manage?"

Eddie threw his head back and roared with raucous laughter. "You think I want to farm this land? Can you see me on the old John Deere, plowing up the fields?" He hooted in mirthless glee.

Fear circled Misty's chest with a tight band, squeezing the breath from her lungs.

Her tormentor suddenly sobered. "You're crazy if you think I wanted to be a farmer. I saw my own father work himself to the bone and then lose it all. When Uncle Levi is dead and all his property comes to me, I will sell it right off." He huffed out a triumphant crow.

"I will have all the green cash money to live like a king. I'll kiss this Podunk town goodbye and go buy me a mansion somewhere nice…where pretty girls appreciate men with money." His gaze was fixed on a place far away that only he could see.

Misty cringed, drawing in upon herself.

He straightened and advanced toward her. "And now I can't let you live, can I?"

"You won't get away with this," she whimpered.

He let out a yowl of laughter. "They can have their suspicions, don't you see? They can think I'm guilty all they want, but they have to prove it." He reached for her, grabbed her arm, and jerked her to her feet. "And I'm about done tying up all the loose ends."

When Colton turned in at the Dalton ranch, he saw his dad's big silver pickup parked close to the house, with the headlights cutting a path into the gloom. Big Jim and Beau were standing outside it, waiting for him. They walked to meet Colt when he pulled up close.

"Nobody here," Beau said.

"It doesn't look like anything's been disturbed," Big Jim said. "I don't think anyone's been here in a while."

Colton's heart sank. He had been hoping Misty might be here, even if it meant confronting her kidnapper.

Big Jim's cell rang, and he answered it. There was a brief exchange, and then Big Jim said, "Colton's right here with me. We're out at the Dalton place, but it's quiet as a tomb."

The words chilled Colt to the bone. He blew out a breath and lifted his gaze to the now fully darkened sky. An almost-full moon played hide-and-seek behind the clouds skittering across the night sky. Colton's fists were clenched, but he felt powerless. He knew he should be doing something but hadn't a clue as to the best course of action.

Big Jim rang off and returned the cell phone to his shirt pocket. "The sheriff says we're to wait for him here. He's on his way."

"Great!" Colt ground out. "I should be doing something instead of just standing around here, waiting."

Big Jim held up a hand. "I know patience is not one of your long suits. It's not one of mine either. But the sheriff said he had the Diaz boy in custody, and his deputies found the other kid who hung around with Eddie Simmons. He'd been shot."

"Are you talking about Stan Lynch?" Beau asked. "Are you telling me Stan's dead too?"

Big Jim emitted a scoffing sound from deep in his throat. "No, I'm telling you this Stan guy has been shot. The doc's with him now. The kid said Eddie Simmons shot him."

"All of those guys were in my class in school. Misty's brother Joe too." Frowning, Beau fisted his hands at his waist. "What a mess."

"It sounds like Eddie is cleaning house," Big Jim said.

Colton absorbed this, trying to hold it together for Misty's sake. She had to be terrified. It wouldn't do her any good if he became paralyzed with fear. "Did you check the barn and outbuildings when you got here?"

"First thing," Big Jim responded.

It occurred to Colt that there was another barn and some outbuildings on the property. The abandoned place

where Paco's truck had been discovered and where Paco
himself had almost been beaten to death. "I'm going to
drive over to check on another place. If she's not there,
I'll be back."

"Wait!" Big Jim's voice sounded loud in the stillness
of the night. "The sheriff said to wait for him."

"I can't, Dad. I have to check this out." Colton was
hoisting himself into his truck.

"Wait for me." Beau scrambled in on the passenger side.

"Strap in, Little Brother." Colton drove away, leaving
Big Jim glaring after them.

"I think you pissed our daddy off big-time," Beau
commented.

"He'll get over it," Colt said. "I hope. Right now, I'm
more concerned about finding Misty alive."

"And you think you might know where she is?"

Colt shook his head. "I'm probably way off base, but
I thought of a place she might be. The same place she
found Paco."

———

In the midst of Misty's fear, a kernel of anger festered.
She cast about for some way to fight back. To resist
Eddie's plan to kill her.

She needed a weapon. Something…anything at all,
but his fingers were digging into her upper arm, and he
was forcing her toward a pile of lumber.

"So, what are you going to do?" she snapped. "Shoot
me like you shot Joe?"

Eddie reached down to remove some of the wood
from the pile. "Heck no. I don't even have to waste a
bullet on the likes of you." He kicked a few more pieces

of lumber to the side, uncovering what looked to be a circle of stones held in place by concrete mortar.

She thought it looked a little like a fire pit. Maybe he was going to burn the evidence after he murdered her. His strong and sinewy hand grasped her arm. She tried to pull away, but he jerked her toward the stone thing. Much to her horror she realized it was a pit or well of some kind. She snatched at one of the broken boards and took a swing at Eddie's head. She missed but cut a slice in his forearm with the jagged wood.

He cursed and lunged for her, snatching her by both wrists.

"You are going to spend a little time with some of my relatives," Eddie said. A sardonic grin spread across his face. "My cousin Nate and my uncle Levi. They went on ahead to get things ready for you...but for now, Misty Dalton, you can go to hell."

With a mighty thrust, he shoved her toward the ominous dark hole.

She fell backward, scraping her lower leg on the jagged edge of the rock circle. She seemed to be falling in slow motion, at least for a few moments...then she slammed into something solid jammed crossways in the shaft. She'd hit with enough force to knock the wind out of her. Pain radiated from the point of impact throughout her body. Gasping for breath, she managed to suck in a lungful of the dank, putrid-smelling air.

Her entire spine and the back of her skull reverberated pain. The thought crossed her mind that she might have crushed her back or neck. Gingerly, she tried to move, discovering in doing so that her fall had been broken by a plank of lumber jammed in the well at an angle. Thankfully, her entire spine seemed to be functional, and she could turn her head.

Releasing a ragged breath, she listened to her heart pounding in her ears. She tried to assess her situation in a logical manner.

First, she wasn't dead. That was a good thing.

However, she was stuck in a deep, dark hole in the ground on an abandoned part of her own property.

Second, she was laid out on a piece of lumber that might give way at any moment, but it was holding for the time being. Gripping the wood with both hands, she tentatively lifted her gaze. The sky was dark, but the full moon outlined the person gazing down into the depths of the well.

"I didn't hear a splash," Eddie called. "I hope whatever you landed on killed you outright because otherwise you're going to starve to death down there. Nighty night, little Misty." He turned away, an echo of raucous laughter trailing behind him.

The next sound she heard was his truck door slamming shut and the motor turning over. There was a revving of his engine, and he roared away, leaving her injured, in pain, and desolate.

She cried out, knowing no one would be able to hear. Tears rushed to spill from her eyes. They rolled unheeded into her hair. She dared not release her grip on the wood lest she fall farther down the well. Apparently, there was water, according to Eddie, but she had been fortunate to land on some obstruction.

"Don't move," a gravelly voice rasped from below her.

The prickle of gooseflesh spiraled along Misty's skin. She was frozen in fear, not trusting herself to draw a breath. "Who—who is it?" she whispered in a shaky tone.

A huge sigh was released in the darkness beneath her. "It's me…Levi Blair. My nephew Eddie shot me and throwed me down here."

"Oh, Mr. Blair," Misty said, all her former fear of the man dissipating. "You're shot?"

"The little weasel got me in the shoulder."

"I'm so sorry," she offered, realizing her words were pointless if they were both going to die down there.

"It's okay," he said mournfully. "It don't hurt much no more."

"That's good," she said. "I landed on a board of some kind. It's stuck at an angle, but it seems to be stable."

"I think I hit that'n on the way down and fell onto another one. There's a whole bunch of crap down here… and…and…" He broke off with a strangled sob. "Eddie told me my boy Nate's down here. He kilt him when he was only fifteen. Then throwed his body down the well. All the time lyin t'me about not knowing nothin'." He let out a mournful grunt. "Now, I got nobody. I always held out hope…but now…"

"That's terrible," Misty said. "Eddie killed my brother too. I hope he doesn't get away with it."

The old man heaved another sigh. "Plumb shame. I've made my peace with God, but you're too young to wind up down here…like my Nate. You got your whole life out in front of you. Plumb shame, little Misty."

Misty silently agreed but felt determined to remain positive. "Maybe we won't die. Maybe someone will find us."

"Ain't likely," the sonorous voice returned. "Nobody's gonna think to search here."

"Maybe they will…I have a fiancé."

Chapter 18

"YOU THINK MISTY MIGHT BE AT THAT OLD FARM-house?" Beau asked.

Colton blew out a deep breath. "Not really, but it's where her hired hand got beaten up. Maybe there's some connection."

His headlights cut into the blackness. There was an almost-full moon, but clouds obscured it intermittently. This far from town or any populace, total darkness surrounded them as they hurtled through the night.

"I hope we find her," Beau offered.

Colt knew this was an olive branch being extended after their exchange of terse words. He was glad he had held his temper and not pounded his younger brother for speaking against Misty. "Thanks. Me too."

Up ahead a vehicle turned onto the road, headed toward them. Not usual to meet any traffic on this stretch of road. As they grew closer to the oncoming headlights, Beau leaned forward. "Truck." And as the vehicle sped by them, he added, "That was Eddie Simmons."

A cold anger settled in Colton's gut. He was torn as to whether to turn around and chase Eddie down or to keep going in hopes of finding Misty. He pulled his cell from his pocket and punched in his father's number. "Dad? Eddie Simmons is headed your way. Will you tell the sheriff so he can catch the asshole?" With Big

Jim's assurances he would relay that information to the sheriff, Colt disconnected.

"I'm surprised you didn't go after him," Beau offered.

"If Eddie is coming from the abandoned farmhouse, there's a good chance he took Misty there. If she's injured, I need to find her. If she's…" He couldn't bring himself to utter the word "dead." *Please don't be dead*.

In a short time, he spotted the group of derelict structures off to the side of the road. Colton pulled in and stopped the truck. He left the headlights on and grabbed a high-powered flashlight from the console.

He and Beau exited the vehicle on opposite sides. The slamming of doors sounded like cannon fire in the stillness of the night.

Feelings of hope and dread duked it out in Colton's chest. "Misty?" he called, but there was no answer. He headed for the barn first while Beau checked the house. Nothing appeared to have been disturbed in the ramshackle remains of the barn since Colton's previous visit, but he checked thoroughly in case Misty might be there, unable to respond.

He went on to the stable, quickly spilling his light into each stall and storage area. It was evident that she was not here. Emerging on the back side, he saw at once that the lumber had been disturbed and was strewn all around. "Beau. Back here," he yelled.

In a matter of seconds, Beau appeared. "What's this?" He indicated the lumber and the well.

Colton's chest tightened when he spotted a smear of blood on the broken edge of the well. "There!"

Beau sucked in a breath. "Damn! Something bad happened here."

Colton saw signs of a struggle, footprints in the soft
dirt, and a broken piece of wood stained with blood on the
jagged edge. He went to the well and shone his light down
into the void. "Hello? Misty? Honey, are you down there?"

A faint reply reached his ears. He fell to his knees, and
leaning farther over, he peered into the darkness. "Misty?"

"Colt?" Her voice echoed off the stone walls.

A rush of relief washed over him. *She's alive.* "Yes,
it's me, baby. Hold on."

Beau had come up behind him. "Is it Misty?"

"She's down there," he said to Beau. "Get us some
help."

Beau pulled his phone out and punched in a number.
"Dad, can you send the sheriff to the old abandoned
property where the road dead-ends onto Reeves Road?
We found Misty." He listened for a while, and Colt
could imagine what Big Jim was saying. "We need an
emergency crew and an ambulance. Misty is down a
well and needs to be extricated." He listened some more
and then disconnected. He dropped to his knees beside
Colton. "The sheriff is there with Dad. He's called for
assistance. He said for us to stay put."

Colton snorted. "You couldn't pry me away with a
forklift." He leaned back over the side of the well. "Help
is on the way. Just hold on."

"Colt?" Her voice sounded hollow and so very far
away as it traveled up the stone walls of the well. "Mr.
Blair is down here below me. He's been shot."

"Levi Blair?"

"Eddie shot him and tossed him down here." There
was a pause. "He threw me down the well too, but I'm
holding onto a piece of wood that's jammed in here."

Colton recalled the lumber he'd broken when he had almost fallen in the unseen well. Maybe that was what she was clinging to. Maybe it had kept her from plunging all the way to the bottom.

From a distance they heard the scream of sirens and saw flashing lights. In a short time, an ambulance and a sheriff's department cruiser rolled onto the property. Beau went out to show them the way.

Colton relayed this information to Misty.

Two EMTs came running up, bearing a stretcher between them. They stopped and peered over the edge.

Beau returned, flanked by two of the sheriff's deputies. "There's more help coming."

One of the EMTs explained that a Life Flight helicopter had been dispatched out of Amarillo. "And a CS crew is on its way out of Langston."

"What is a CS crew?" Colton asked.

"Confined space team. They have all the equipment and training to get the job done."

Colton tried to assimilate that information, judging how long it would take for real help to arrive. He alternated calling down to Misty and pacing.

In a short time, another siren was heard, and a fire truck pulled into the clearing and around back to the site of the well. Several firefighters emerged from the truck almost immediately and began setting up equipment.

"Step back, sir," a female voice ordered.

Colton responded to the hand on his arm. Turning, he saw a slim young woman in coveralls. She was donning some kind of helmet while the others arranged a tripod of sorts above the opening to the well. Now she was stepping into a harness.

"Oh no," Colton murmured. "She's not going down after Misty, is she?"

The woman turned, eyeing him coolly. "What's your problem?"

Colton swallowed hard. "I just mean, you're so small. How can you lift her out? Let me go down."

Her eyes raked over him from head to toe. "What do you weigh? Well over two hundred pounds, I'm sure."

"Two and a quarter," he replied.

The young woman glanced toward the sheriff's men. "Deputies, I want you to restrain this man if he steps close to the well." Without another word, she buckled into the harness, adjusted her helmet, and swung herself over the side. Giving a signal, she disappeared down into the well as the winch motor whined.

"What?" Colton said. "I don't need to be restrained. Tell them, Beau."

The deputies closed in on either side of him.

Beau shook his head. "My brother is crazy in love with that girl down there, but between the three of us, I'll bet we can keep him from jumping in after her."

Misty could see lights above her and heard a lot of commotion, but now something or someone was being lowered down on top of her. She held her breath, trying to keep her panic level from reaching hysteria. *I'm just barely hanging on here. Don't knock me off.*

In a matter of seconds, a bright light shone in her face and someone was hovering right over her. "Hello. I'm Stephanie. Can you tell me your name?"

"Misty," she gasped out.

"Where are you injured?"

"I don't know. I hit this piece of wood with my back. I've been hanging on for dear life. There's a man down below me. He's been shot."

"We have to get you out first," Stephanie responded. "Show me if you can move all your extremities. This foot first." Stephanie tapped her left leg and then her right. She repeated the process with her arms, although it was terrifying for Misty to let go of the board, even for an instant. Finally, Stephanie asked Misty to lift her head, and when she did, she got a thumbs-up.

Stephanie was reaching across her and looping some kind of harness over her arm. She repeated the process, gently lifting Misty's head. She secured the harness and then, using a handheld control, lifted Misty off the board. "Hold on to me," she instructed, and the two of them rose straight up and out of the well.

When her head reached above the level of the well, she was momentarily blinded by the bright lights.

"Misty!" It was Colton's voice she heard, followed by a chorus of "Stay back, sir."

"Easy, now." Stephanie was holding her, but other hands were reaching for them. They were swung over to one side where Misty was released from the harness and gently lowered onto a stretcher. A circle of anxious faces bent over her.

"Mr. Blair…" Misty said.

"I'm going back down for the other victim." Stephanie threw her leg back over the side of the well. "She said he's been shot, so send down the basket when I ask for it."

The whining sound again as Stephanie lowered herself into the well with the winch.

"Baby, are you all right?"

She was able to focus on Colton's worried face hovering over her. "Colt," she breathed. The EMTs raised the stretcher with a jolt and rolled her into the waiting ambulance. She was aware that Colton stood outside the open doors of the vehicle. He looked worried. That made her feel grateful. Glad to have someone who cared.

The EMTs began examining her.

"Is she okay?" Colton asked.

"That's what we're trying to ascertain, sir."

In a matter of minutes, she heard the rotors of a helicopter.

"That's your ride," one of the EMTs announced. When they transported her to the helicopter, Levi Blair had already been loaded. He looked ashen.

"Misty, I'll be at the hospital as soon as I can get there." Colton's distraught face tore at her heart.

"I'm pretty sure I'm okay," she said. "They want to take X-rays and run some tests."

"Whatever it takes." He was hustled out of the way as the Life Flight crew took over.

The helicopter lifted off, and Misty tried not to think of how high off the ground they were. She tried to look at Levi Blair, but the EMTs had fitted her with some kind of device that immobilized her neck. "Is Mr. Blair okay?" she asked the person who was taking her blood pressure. Misty read his name tag and that he was an RN.

"He's lost a lot of blood," the man said. "Are you a relative?"

Misty sat up halfway so she could see Levi Blair at the same moment he opened his dark eyes to stare at her. "Yes," she asserted. "I'm his relative."

A ghost of a smile flickered across his mouth and then vanished.

"Do you know his blood type?" the nurse asked.

"No, but mine is O positive. Universal donor here. Just let me know if he needs some of mine."

Colton stood for a minute staring up at the helicopter after it lifted up and flew in a straight line toward Amarillo.

The sheriff's car pulled around the side of the stable. Colt was surprised to see his father riding in the passenger seat. Big Jim climbed out, his face grim.

The sheriff got out and came around. "What's happened here?"

"Misty and Levi Blair are on their way to the hospital in Amarillo. Eddie shot Levi and threw him down there and then kidnapped Misty. Thankfully, he didn't shoot her before throwing her in the well. She said Nate Blair's remains are down there too."

Big Jim stared at him morosely.

"Don't worry," the sheriff said. "We'll dredge up this whole thing to make sure we recover Nate's remains and anyone else that might be down there."

"Dad, are you okay?" Colton asked.

"My truck," Big Jim pronounced.

Colton looked around. "Where is your truck?"

"Gone."

The sheriff slapped Big Jim on the back. "Your dad is a hero, boys. When you called to tell him Eddie had passed you, he drove his truck across the road to form a barricade. Eddie must not have seen him because he broadsided your dad's truck and went airborne. Landed upside down in the field."

Big Jim's face was a mask of tragedy. "My truck."

"What happened to Eddie?" Beau asked. "Is he dead?"

"Nope," the sheriff said. "He climbed out and took off running across the field. I have deputies out looking for him."

"I'm headed to the hospital in Amarillo," Colton said. "I want to be there for Misty. I can drop you two off at the house, or you can come along."

"I'm a-coming," Beau announced.

Big Jim sucked in a deep breath and released it. "Me too."

~~~

Misty went through a battery of tests. She was X-rayed and run through an MRI machine. Her blood was drawn, and she peed in a cup. Since her clothing had been demolished when it had been cut away, she wore a hospital gown with another one on the wrong way to cover her backside. She was sitting up sipping apple juice in the ICU outside the treatment room where Levi Blair was being attended.

She was extremely sore and wore a mass of scrapes and bruises, but the many tests had revealed that she'd suffered no broken bones or internal injuries. The scrape on the back of her calf had been cleaned and bandaged as had another scrape on the back of her shoulder. Her entire spine was bruised, and she had a knot on the back of her head.

"You are very lucky, young lady," the ER doctor pronounced.

"Yeah, lucky." She thought of all the misery caused by Eddie Simmons. "I guess I am at that."

When a doctor emerged from behind the door to Levi's room, she stopped him, climbing painfully to her feet. "Mr. Blair, how is he?"

The doctor shook his head. "Touch and go. He's lost a lot of blood."

"I want to donate," she said. "I've given blood in the past. My dad was a cancer patient."

The doctor raised a brow and fisted his hands at his waist. "You'll pardon me for saying so, but you don't look like a prime candidate to give blood."

With effort, she drew herself upright. "I'm just a little banged up, but I'm very healthy."

The doctor agreed and called for a tech to take her to the lab. Quickly, a lab tech arrived with a wheelchair to transport her. It was determined that Misty could, indeed, donate blood for Mr. Levi Blair, and so it was drawn. It was more painful than Misty remembered, but that was probably because generally she hurt all over.

When she was wheeled back to the ICU, she was met by the three Garrett men at the nurses' station. All of them surveyed her anxiously, but Colton's expression caused her heart to flutter in her chest.

She grinned, aware that her appearance might be frightening. "I'm better than I look."

The nurse put a fresh ice pack in her hand, and she held it gingerly to the knot on her head. "I tried to check on Paco, but he's not here. The clerk at the information desk couldn't tell me what happened to him." She felt her lips tremble. "She said I would have to call tomorrow. I hope he isn't dead."

"I hope not either." Colton's brows drew together. "We'll find out tomorrow, first thing." He squatted down beside her. "Baby, you look rough." His fingers gently caressed her cheek. "You have a bruise here."

"That's where Eddie hit me."

Colt flinched. "He'd better keep running."

"Don't worry. Nothing's broken. No internal injuries. I'm just covered with cuts and scrapes. Bruised everywhere." She heaved a sigh. "But I'm alive."

"Yeah," he said, softly stroking her cheek.

"Glad you made it," Big Jim Garrett said gruffly. He pointed to her arm where the blood had been drawn and a cute bandage announced "I gave." "What happened here?"

"Um, I donated blood for Mr. Blair." She shrugged at Colton's concerned expression. "I thought he needed some Dalton blood."

"Is that so?" Big Jim frowned down at her. "Well, he for sure needs some Garrett blood. That might soften up the old coot." He started rolling up his sleeve and cocked his head at the lab tech. "Come on, young lady. I'll donate for Levi."

"Me too," Beau announced. Two of the Garrett men were led off to the lab.

Colton remained beside Misty. "You really scared me," he said. "I thought for sure I had lost you." He reached for her hand.

"I'm not letting you off that easy. You promised me jewelry." She held out her left hand, waggling her ring finger at him.

For the first time, the tension around Colton's eyes relaxed, and he chuckled. "I'll pay up. Don't worry about that."

She eased herself out of the wheelchair and took up her station outside Levi Blair's room. Peeking in when the door opened, she had to duck out of the way when the doctor came hurrying out. She noted that Levi's color looked a little better.

The doctor closed the door behind himself and stopped to speak to her. "We're taking him to surgery to remove the bullet. He wants to see you."

Misty glanced back at Colton's puzzled expression and then entered the small room. Levi Blair was hooked up to several beeping machines with various lights blinking. She stepped closer, and he opened his eyes. "Hey," she said with a smile. "They're going to take that bullet out."

"So I heard." Levi's voice was just a whisper. "I wanted to say thanks."

"For what? I told you there might be someone looking for us."

"Looking for you," he said. "You gave me hope when I was ready to give up." He reached toward her. "I was ready to let go of that board and let the well take me. I kept thinking that at least I would be with my boy, Nate."

"I'm glad you held on." She gathered his hand in hers. "Did you know my daddy, Mr. Blair?"

"As a matter of fact I did. Arnie and me used to go fishing when we was kids."

"Well, my daddy passed recently. And my only blood relative is my twelve-year-old brother."

"I'm so sorry, young lady." His gaze softened.

"I'm going to get married, and I sure would like it if you would walk me down the aisle. Maybe then neither of us would be so lonely."

Levi's dark eyes assessed her. "Misty, if I survive this surgery, I would be right honored to walk you down the aisle."

She leaned over and gently kissed him on his scruffy cheek. "You'll be just fine. I promise."

All of the Garretts waited with Misty until Levi was out of surgery. The doctor came by to inform her that the surgery had gone well and Mr. Blair was in recovery.

"I'm taking her home to get a little rest," Colton said. "We'll be back to see Mr. Blair tomorrow."

Reluctantly, Misty allowed Colton to convince her to accompany him back to the Garrett ranch.

She was forced to ride to the portico in the wheelchair pushed by a less-than-enthusiastic orderly. Colton and Big Jim were standing beside Colton's truck. Colt assisted her up into the cab and then went around to climb in on the driver's side. Big Jim climbed in beside her while Beau took over the back seat, slouching down and closing his eyes.

She clutched a plastic bag containing her torn and bloodied clothing. "Thanks for coming to get me."

Colt tossed the bag in the back seat before planting a kiss on her upturned face. "Didn't you know I would?"

"Yes." She nodded happily. *Yes, he will always be there for me*.

Colton drove out of town, and as soon as they left the bright lights of the city, Misty's head dropped onto his shoulder, and she was fast asleep.

Colton was exhausted. It had been a long and tough day. He remained aware of the precious person resting against his shoulder. His jaw was still tight from the grueling search and the frightening rescue. *But I got her back*. All the agony of the search had been worth the results.

"Who's going to tell Leah that her old beater of a car is toast?" Beau mumbled from the back seat.

Colt made a scoffing sound in his throat. "I'm pretty sure that would be me."

"She loved that old wreck." Beau removed his hat and raked his fingers through his thick crop of hair.

"Don't rub it in. I don't think the car is worth the repair bill."

Beau let out a derisive snort. "I would advise you not to tell her that."

When Colton pulled in through the horseshoe-shaped gate, he felt an easing of the tension in his gut. This was a safe haven. A place where his loved ones could hole up and lick their wounds. Although the only one with physical wounds was the woman beside him, his emotions were raw from the torment of his search. Not knowing if Misty was alive or dead had been agony.

He pulled up to the house and put the truck in Park as quietly as possible. Beau and Big Jim climbed out and opened the door to the house, leaving it ajar for Colt to follow.

Stepping out of the truck, Colt gently unfastened Misty's seat belt and eased her into his arms. She stirred, settling her head on his shoulder as he carried her into the house.

Beau closed and locked the front door behind them and headed toward his own room. It was very late—or very early, depending on how you were looking at it.

Colton stepped into the guest room Misty had been

using. His throat tightened when he saw that Leah had left the lamp turned on for them atop the bedside table and had folded the bedding down as well. Everything looked comfortable and inviting. He was extremely glad his middle brother had married such a gem.

He placed Misty on the fresh sheets and gently slipped his arms out from under her. Arranging her head on the pillow, he then removed her shoes and tenderly slipped the outer hospital gown off. She looked pale and fragile. Her bruised cheek and the dark smudges beneath her eyes gave silent testimony to what she had been through. He started to arrange the cover over her but was surprised to find her large dark eyes regarding him steadily.

"I hope you're not planning to leave me in here all by myself."

"Well, I...I thought you needed to sleep."

"Nooo." Her denial came out like a moan. "What I need is for the man who loves me to wrap his arms around me and never let me go. I can't get the dark images of Eddie Simmons out of my head." Her lower lip trembled. "Please, Colt. I—I need you." She unsnapped the shoulders of the remaining hospital gown, letting it fall to bare her lovely bosom.

The flame of desire licked his insides. "I don't have to go." Colton unbuttoned his shirt and closed the door. The house was quiet, and he was pretty sure everyone was either fast asleep or well on their way. He didn't want to cause a problem, but he couldn't leave her...not tonight. He arranged his shirt over the back of a chair and slipped off his boots. "I'd love to hold you in my arms, all night long, if you need me."

As quickly as humanly possible, he shed the rest

of his clothing and turned off the lamp on the bedside table, so that the room was bathed in moonlight filtering through the lace curtains at the windows.

Misty reached for him, and he lost no time in climbing onto the bed beside her. Her arms drew him closer as she arched against him. Her breasts grazed his chest, erasing any doubt as to what she wanted.

"Are you sure you're up for this?" he whispered against her ear. "You've been through a lot, and you have some injuries."

She chuckled deep in her throat. "Yes, I have, but I'm still alive. I can't think of any better way to celebrate than to make love with you."

Colton eased her onto her back and pressed a kiss against her lips. "In that case, you should relax and let me show you how much I love you."

A grin spread across her face.

"I'm going to devour you like a starving man at a banquet."

"Is that a threat?" She laughed and then winced in pain.

"First, I'm going to snack on your soft lips." He kissed her deeply, probing her mouth with his tongue. "And then I'll have a little bite of your neck." He kissed his way from her neck to her shoulder. He nuzzled his way to her breasts. "Oh, my favorite."

Misty giggled and squirmed as he licked and suckled each breast. He worked his way down her ribs to her navel, sticking his tongue in and wiggling it around.

He had to quell his desire to crush her to him. "And now for the main course." He trailed his tongue lower, and she spread her thighs. He heard a soft intake of breath as he lowered his mouth to take possession of her mound. All he wanted to do was please her and heal her wounds. He took his time, making sure to satisfy her needs. When he started to move away, she pulled him closer.

"Don't stop," she said, her voice ragged with desire. "I want more."

"Yes, ma'am." He donned a condom and entered as gently as possible, but he needn't have bothered because she wrapped both thighs around him and writhed hard against him. He held his weight off her but had no defense against her rage of passion. His thrusts were met with equal enthusiasm, sending them both into a deep abyss of ecstasy. When they lay tangled in each other's limbs, spent and breathing hard, he reflected that they were perfect together.

In a matter of seconds, she expelled a deep breath and fell asleep.

He smiled in the dim moonlight. *One satisfied customer. Job well done.*

He tried not to disturb Misty, but considering how deeply she slept, he doubted if a tornado could have disturbed her.

He stretched across her and pulled the coverlet over both of them, not intending to wake her, but she turned toward him, and he gathered her in his arms. Yes, this was the way it was meant to be. The perfect way to end a hard day is to hold the one you love in your arms. To hear her soft intake of breath. To feel her hand against his bare chest. *Yes, I'm here for you. I always will be.*

Chapter 19

IN THE MORNING, LEAH KNOCKED GENTLY ON THE door. "Misty, can I come in?" At the same time she asked, she pushed the door open. *Oh my!*

Her oldest brother-in-law was curled up with Misty, cradling her in his arms.

It wasn't that Leah was shocked to have walked in on them together but that she didn't want to disturb them. Certainly she and Tyler had shared many passionate nights before they were married, but this was different. With Misty's bruised face nestled against Colton's chest, it appeared to be a portrait of tender caring. She smiled and quietly set the tray down on the bedside table. Time enough for food when they were both rested.

She stole carefully out of the room. Silently, she twisted the knob to close the door behind her.

In the big, cheery kitchen, sunlight streamed through the bank of windows on the patio side. Just gazing out at the plants, fiercely blooming in huge ceramic pots arranged around the patio, was like looking at a page from a garden magazine. *Really beautiful*.

She sucked in a deep breath and released it.

Mark and Gracie were at the table, just finishing their breakfast of scrambled eggs, biscuits, and ham with red-eye gravy.

"Something smells great." Big Jim strode into the kitchen, fastening the buttons on the cuffs of his Western shirt as he walked.

She gave him a grin. "Help yourself to coffee, and I'll scramble up some fresh eggs just for you."

Big Jim went behind the kitchen counter and selected a mug from the cabinet, carrying it to the coffeepot. "Thanks a lot, Leah."

Beau came in next, and Leah broke more eggs into the skillet. "Scrambled eggs, coming right up."

Beau thanked her and grabbed a cup for himself. He held it out for Big Jim to fill. "Morning, Dad. Have you recovered from the loss of your truck?"

Leah turned to gaze at Big Jim in surprise. "You lost your truck?"

Big Jim emitted a less-than-polite snort. "My truck was murdered."

Beau settled on a stool by the granite breakfast bar. "You can say that again. In fact, there were two vehicular murders last night, and the same guy was responsible for both."

Big Jim's brows drew together as he glared at his youngest son.

"Vehicular murders?" Leah frowned. "What does that mean? Two people were killed by a vehicle?"

Beau was grinning now. "Nope. Two different vehicles were totaled last night by the same idiot."

Big Jim shook his head before casting another cool glare in Beau's direction. "The creep ran smack into the side of my truck. Crushed in the driver's side, bent the frame and axle. Not worth the repair bill. They never handle right after a wreck."

Beau gave Leah a knowing look. "I think my dad will be visiting the truck dealership today."

"Danged right." Big Jim took a swig of his coffee.

Leah slid two filled plates onto the countertop. "Another vehicle was totaled? That must have been the one this so-called 'creep' was driving."

"Um, yeah," Big Jim said. "The creep's truck makes three."

Leah looked from father to son. "I don't understand. What other vehicle was totaled?"

Carefully, Big Jim set his cup down. "Look, Leah, this Eddie Simmons sideswiped Misty when she was on the way home, and your car pretty much bought the farm."

Leah's breath was sucked right out of her lungs. "My car?" she gasped.

Beau paused, his fork full of scrambled eggs halfway to his mouth. "Do you have insurance on your old beater?"

"My car?" Leah stared from man to man. "My car is gone?"

"Aw, I know how you feel," Big Jim said. "But was it insured?"

"Only liability," Leah replied. "I know it wasn't worth much. It's just that…Gracie and I made our escape from Oklahoma in that car. It brought us all the way here with our meager possessions." To her consternation, a tear trickled down one cheek and fell onto her blouse.

Big Jim reached out to pat her hand. "I think you and I need to go to Amarillo to look at something new for you to drive."

She heaved a sigh. "I have the use of Ty's truck. I guess that's all we need. I'm just being silly." Swiping the tears away, she turned to find Gracie and Mark standing beside her. Each held their empty plate and eating utensils.

"What's wrong, Mommy?" Gracie asked, concern written on her face.

"Somebody ran into our car last night," she said. "It's okay. Mommy was just a little sad, that's all." She took the plates and utensils, rinsing and stacking them in the sink, ready to be loaded into the dishwasher. "You two run along now. You have this beautiful Saturday to enjoy." She smiled, watching them head out to the patio.

Big Jim's phone sounded, and he retrieved it from his shirt pocket. He glanced at the caller ID before accepting the call. "Hello, Sheriff." He listened and then said, "Yes, we're all here at the ranch. The hospital kept Levi Blair after they removed the bullet from his shoulder. Have you captured that asshole Eddie Simmons yet?"

Beau scooped the last of his eggs into his mouth and reached for another biscuit to sop up the remains of the gravy on his plate.

"Good to know," Big Jim said into his phone. "Keep us informed, Sheriff. I want to know when you catch that sumbitch." He rang off and slipped the phone back in his shirt pocket before tucking into his food again.

"Well?" Beau cocked his head to one side. "Are you going to tell us, or do I have to ask what the sheriff had to say?"

Big Jim flashed a mischievous grin. "Go ahead. Ask me."

"I'll ask you," Leah said. "What did the sheriff say?"

Big Jim took his time scooping another bite into his mouth and carefully chewed before he answered. "The sheriff said that Misty's ranch hand, Paco, was released from the hospital some time yesterday and is now in a rehab center to recuperate, so he's made a turn for the better."

Leah leaned her elbows on the countertop. "That will make Misty's day. I know she's been so worried about him."

Beau continued to stare at Big Jim, a bemused expression on his face. "C'mon, Dad. You're holding out on us."

Big Jim shrugged. "Well, the sheriff did happen to mention that Paco identified Eddie Simmons and his pal Stan Lynch as his attackers."

"Stan?" Beau heaved a sigh. "Damn! I just don't know what kind of hold Eddie has over those guys."

Big Jim finished cleaning his plate. "And then Eddie shot Stan. That's a helluva note."

Leah blew out a huff of air. "Okay, I'm over it. I don't care if my car was totaled. I only care that Misty is back home and everyone I love is safe."

"Me too," Big Jim said. "And just you make yourself comfortable with the fact that I am going to take you to Amarillo and buy you a brand-new car. Maybe a Jeep or a Hummer. Something big and strong to protect you." He gave a nod as though that completely settled the matter.

———

When Colton opened his eyes, all the events of the previous evening came flooding back into his consciousness. He was stunned to see how dark the bruise on the side of Misty's face had become.

Releasing his breath carefully, he didn't want to awaken her. Dark smudges beneath her eyes bespoke her exhaustion.

A soft tap sounded at the door, and Leah poked her

head in. She made a shushing gesture but motioned for him to get up.

Carefully, he slipped his arm out from under Misty's neck and sat up, clutching the coverlet to cover his nakedness. He glanced again at Leah. She was grinning from ear to ear and motioned for him to hurry before quietly closing the door.

Obediently, Colton donned his Wranglers, pulled on his boots, and reached for his shirt. He needed a shower, and his shirt was desperately in need of a wash. He slipped it on but left it unbuttoned, the easier to strip off once he found out what had his sister-in-law so excited.

Hearing raised voices in the kitchen, he rounded the corner, delighted to see his middle brother, Tyler, holding court. He stood with an arm around Leah while Beau and Big Jim clustered around him.

"Whoa! Look who's home," Colt said. "The rambling man found his way back." He opened his arms, and Ty grabbed him in a bear hug. The two exchanged a hearty round of back-thumping.

"Good to be home," Ty declared. "I missed everyone. Even you, Bubba."

Colton guffawed. "Don't call me that."

They gravitated as a group to the table and took seats all around.

"So, what have I missed?" Ty asked.

Big Jim snorted. "We've been keeping busy since you went on tour, Son."

"Colton's in love," Beau announced in a singsong voice.

Ty's face split into a grin. "So Leah's been telling me. Well, where is this amazing young woman who hog-tied my big brother?"

"Let her sleep," Colton said. "She's been through a lot in the past twenty-four hours."

"Plenty of time." Big Jim shook his head. "Plenty of time."

"Are you home for a while?" Colt asked.

"Until the album comes out. Still need a few more songs." He pulled Leah onto his lap. "I needed some inspiration. Besides, I'm hoping to move my bride into our own home in about a month, so I want to be on hand for the final construction."

"Oh, there's plenty to do," Leah assured him.

Gracie burst into the kitchen, red-faced and out of breath.

Ty stood up, still clutching Leah in one arm and holding out his other to Gracie. "There's my girl!" Gracie threw herself at him, and he caught her. "What's the matter, baby girl?"

Leah wrapped both arms around her daughter and brushed her hair away from her face.

Colt noticed Gracie was whimpering, and tears streamed down her cheeks. He stood up. "Are you hurt?"

"No-o-o," she drew out, shaking her head vehemently. "There's a man. He's got Mark."

Colton's stomach did a flip-flop. "What does he look like?" His gaze narrowed. "Is this man tall? Kind of red-faced and wiry?"

Wide-eyed with fear, Gracie nodded. "He has a gun, and he's talking funny."

Big Jim and Beau scrambled to their feet.

"Damnation!" Big Jim thundered. "Eddie Simmons is here?" He pulled his phone out of his shirt pocket and hit redial, beginning a rapid conversation with the sheriff almost immediately.

"He was in the stable. I went out to watch Mark take care of the horses."

Colt was already through the front door and headed toward the stables when he stopped cold.

Eddie stood between Colton's and Beau's trucks. He had a gash across his forehead and another down his cheek. His shirt was covered in blood, and he had a shotgun aimed at Mark's head. "Hey, Beau. Tell your big brother to slow down, or it's gonna get a little messy around here."

Colt's teeth gritted together. "What do you want, Eddie?" he demanded.

Eddie laughed. "I want the keys to one of these Garrett trucks." He nodded toward Tyler's red extended-cab pickup. "Not that one. Too noticeable. Gimme the keys to this nice gray one." He smacked his hand against Beau's silver truck.

"And then what?" Big Jim asked.

Eddie nodded toward Mark. "Then me and Joe's little brother are going to take a ride. I'll let him go when I'm clear."

That thought chilled Colton to the bone. He had no intention of allowing Eddie to take Mark anywhere. Mark looked terrified, but his gaze was locked on Colton.

"You can have mine," Colton ground out. He dug his keys out of his pocket, jangling them to draw Eddie's attention. "It's filled with diesel and ready to go."

Eddie shifted his attention to Colton. "Look who it is! Big brother here to save the day." He turned to Beau. "I think I want your truck, Beau. Why don't you hand over the keys real nice-like, and we can get this over with."

Beau caught Colton's eye and turned back to Eddie. "I'm almost out of gas, Eddie. You might make it as far as town, but I'm running on fumes."

A shriek split the air. "No! Don't hurt him!"

Everyone turned to see Misty run from the house. She was still wearing the hospital gown. Barefoot, she ran straight at Eddie Simmons, who raised the barrel of the shotgun to level it at her.

Colt held out his arms and caught her as she tried to evade his reach. He lifted her high in an arc and brought her back down to earth. "No you don't," he said sternly. "Beau, take care of Misty for me." He handed her off to Beau, trying to ignore her agonized expression. He heard her protests as Beau carried her back to where Leah was standing. Leah opened her arms, and the two women clung to each other.

Tyler came to stand beside Colton, propping his forearm on Colt's shoulder. "So, Eddie, you're the asshole who wrecked my dad's truck? Colt, I don't think you should trust this guy with yours. I sure as hell don't intend to give him mine."

Colton caught the look in Ty's eyes as he cocked his head to where Eddie stood, clutching the shotgun in one hand and Mark in the other. "Well, I do see your point, Ty. Perhaps you're right."

"No, wait," Eddie said. "Gimme the keys to your truck, Colton. That will do just fine." He juggled the shotgun and let go of Mark, reaching out as if ready to catch the keys.

"I'll go high, you go low," Colt said in a soft voice.

Ty gave an almost inaudible grunt of assent.

Colton didn't even look at Ty but held out the keys.

"Okay, here you go, Eddie. Catch." He tossed the keys in a high arc, and as Eddie stretched up to snag them, Colton launched himself at his target.

Ty raced toward Mark, grabbing the boy and rolling away, just as Colton slammed into Eddie with his shoulder catching him in the gut. Colt fell on top of Eddie, shoving the shotgun to the side and pinning him to the ground. He swung a fist, connecting with Eddie's jaw. It sounded like a ball player slamming one out of the park. "That's for hitting Misty, and this—" He delivered a resounding blow with his other fist. "—is for throwing her down the well."

Large hands grabbed Colton by the shoulders, pulling him backward. "Leave it," Big Jim growled. "Don't kill this piece of crap. The sheriff is on his way."

Eddie wasn't moving. A trickle of blood ran from his lip toward his jaw. His eyes were glazed, and he moaned softly.

Scrambling to his feet, Colt took a deep breath and blew it out. "Damn!"

"You can say that again." Big Jim gave him a slap on the back. "Proud of you, boys."

Tyler got to his feet and reached a hand out to lift Mark off the ground. "You okay?"

Mark nodded, tears spilling down his cheeks.

Colton turned and sought out Misty's face. He started walking toward her.

Misty broke away from Leah and Beau and began running to meet Colt. Her beautiful face was contorted in a grimace, but she ran straight at him. He heard her whimper when she threw herself into his arms. "Oh, Colt. I was so afraid he was going to kill you." She cupped his face in her hands, raining kisses on his mouth and face. "I can't believe you ran right at a crazy man holding a gun."

He held her tight, unable to explain why he would take such a risk. "I would have given him the truck, but I couldn't let him take Mark."

The sound of sirens split the air, and in no time, the sheriff's vehicle turned in along with a second department car. The sheriff rolled out, hand on his weapon, with two deputies on his tail. "You got him?"

"My sons did," Big Jim acknowledged, a tinge of pride in his voice as he stood with his hand on Mark's shoulder. He gestured to where Eddie was sitting on the ground with Ty standing guard.

The sheriff nodded to his deputies, who rushed forward to cuff and take charge of the prisoner. They loaded Eddie into the rear of the deputy's car with the sheriff's instructions to take him in with the charge of three counts of first degree murder, three counts of attempted murder, and one count of attempted kidnapping.

Colton couldn't seem to let go of Misty, nor she him. When the sheriff finally drove away, Colt and Misty stood with an anxious yet relieved Mark by their side.

"I—I better get dressed." Misty glanced around self-consciously, gathering the gown close around her.

Considering her bare feet, Colt lifted her in his arms and carried her toward the ranch house. "I'll give you a ride."

Once in the house, Misty protested that she could walk, but Colt insisted on carrying her all the way to the bedroom she had been staying in. He set her on her feet, the soft carpet a welcome change from the caliche driveway she had been on.

"Thanks," she said, but he drew her into his arms and kissed her.

"Let's get married," he said.

Misty had to giggle at that. "Yes… I already said yes."

Wrapping both arms around her, he lifted her and spun around in a circle. "Now. I want to get married now."

Squeezing his neck with her arms, she nodded. "It's okay with me. You can work out the details. Just tell me when to show up."

He released her, but not before his hand caressed her bottom.

"You get dressed and we can go talk to the pastor about the church and drive into Amarillo to look at rings today."

"Really?" She was almost afraid to look at him. Afraid he was joking.

"Really." He gave her another little squeeze on the butt. "We can have dinner in the big city before we come home."

She closed her eyes. "Home. I'm not sure where that is right now."

He pulled her back into his arms. "It's wherever we're together."

"Colton, I had the best dream last night. I dreamed you held me all night long. I felt so safe and…loved."

"I slept here, holding you. You don't think I could let go of you after everything that happened, do you?"

She gazed up at him. "Never let me go, Colt."

"Never." He kissed her nose and backed out of the room, making a hurry-up gesture.

As the door closed softly behind him, Misty quickly

gathered her clothes and grooming essentials and headed for the bathroom.

Keeping in mind the doctor's warning to keep her bandages dry, she filled the tub and gently slipped into the water. Carefully, she arranged her calf atop the rim of the old-fashioned claw-foot tub and managed to bathe herself all over without dousing her calf or shoulder. While luxuriating in the warm water, she thought about all that had transpired in the past few days. She examined her minor cuts and scrapes as though discovering them for the first time. "I'm alive," she whispered. "You didn't kill me, Eddie. My Colton found me." A little shiver of contentment ran through her. She knew whatever course her life took from that moment onward, Colt would be by her side.

When she had dressed and applied a swipe of makeup over the bruise on her cheek, she presented herself to Colton in the kitchen.

His hair was still damp from his shower, but he was dressed in his usual attire of freshly ironed Wranglers, a Western shirt and belt, and, of course, highly polished boots. He stroked his palm over her bruised cheek, his lips tightening as he gazed at her. "You look gorgeous, baby."

She grinned. "That's what you say now, but give me a week to heal, and I'll be back to normal...whatever that is."

"You two sit down right now and eat a little lunch before you make that drive." Leah scooped chili into two bowls and laid a slab of cornbread alongside each. "This should keep you going for a while."

Colton pulled out a chair for her and seated himself beside her. "This looks great, Leah."

Mark slid into the chair across from where Misty sat. "Man, that is some bruise," he declared.

"Thanks ever so," Misty said, spooning up a bite of the fabulous-smelling chili. She made a sound when it first hit her tongue, savoring the rich, meaty stew. "Delicious."

Leah smiled as she settled onto a kitchen stool at the breakfast bar next to her husband, Ty.

Now, as Misty stole a glance at Tyler with his Leah, she thought he was very handsome, but not nearly as handsome as Colton. While all four of the Garrett men shared the same broad-shouldered stature and intense blue eyes, Colt was the only man she could see in the room. Big Jim shared the same breadth of chest and had probably looked a lot like Colton in his younger days. The silver-haired patriarch stood looking on at his brood, wearing a contented expression she had not seen before.

Colt stuffed his face with chili and cornbread, then washed it down with a large glass of iced tea. "Eat up, baby."

When they got on the road, Misty felt like a kid at Christmastime. Anticipation took the place of all the fear that had controlled her emotions.

They went to the church first, and sure enough, the pastor found an available date for their wedding. She and Colton almost ran down the church steps to the truck.

"I hope Amarillo has a ring you like." Colt reached over to squeeze her hand.

Misty had been thinking of a modest engagement ring with a plain gold band. No, that wasn't what Colton had in mind. When they entered the jewelry store, he instructed the jeweler to bring trays of engagement rings

from the back. He placed one after another on her finger
and watched her expression with each one. "This one
okay with you?" He indicated a much larger stone surrounded by a circle of smaller diamonds, and a wedding
band made up of a circlet of diamonds all around. The
jeweler stepped away to allow them privacy.

"Oh, Colton," she whispered. "This is so extravagant.
I really don't need anything this fancy."

Colton let out a snort of laughter. "Baby, I'm only
going to do this one time. Let's get it right."

She grinned and nodded. "In that case...wow! This
is a gorgeous ring, and I would be proud to wear it,
Mr. Garrett."

They left the rings to be sized, and Colton drove her
to the private care facility where Paco was receiving
physical and occupational therapy. He was delighted to
see them. Reclining on the bed, he was watching the
news on television. They chatted for a while and then
left after the therapist assured them Paco was making a
slow but steady recovery.

The next stop was the hospital, where Misty would be
able to visit with Levi Blair. He was no longer in the inten-
sive care unit and had been upgraded to a regular room.

Misty chose a bouquet from the hospital gift shop.

Colton gave her a wry smile. "Aw, baby. Guys don't
like flowers."

"Yes, but girls do, and I'm a girl." She chose a cheery
arrangement of daisies, gladioli, and asters.

When she entered Levi's room, he was watching
television but quickly switched it off. "Danged idiot TV
shows rot the brain."

Misty grinned. "Well, Colton tells me guys don't

like flowers, but I figured you were man enough to hang out with these." She placed the vase on his bedside table.

"Well, ain't that nice." A grin spread across his face. "They's almost as purty as you, little missy."

She told him the date selected for the wedding. "You better be there, ready to give me away."

Levi raised one of his bushy brows, skewering Colton with his gaze. "You okay with that, Garrett?"

Colton stepped forward and extended his hand. "Very okay with that. After all, the two of you survived together. I think it's extremely appropriate that you two stick together."

Levi clasped Colton's hand, and the two men exchanged a hearty handshake.

"I understand that old rascal Jim Garrett donated blood for me?"

Colton nodded. "My little brother and Misty, too."

A sly grin spread across Levi's face. "But not you?"

Colt let out a snort of laughter. "No, sir. I was too busy holding on to this little one. I couldn't let her out of my sight." He slipped his arm around Misty's shoulders.

"Don't blame you none." He turned back to Misty. "Well, I'll be there. My doc assures me I'll be going home in a couple of days, so I will definitely be on hand to walk you down the aisle."

Misty leaned over to place a kiss on his cheek. "I'm just glad we survived."

Colt saddled two horses and took Misty for a ride early the next morning, just after breakfast. They went to the section of land where the creek curved around in an arc. His favorite spot on the ranch.

Stopping beside the creek, he smiled as he observed her face.

She leaned forward in the saddle, inhaling the clean country air. "This is really beautiful, Colt. It's so peaceful. Just what I needed to try to forget all the bad things that have happened recently."

He shook his head. "I'm pretty sure none of us will ever forget the events of the past few weeks, but we can try to put them behind us."

She glanced at him and grinned. "I'm ready for that."

He dismounted and walked over to where Misty remained astride the horse. "Let's take a walk." He held the reins while she climbed out of the saddle in one lithe move.

She smiled up at him, slipping her hand in his.

He led her to the creek's edge, where it curved. A mesquite grew nearby, its gnarled trunk twisted into a graceful arc. "What do you think about this place?"

"It's gorgeous. What else would I think?" She placed a hand against the trunk.

"I was thinking about building our home here. Would you like that?"

She caught her breath. "Oh, Colton. I thought maybe we could move back to my place...the Dalton place." She faltered. "I mean, it's already built and available."

"I know," he said kindly. "But that house holds so many sad memories for you and for Mark. If we're going to put the past behind us, I'd like to start with a brand-new home that we design to meet our future needs." He watched as she absorbed his words, barely breathing. "Besides, Rosa and Paco will be living there as soon as he is able. I know you want to continue to provide for them."

"Yes, I do."

"And the Dalton house also belongs to your brother Mark. We can keep the house repaired so he can live there in the future if he chooses."

"That's true." She gazed around at the scenic landscape. "It is incredibly beautiful here."

"And most of all," he said, "I want to build the perfect home for my bride. Whatever it takes to make her dreams come true."

When she gazed up at him, her lashes were spangled with tears.

"Aw, baby...I didn't mean to make you unhappy." He drew her into his arms. "We can live at your house if that's what you want."

"No. I like your plan. I'm just happy. I can't ever remember being this happy. I'm pretty sure living with you right here in this beautiful spot will be like heaven on earth." She sobered. "You're sure you're okay with Mark living with us?"

"Of course," Colton said. "Mark is a part of you. He's a great kid, and I intend to always be there for him. Besides, my old man is pretty fond of him as well."

"How could I not be in love with you?" She gave him a radiant grin.

"How indeed?" He kissed her, delighted with the affirmation that she loved him. Happy their wedding was to take place in less than a month, and relieved he could put an end to her sadness. "From now on, I promise you a lifetime of love and happiness."

"That's enough, Colton. That's just long enough."

Want to know more about Beau? Read on for an
excerpt from *Full Throttle Cowboy*, next in the
Dark Horse Cowboys series by June Faver

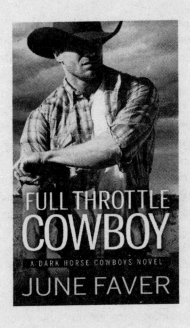

Available April 2019
from Sourcebooks Casablanca

Chapter 1

"YOU'RE BEAU GARRETT?"

Beau turned, eyeing the speaker, a man about his own age, mid-twenties. The man was not as tall as Beau, but he was beefy, wearing a T-shirt advertising a gym in Dallas.

"That's right." Beau put forth his hand, offering to shake with the stranger.

"You sonovabitch!" This pronouncement was followed by a rushing behemoth whose shoulder to Beau's gut took them both to the sidewalk.

Ahh, shit! Beau's freshly starched Western shirt was being ground into the dirt as his attacker prepared to take a swing. Beau dodged to one side, and the oncoming fist smacked into the concrete sidewalk.

A howl of pain and rage burst from his assailant.

Beau scrambled to his feet and swung a fist of his own, catching the man square in the nose. "Who the hell are you, asshole?" he demanded.

Blood streaming from his nose, but unfazed by the punch, the man sprang to his feet. He swung his uninjured fist, grazing Beau's chin as he tried to dodge.

A kernel of anger burst in Beau's chest like an incendiary device being detonated. He set on the man, both fists delivering well-placed blows, mostly to the head and gut.

"Beau Garrett, you stop that right now."

The feminine voice sounded vaguely familiar, but Beau managed to deliver one more punch that sent his foe to the sidewalk in a heap. Beau dropped his fists and turned to face the woman who had spoken, only to receive a roundhouse blow to his cheekbone. He staggered backward, barely avoiding falling over the man on the ground. "Dixie?" he asked when his vision cleared enough to focus.

The irate redhead stood with both fists cocked. "What have you done?" she demanded. "Why did you attack my friend?" She glowered at Beau before going to hover over the man on the sidewalk. "Scott, are you okay? Let me help you."

"Dixie?" Beau repeated as though in a daze. His cheek and eye socket throbbed from her punch. "What are you doing here?"

She paused in her ministrations to the fallen man and glared up at him. "Well, in case you hadn't heard, my father died, and I'm here to make arrangements for his funeral."

"Oh, I'm sorry," Beau muttered. "I didn't know your dad was ill."

"He wasn't," she snapped. "Somebody shot him dead last night while he was closing up the store. Sheriff thinks it was a robbery. His bank deposit bag was missing."

"Sorry," Beau said again, feeling completely inadequate. "I—ah."

Dixie helped the aforementioned Scott to his feet. Offering soothing comments, she led him toward a vehicle parked at the curb. "I'm going to take you to the local doctor. She'll fix you right up."

Beau watched as Dixie loaded the guy into the SUV and then took off in the direction of the doctor's office.

He huffed out a huge sigh, turning toward the store that had been his intended destination that morning. In his pocket was a check made out to Moore's Feed and Seed Store meant to pay the Garrett ranch tab for the previous month. Beau's father, Big Jim Garrett, had sat in his study the night before, writing checks to keep all the accounts current.

Sure enough, there was a hand-lettered sign in the feed store window that read CLOSED DUE TO DEATH IN THE FAMILY.

Beau swallowed hard. He found it difficult to accept that Mr. Moore had been killed. There had always been a Mr. Moore. When he was a boy, his dad had taken him into the feed store, and Vernon Moore had always been there. Later, when he was in grade school, he recalled being instantly enamored of the little girl with the bright red curls. They had played together like puppies, Dixie being a complete tomboy and more ready to wrestle or climb a tree than sit down to a tea party with dolls.

"Dixie Moore," Beau intoned softly. His first crush. His first girlfriend. His first sexual partner. His shoulders sagged.

And then she was gone.

In the middle of their senior year, Dixie's mother had suddenly left town with Dixie. There had been no warning. No goodbyes. No way to keep in touch.

Losing Dixie had torn a hole in Beau's heart. He had never quite recovered and never found anyone to replace her. He'd gone to the prom alone and come home early.

Beau stared at the closed-up store. Someone would have to open the doors soon. All the ranchers in the area depended on Moore's Feed and Seed. It couldn't just cease to serve the community.

He climbed in his truck and drove back to the Garrett ranch. He was sure Big Jim would have something to say about the morning's events.

～～～

Frowning, Big Jim Garrett stared at his youngest son. "Better get some ice on that. You're going to have a beaut of a shiner."

Beau slouched at the granite countertop in the Garret kitchen. "I swear, he just called my name and then came at me."

Having raised three sons, Big Jim was used to mishaps that required ice. He kept several ice packs in the freezer just for such occasions. Selecting one, he tossed it on the wooden cutting board and pounded it with his fist to break up the chunks. "Here you go." He flung it on the countertop near his son's elbow.

Beau grunted and reached for the pack, placing it gingerly against his cheek. It was already swollen and turning purple.

"Nice job," Big Jim murmured. "And you said it was Dixie Moore who punched you?"

Beau nodded. "First, her boyfriend attacked me out of the blue, and then Dixie got off a shot. What is this? Beat on Beau Garrett day?"

Big Jim snorted. "Sounds like you got in a few punches of your own."

A wry grin spread across Beau's face. "That I did. We Garretts aren't exactly known for turning the other cheek."

Big Jim exploded with laughter. "That's for damn sure."

"What happened to you, Little Bro?" Tyler, Big Jim's middle son, entered the kitchen and slid onto the stool next to Beau. "That's quite a shiner you've got working there."

"Shut up," Beau responded.

"Remember Dixie Moore?" Big Jim asked. "She gave him that one."

"No way!" Ty grinned at Beau. "I remember her as a scrappy little hellion. What did you do to piss her off?"

"Not a damned thing." Beau tossed the ice pack down on the countertop and pounded it a few times with the side of his fist before gently applying it to his face again.

Tyler's face sobered. "I heard her dad was killed last night. It's on the news."

Big Jim frowned. "That's what Beau was telling me. It seems little Miss Dixie is here to bury Vern."

Ty's brows drew together. "I wonder what she's going to do with the store."

"Well, for damned sure there has to be a feed store in Langston," Big Jim thundered. "Too many people around here depend on it."

Dixie had taken Scott to see the local doctor. Scott had sustained a broken nose and fractured two bones in his right hand when his fist impacted the pavement instead of Beau's face.

Now, Scott looked almost comic, with his right hand in a cast and the entire arm immobilized in a sling to remind him not to use it. He also had rolled-up gauze stuffed in his nasal cavities, and both eyes were turn-ing black with bruising. In all, he looked like a petulant walrus with his two gauze tusks.

"Whatever were you thinking?" Dixie glanced over at Scott as he slouched in the passenger seat of her bur-gundy SUV. "I could have told you Beau would whip your ass."

"You know why," Scott said. Due to the gauze up his nose, he was mouth-breathing, and his voice was raspy and nasal.

Dixie figured Scott recognized Beau from the high-school photos she had of him in her apartment. Somehow, she just couldn't put them away. And seeing him again was like stabbing her straight in the heart. He was even better looking as a man than he had been as a teen. His shoulders were broader and his tall, lanky teen form had filled in with a solid bank of muscle.

She swallowed hard. It was the eyes that got her. *Those killer Garrett eyes.* Beau's hair was a little lighter than his two older brothers, but they all had those incredible blue eyes. Almost turquoise, ringed with black lashes all around.

When Scott and Beau had been fighting, she knew Scott was the underdog. Although he had greater muscle mass and was much heavier, he didn't stand a chance against Beau Garrett. And there was the fact that Scott had started the fight, so he had the element of surprise on his side. He would never think of himself as a loser… but in this match, he was far outclassed.

Beau Garret could always whip his weight in wild cats and had done so, on occasion, while defending Dixie's honor.

She fought to control the smile threatening to break out as she recalled how valiant Beau had been. Always her hero. *Well, almost always...*

And now she had her friend Scott trying to defend her honor against her former hero. *How sad is that?* She glanced over at her sullen protector and reached out to give him a pat on the arm.

"You're sweet, you know?"

"I'm a dumbass, apparently." Scott placed his good hand on top of hers. "But I love you, you know?"

"I know. Love you too. You're my best friend in the whole wide world."

He nodded. "I don't know what I would do without you...and Roger, of course."

Dixie smiled at the mention of Scott's lover and soon-to-be groom. "I'll have to thank him for letting you come with me. I don't think I could face this ordeal without you."

"I'm always here for you. It's terrible that your father was murdered." He shook his head. "This little town doesn't exactly look like a hot bed of crime."

She pressed her lips together, strengthening her resolve to tie up loose ends as fast as possible and try not to get caught up in whatever happened to Vernon Moore. She couldn't imagine her mild-mannered father getting involved in anything that would get him killed. But then again, maybe she didn't know him at all anymore. She had been gone a long time. "Yeah," she intoned. "I'm sure the sheriff will deal with it."

He wagged his head from side to side, the tusks making a wide arc. "I don't understand," he said. "I can take anybody at the gym. I was on the boxing team in college. How come this punk cowboy can chew me up and spit me out?"

"Don't feel bad," she said. "He's no punk. That cowboy works hard every day. He's just one big muscle. And if memory serves, just the mention of a fight would have all the Garretts jumping in." Shaking her head, she let out a chortle. "It wasn't the same kind of fight as in a gym with a referee. Those Garrett boys knew how to fight."

Scott made a guttural noise in the back of his throat. "One of them still does."

<center>~~~</center>

Beau saw the SUV around town, but Dixie always had her goon boyfriend with her. He ached to talk to her. To have a real conversation. He wanted to know why she and her mother had left town so abruptly and why she never contacted him. She knew he was in love with her. She knew he was serious about her. She knew...

Vernon Moore had always opened and closed his own store, but he had a full-time helper who had been pressed into service to keep the feed store in operation.

Beau pushed the door open and approached the counter. Pete, the clerk, looked tired and maybe a little dazed. Beau gave him the check he had been tasked to deliver from Big Jim. "How are things going?" he asked.

Pete shook his head. "Terrible. I can't believe old man Moore is gone. Somebody just shot him...right outside the door when he was locking up." Pete gave an exaggerated shudder. "Gives me the heebie-jeebies every night when I'm trying to close the store."

"I guess so," Beau agreed. "Isn't there another guy who works here?"

Pete grimaced. "Josh Miller, my cousin. He's been working part-time since he was in high school. He's a big guy, and he could handle the heavy lifting when it got to be too much for Mr. Moore." He shook his head. "Vern kept him on because he felt sorry for Josh's mother."

"Yeah?"

"My aunt is a widow. Nice lady, but having a hard time getting by." He scratched his head, thoughtfully. "Mostly, Josh works in the big shed out back. He receives shipments and rotates the stock so we can keep it fresh...does inventory. He loads the orders into customer trucks. That sort of thing." He shrugged, "You know Vern. Always a soft touch."

Beau nodded. Vern was known to allow some of the local ranchers to stretch their credit quite thin during a bad spell. "When is the funeral going to be held? I haven't heard anything about it."

Pete looked both ways as though about to spill a secret, but the only other customer was a lady pawing through the vegetable seed packets, and her two kids were squatted down petting the baby bunnies. "The medical examiner hasn't released the body yet. It was a murder, you know?"

Beau nodded, his patience wearing thin. "How about Vern's daughter, Dixie? Has she said what she plans to do with the place?" His casual question was tossed out in hopes Pete would tell him she planned to move back to Langston.

Pete shook his head, his expression dour. "Lil' Miss Dixie—she said she would put everything on the market. She can't wait to get back to Dallas." He shrugged.

"Who would have thought our little Dixie Moore would turn out to be a city girl?"

"Yeah," Beau said. "Who would have thought?" He huffed out a sigh and left the store, distinctly dissatisfied.

He stood for a moment, blinking in the sunlight after the dimness of the store. He couldn't imagine why Mr. Moore had been targeted, but he guessed someone had been desperate enough to rob an old man and shoot him.

He climbed into his truck and started it up. The big diesel motor gave a little roar as he revved it. Slipping into gear, he backed out and pulled onto the main drag. Moore's Feed and Seed was located on the outskirts of town, the opposite direction from the Garrett ranch.

Beau drove slow, taking in everything but keeping an eye out for the maroon SUV. He spied his new sister-in-law's Jeep parked in front of the law office where she worked. His oldest brother Colton had married Misty just a few months ago, and the vehicle was a present he bought for her. Beau could have killed some time by pulling in and chatting with her, but he figured she had work to do, and he would just be in the way.

At the next intersection, he glanced down the street and located Dixie's automobile in front of the church. He sucked in a breath and blew it out, puffing his cheeks as he did so.

Might as well give it a try. Surely she won't punch me in church.

He pulled in beside her car and stepped out. What if her boyfriend was with her? Beau squared his shoulders. *So what? That guy would be an idiot to go after me again.* He climbed out and pocketed the keys.

Although his footsteps appeared sure and confident,

Beau's gut was doing flip-flops. He had no idea why he was anxious about seeing Dixie again. Taking a deep breath as he sprinted up the steps, he paused with his hand on the brass door to consider what he might say to the girl who had left him and never looked back. He swung the door open and stepped into the cool darkness. It took a moment for his eyes to adjust. Walking deeper into the interior, he made his way to the back hall that led to the church office and various rooms used for Sunday school classes, Boy Scout and Girl Scout meetings, and other gatherings.

There was a certain lemony smell to the church. It was always clean, immaculately so. Everything was polished and ready for the next group, class, or sermon to commence. As he strode toward the church offices, he was glad the hallway was carpeted. At least his arrival wouldn't be announced. Nearing the open doorway, he peeked inside, but the church secretary was not at her desk. He heard voices coming from the pastor's office. He recognized the sonorous voice belonging to the minister and Dixie's lighter, feminine tone.

Beau leaned against the wall outside the doorway, not able to hear the words spoken, but he gathered Dixie was making arrangements for Vern's funeral. In a few minutes, he could tell the voices seemed to be concluding their business, and it appeared the pastor was walking her to the door. Beau hoped the irate Scott wasn't in attendance.

"Thank you so much," Dixie said. "I'm sure the service will be lovely."

"I hope to see you at Sunday services soon, young lady."

"I'm afraid we won't be staying in town. I'll return to Dallas after the reading of the will."

The pastor murmured some comforting words, and Dixie stepped through the door. The big smile on her lips evaporated as soon as her eyes locked on Beau. "You! What are you doing here?"

He shrugged, all the while preparing to duck if she swung a fist. "This is my church. I show up here every Sunday with my whole family."

Dixie's green eyes narrowed, and she let out a derisive snort. "Not all of your family."

Puzzled, he spread his hands. "Yes, unless somebody's sick, we all show up."

Her mouth curved up in a sneering farce of a smile. "Well, isn't that just like you Garretts. You get to pick and choose who you call 'family.'" She gave him a glare that would have killed him dead, had it been a weapon, before she sailed past him down the hallway.

Feeling as though he had been struck again, Beau watched her depart. "Wait! What are you talking about?" He hurried to catch up with her.

She ignored him. Head held high, she strode through the church, placing both hands on the exit door, but Beau grabbed the big brass handle and held it fast.

"I mean it, Dixie. What are you talking about?"

He watched her profile as a series of emotions played out across her face. "You know," she said in a whisper.

"No, I don't know. Please talk to me."

Heaving a sigh, she finally met his gaze. "We have nothing left to say to each other, Beau. Nothing at all." With that, she shoved him aside and pushed through the door.

Beau trailed after her, watching as she opened her car with the remote and swung up into the driver's seat. In an instant, she had backed out and driven off in the direction of the Moore ranch.

He could follow her if he wanted, but he couldn't bring himself to do so, since it was pretty clear he was *persona non grata* to one Miss Dixie Moore.

Hearing a noise behind him, he turned to see the pastor exiting the church. "Oh, hello, Beauregard. I didn't know you were here. Did you need to see me about something?"

"Um, no—yes sir. When is Vernon Moore's funeral going to be held?"

"This coming Tuesday at ten in the morning. The viewing will be the day before from two to six p.m. I hope the Garrett family will come to pay their respects."

Beau nodded curtly. "You can count on it, sir."

～～～

Dixie drove toward her childhood home, tears flowing down her cheeks. "How could he? How—how could he?" She hiccupped. "Damn you, Beau Garrett. How dare you act the innocent?"

Heaving a sigh, she pawed through her handbag with one hand, searching for a tissue. She mopped at her face and gave her nose a hearty blow. "Enough of that. I will not allow Beau Garrett to cause me to shed another single tear." Straightening her shoulders, she clasped the steering wheel with both hands.

She had grown up on the Moore family ranch, located about ten miles east of town. Her father raised Charolais and Black Angus beef cattle and grew some of the feed for his herd. He had never considered himself a farmer but rather a storeowner and a gentleman rancher.

And someone killed him. An involuntary shiver snaked down her spine. How could someone have murdered her father? She tried to moisten her suddenly dry lips. Now she would never have a chance to confront him…to ask him why…to make things right. She had always thought there would come a time when they would see each other again.

Dixie slowed the vehicle and turned in at the farm-to-market road leading to the ranch house. Seeing the house brought the ache of tears back to her throat. She swallowed hard, remembering how happy this view had made her as a child. Riding the bus after school, she always felt a little tug of joy when first sighting her home. Her mother would be inside waiting for her with a hug. There would be a snack spread out on the kitchen table to fortify Dixie for homework. And her mom always asked her about her day, who she had played with, and what her teacher had to say. Those early mother-daughter after-school chats had bonded them, making her mom the person Dixie could pour her heart out to. Whenever she had needed her mom, she was always there for her.

But now, her mom remained in the city, unwilling to attend the funeral of the man she had been married to since she'd been a teenager herself.

When her mother had first taken her to Dallas, she thought it would be a temporary arrangement, but her mother purchased a condo and settled in.

At first, Dixie kept expecting to hear from Beau, or at least from her dad, but apparently he had no use for her either.

Her mother filed for divorce a few months later, she said because her husband had disowned Dixie. Being abandoned by her father had left a huge void in her life. Where was the man who had treated her like a princess when she was young, who had attended her basketball games and track events, who had applauded when the calf she raised got a ribbon at the county fair?

Dixie choked back tears as she pulled into the drive leading to the house. Her father had planted pecan trees along the driveway when Dixie was a child. Now they had grown to be tall and seemed to be covered with clusters of green pecans in shells. Soon they would be ready for harvest, but Dixie was certain she would be back in Dallas by that time. After all, she had her business, and as the sole owner, she had to be present to make sure it was running right.

She pulled up close to the house and turned off the motor. *Who am I kidding? I can run everything online.* Her craft store was more of a hobby than an actual business, but she did turn a profit and had regular customers. Promoting it and filling orders via computer took up very little time but provided a healthy payday.

She got out and slammed the door with a vengeance. Truth was, she couldn't wait to get back home to Dallas, where everything she held dear was waiting for her.

About the Author

June Faver loves Texas, from the Gulf coast to the panhandle, from the Mexican border to the Piney Woods. Her novels embrace the heart and soul of the state and the larger-than-life Texans who romp across her pages. A former teacher and healthcare professional, she lives and writes in the Texas Hill Country.

Also by June Faver

DARK HORSE COWBOYS
Do or Die Cowboy